Appeals in
Modern
Rhetoric

Appeals in Modern Rhetoric

An Ordinary-Language Approach

M. Jimmie Killingsworth

Southern Illinois University Press
Carbondale

Library of Congress Cataloging-in-Publication Data

Killingsworth, M. Jimmie.
  Appeals in modern rhetoric : an ordinary-language approach / M. Jimmie
Killingsworth.
    p. cm.
  Includes bibliographical references and index.
1. English language—Rhetoric. 2. Persuasion (Rhetoric). 3. Report writing. I. Title.

PE1431.K55 2005
808'.042—dc22
ISBN 0-8093-2662-0 (cloth : alk. paper)
ISBN 0-8093-2663-9 (pbk. : alk. paper)   2005003751

Printed on recycled paper. ♻

The paper used in this publication meets the minimum requirements of
American National Standard for Information Sciences—Permanence of Paper
for Printed Library Materials, ANSI Z39.48-1992. ∞

Contents

Preface   vii

Acknowledgments   xiii

1. A General Introduction to Rhetorical Appeals   1

2. Appeals to Authority and Evidence   11

3. Rhetorical Situations   24

4. Appeals to Time   38

5. Appeals to Place   52

6. Appeals to the Body   68

7. Appeals to Gender   85

8. Appeals to Race   98

9. Appeal Through Tropes   121

10. The Appeal of Narrative   136

Notes   153

Works Cited   159

Index   165

Preface

This book arises like all communications out of a particular situation. I found myself in a fix (as we say in the South)—as if I were walking in the woods and came to the end of the path before I had gone a hundred steps, or found so many paths that I couldn't decide among them. Every path I tried took me some place I didn't want to go—a dead end, a crowded town, a stinking landfill.

I kept trying to teach a course in modern rhetoric to undergraduate students and finding no text they could understand and easily apply to their lives and work. I could barely coerce my graduate students to read the likes of Kenneth Burke and Wayne Booth, authors whom I dearly love but whose books are so drenched in tradition and erudition that you need a PhD to read them. There were plenty of good books that introduced ancient rhetoric, in the mold of Edward P. J. Corbett's *Classical Rhetoric for the Modern Student*, but nothing with a title like "Modern Rhetoric for the Modern Student." Judging from the textbooks available, it would be easy to think that no work has been done in rhetoric since the time of St. Augustine or that contemporary students ought to be able easily to comprehend the work written more recently. My experience said no to both suggestions.

What I needed, then, was a place to start. Convinced that rhetoric remains relevant in our times, I came up with an idea that would allow me to introduce the subject in ordinary language for people with no background in the tradition and no patience for reading tomes like Bizzell and Herzberg's *The Rhetorical Tradition*, which after a couple of thousand pages only gets the reader to the edge of the woods anyway.

The idea I landed upon was to introduce the topic through the concept of the *appeal*. Everybody knows what *appeal* means in ordinary language, and we can build on that common knowledge and get quickly into the deep woods of rhetorical theory and practice. In an earlier work, I had defined rhetorical appeals as "efforts to overcome oppositions and divisions either by forming new solidarities, by reinforcing old ones, or by revealing distances and likenesses in order to transform attitudinal conflicts into [communal forms of] action" (Killingsworth and Palmer 17). I felt I could do better than that, so I went to the library and looked up the word in the indexes of whole shelves of books on rhetoric to see what others had to say. To my wonder, I found no listing for "appeals, rhetorical" in the indexes. After an initial moment of panic and then one of glee—for scholars love to find a gap that needs filling—I had to conclude that the rhetorical appeal is a concept whose meaning is rarely explained in the scholarly literature.

No doubt for many authors in the field, the meaning of *appeal* is tacitly understood, so there is no need to explain. But this kind of background knowledge is lacking for beginners in the field. And my further reading revealed that there is some chance that, even for specialists, who may have assumed too quickly that Aristotle had the last word on appeals, the concept has been "undertheorized," as we say in academic jargon these days. On that chance, I decided to try to write a book for students and their teachers, with the idea of helping novices in rhetoric to use their everyday understanding of what *appeal* means as an entry point into the study of rhetoric and at the same time urging scholars and teachers in the field to refine and articulate their own understanding of this central concept.

So here we are, standing at the edge of the woods with a modest path-opening device—the idea of *the appeal*. It has two significant common meanings. In the first definition, an appeal is a kind of attraction. When you find something *appealing*—a book or movie or dinner or person—you say "that one has appeal" or "that one appeals to me." In the second definition, an appeal is a way of approaching an audience. In this sense, you "*appeal to* a higher authority," such as God or Nature or the Supreme Court. An author may appeal to evidence, values, experience, or any number of cultural constructs—time, place, gender, or race, for example.

The two definitions are related in special ways explored in chapter 1. The main idea is that in *appealing to* something or somebody, an author must create an *appealing* text. In the terms that come down to us from Cicero, we must *please* the members of our audience in order to *teach* or *move* them. Rhetoric is all about bringing these three purposes—to please *(delectare)*, to teach *(docere)*, and to move *(movere)*—into harmony (Barilli ix).

The ten chapters presented here were originally given as weekly lectures in my courses on modern rhetoric. I have tried to retain something of the flavor of the lectures and the quality of the original aim: to provide an entry into rhetoric by way of this double-edged concept of the appeal, pointing out related paths along the way and sources in the rhetorical tradition, and showing how a model of appeals can be used to analyze and create texts. I also try to make the explanations comprehensible by paying attention to the two things that, according to my students, make specialized academic prose most difficult for them: "jargon" and "name-dropping." I use terms like *appeal* and other instances of ordinary language wherever I can and take time to explain specialized terms whenever I need to cross intersections with the rhetorical tradition and its sometimes confounding language. As for the "name-dropping"—our habit of citing hundreds of authorities and exhausting every possibility of reference—I experiment here with keeping references to a minimum in the text and using brief citations and bibliography to cover at least the majority of my debts. I doubt that my colleagues in rhetoric will appreciate this approach, but I'm sticking with it to keep the book accessible to the widest possible audience. My dearest hope is that scholars in rhetorical studies will also find the book easy to read and respond to. If they feel that the work remains too superficial to make a strong contribution to rhetorical theory, perhaps they will at least be able to recommend it to their students as a point of departure in modern rhetorical studies.

I feel confident at least in claiming that the approach offered here is not only easier to comprehend but also goes deeper into rhetoric than the usual textbook on argument, which typically chooses material too advanced for most contemporary students and then in an effort to make it usable, dumbs it down to the point of inanity. As an alternative, I offer an ordinary-language approach to rhetoric, the goal of which conforms to the goal of rhetoric since ancient times: *to understand and create informal arguments for use in public forums among nonspecialists.*

My Examples and Topics—and My Own Appeal

In choosing examples to illustrate my position, I reveal much about who I am and where I'm coming from. I show that I'm a scholar in American rhetoric, literature, and culture with special interests in the discourse of environmentalism, lyric poetry, science fiction, and social movements. I also appear as a person of a particular generation, somebody who came of age in the second half of the twentieth century, graduated from college in 1974, and took his first professorial job in 1980. My examples arise from my scholarly and personal experience, and though I try to appeal to a range of generations, many sample texts are likely to seem dated to students and younger readers. In my defense, I can only say that I recall how embarrassing it always seemed when my own teachers tried to keep their examples up to date, referring to what they thought were our favorite songs, movies, and slang terms. We always said they were "trying too hard to be cool." They never quite pulled it off.

I also keep my analysis of the examples brief. This way, I can increase the diversity of the examples and accommodate the novice audience by not going too deep too fast. I can also preserve a focus on the theory rather than the practice of rhetorical criticism and keep the book short—a crucial consideration. Some chapters do offer longer examples of analysis—the authority chapter, the gender chapter, and especially the race chapter—to show how to elaborate and complicate rhetorical analysis.

The topics that make up my chapter titles—authority, evidence, situation, time, place, body, gender, and race—do not come close to exhausting the range of appeals in modern rhetoric. My goal is to open the path. Where you choose ultimately to go is up to you. I hope I can make my choices and my position appealing by finding the common ground, what Kenneth Burke calls the "sub-stance," that connects our examples, our understanding of rhetoric, and our life stories. That will be the test of not only my theories, but also my own rhetorical practice.

What Is Rhetoric?

The problem of finding a good definition of rhetoric nags at newcomers and specialists alike, especially since the trend in modern rhetoric has been to expand the range of study into such fields as communication, psychology, linguistics, the philosophy of language, discourse theory, and other disciplines that did not exist, or existed under different names, in ancient times when rhetoric was first defined. My solution to the problem is to develop a more or less traditional working definition and refine it and complicate it as we go.

So for now, I will define rhetoric as *a concern for audience manifested in the situation and form of a communication. Concern for audience* can involve the desire to persuade (Aristotle); to teach, to move, and to please (Cicero); to identify (Kenneth Burke); or generally to communicate with an audience (I. A. Richards). *Situation and form* include attention to the five classical canons of rhetoric—invention, arrangement, style, memory, and delivery— or to the genre and mode of communication; to the social and historical context in general; or to the rhetorical situation as defined in modern studies, with such elements as exigence, audience, and constraints (Bitzer). One of the claims I am making is that the concept of rhetorical appeals suggests new insights into rhetorical situations and forms.

The Plan of the Book

Chapter 1 provides a model of appeals built on three key positions that appear in every rhetorical situation—author, audience, and value. Brief examples from social criticism, popular cinema, and advertising show how the model works. Every model is an oversimplification, and this one is no exception. Rather than trying to be comprehensive and exhaustive (or exhausting), trying to do everything in the first chapter, I provide a rudimentary starting point. Each chapter that follows offers elaborations and refinements of the model.

Chapter 2 shows how the model accommodates traditional appeals to authority and evidence, comparing authority-based arguments (the kind used in preaching) to data-based arguments (the kind used in science). Everything changes from one system to the other—author, audience, and values—so that the two systems can never be fully reconciled. I introduce the important distinction between insider audiences and audiences that mix insiders and outsiders to explain how modern rhetoric faces a grave challenge in crafting appeals for wildly varying populations. (To get a quick sense of the problem, we could compare the audience of Aristotle's students— Athenian, male, free citizens in a relatively small world—to the millions of people around the big modern world who watch a television broadcast.)

Chapter 3 shows how to use the appeals model to understand and frame rhetorical situations. Authors place themselves in relation to audiences and values and then attempt to bring the three positions into alignment. Their success often depends upon how they introduce a topic and connect it to larger contexts. We look at several examples of introductions to get a sense of situational awareness and contextual sensitivity in modern rhetoric.

Chapters 4, 5, and 6 apply the general appeals model to three common types of appeals: appeals to time, place, and the body. These appeals strike me as not only common in modern rhetoric but fundamental. Other appeals keep coming back to them and building upon them. The reason is that people in modern societies pretty much obsess over these topics. "Time is money," we say, indicating the value we place upon it. Place becomes a problem for people in a life that is mobile and globalized: how can I find common ground when my own place keeps changing and when my audience spreads over the whole planet? And does the possibility of a public forum—a place to debate issues of common interest—still exist anymore? The body presents us with a common denominator for communication, but our ways of understanding physical difference shift from culture to culture, female to male, and even person to person. Faced with these challenges on even the most fundamental topics, rhetorical appeals strive to work through difference and breed understanding.

Chapters 7 and 8 deal with the efforts of authors to communicate with their "others" on two of the most troubled topics in modern times—gender and race. In appeals involving gender and race, identity struggles with difference on a daily basis. The temptation to give up and say "you'll never understand—we're just too different" is always present in a world of identity politics and polarized communities. The practice of rhetoric offers a way to resist that temptation.

Chapters 9 and 10 go deeper into the question of *how*. Chapter 9 uses a discussion of figurative language to talk about rhetorical strategies that begin at the level of the word or phrase but end up offering new ways of thinking, new twists and turns on conventional definitions of words and habitual patterns of thought. The topic is the *trope*, which literally means "a turn." We want to know how a turn of phrase can turn our heads to new ways of thinking and being, new attitudes. Chapter 10 discusses the perennial appeal of narratives and the special functions of storytelling in a modern democracy.

My goal in all of these chapters is to stimulate stronger questions about readings and deeper thinking about how to craft appealing prose that adjusts itself to a variety of audiences and communication settings, that combats boredom and apathy, that gets to the heart of issues, that goes beyond formulas, that comes alive and makes a difference.

Acknowledgments

I am grateful to many people for making this work possible, most notably the students at Texas A&M University in my undergraduate course and graduate seminar in modern rhetoric. Georgina Kennedy was particularly helpful at the beginning of the project, and my former colleague and good friend Professor Chris Holcomb, of the University of South Carolina, has been a trusted adviser throughout the project, as have my colleagues in rhetoric at Texas A&M, Professors Valerie Balester, Joanna Gibson, and Jan Swearingen. For support both monetary and moral, I thank my department head Paul Parrish and former department head Larry Mitchell. My wife and frequent coauthor Jacqueline S. Palmer read the first draft of the manuscript and offered important suggestions, as did our daughter Myrth Killingsworth.

At Southern Illinois University Press, acting editorial director Karl Kageff and the excellent staff, as well as the two manuscript referees—Professor David J. Tietge of Monmouth University and Professor Stephen H. Browne of Penn State—provided outstanding encouragement and good advice in making the book a reality. This is my second book with SIU Press, so I am doubly grateful.

A somewhat different version of chapter 1 appears as "Rhetorical Appeals: A Revision" in a recent issue of *Rhetoric Review*. I thank the editor, Theresa Enos, and Erlbaum Publishing for permission to reprint.

Appeals in
Modern
Rhetoric

1 ▸ A General Introduction to Rhetorical Appeals

This book develops a model of appeals that draws upon the rhetorical tradition but also reinterprets it for contemporary uses. The model applies to a wide range of rhetorical situations and includes all forms of discourse: speech, writing, "body language," electronic broadcasts, and symbolic actions such as protests and terrorism. It covers artistic productions such as feature films and "creative writing" as well as the usual objects of rhetorical study—political speeches, sermons, legal briefs, academic arguments, and advertising.

My claim is that the most common starting place for studying these forms and situations in courses like freshman composition—the study of formal systems of argument, such as those of Aristotle, Toulmin, and Rogers—ends up being a long diversion from the actual work of rhetorical analysis and practice. We can get into the work faster, with no loss of intellectual rigor, by teasing out the meanings of such expressions as "appeal to an audience," "the appeal to Nature," or "the film's appeal" as they are used in ordinary language. Then we can link those implications to rhetorical concepts that lend them new interpretive and productive power.

The Model

The model I'm proposing involves at least four elements—three positions and a medium of exchange. The three positions are

- the position of the *author* (or agent of production),
- the position of the *audience* (the reader, viewer, user, judge, jury),
- a position of *value* to which the author refers (such as economic well-being, moral goodness, physical health, spiritual enlightenment, family attachment, community solidarity, amusement and diversion, anything that has worth or *value* in one's life).

Authors communicate to an audience through a *medium* such as spoken language, writing, radio, television, or e-mail, working indirectly by appealing to the position of value. Successful appeals *move* the audience, the result of which is the alignment of the three positions.

The best place to get a purchase on appeals is probably not the classical fountainhead of Aristotle's *Rhetoric*, with its famous notion of the three appeals—ethos (appeal to character), logos (appeal to reason), and pathos (appeal to feeling). This notion dominates most discussions of appeals found in rhetoric textbooks, but it tends to categorize before it defines. It gives us the three appeals before giving a definition of the general concept of appeal. In fact, Aristotle's "appeals" may not be appeals at all as we define the term in ordinary language these days. The most literal translation of the concept that links ethos, pathos, and logos in Aristotle's system is not "appeal" but rather "mode of persuasion" or "means of persuasion," or simply "proof."[1]

In the everyday world of television news, courtroom interchange, and commercial discourse, "appeal" means one of two things:

1. *Appeal* can mean "to plead one's case," usually before a higher authority. We can thus appeal to the Supreme Court, for example—or in a more metaphysical vein, we can appeal to Nature, to God, or to some other supreme being.

2. *Appeal* can mean "to please," as when a product appeals to a customer, or a person appeals to a lover: product appeal or sex appeal.

In ordinary language, to appeal thus means *to plead* or *to please*. Consider the original meanings of the two key terms:

1. *To plead* derives from the Old French word for "to go to law or sue," and to a related term in Latin for "that which is agreed upon, a decision, or decree."[2]

2. *To please* is derived from the Latin term for "pleasing" or "agreeable" and a related term meaning "to calm" or "to soothe."

The Indo-European root for all these words points to an interesting meaning: "to be calm (as of the flat sea)."

Etymologically, then, to appeal to an audience—whether to plead or to please—means to promote agreement or harmony, to smooth the waters between author and audience or any two positions. The slight distinction I'm making between "author and audience" and "any two positions" is important. An appeal is always directed to an audience in some sense, but one interesting thing about appeals is that they tend to proceed indirectly toward their goal. Thus when the poet says that the very skies cry out at an offense against the hero, we have an appeal to Nature that the ideal audience will find appealing. If an accused thief says, "As God is my witness, I did not do it," the appeal to the higher power is meant to sway the audience of police or jury. In these cases, the appeal goes toward the audience by way of the third position, God or Nature. The author is trying to align the three positions: the author's position, the position of authority or value, and the audience's position.

This triadic quality of appeals—the attempt to align the three positions—is also suggested by the nautical imagery within the etymology of "plead" and "please"—the part about calming the seas—which in turn resonates in a special way with one strand in the etymology of the word *appeal* itself:

> appeal (v.) - early 14c., from Anglo-Fr. apeler "to call upon, accuse," from L. appellare "to accost," iterative of appellere "to prepare," from ad- "to" + pellere "to beat, drive," probably a metaphoric extension of a nautical term for "driving a ship toward a particular landing." (Harper)

The act of navigation, implied in driving a ship into port, depends upon *triangulation*. Sailors navigate by the stars. The ship goes from launch to landing, but the direction is guided by the stars. Appeals go from author to audience but their success may well be determined by some association the author forms with a third entity, the metaphorical equivalent of the stars. When the accused criminal says "as God is my witness," the appeal goes toward the audience by way of the higher power. An appeal generally follows such a triangulating path, at least in its basic form.

When Kenneth Burke claims in *A Rhetoric of Motives* that rhetoric is founded upon the act of identification, he hints at the triangulating movement of the appeal. In Burke's example, a politician claims to have grown up as a farmer when he addresses an audience of farmers. He appeals to the common ground (sub-stance) of past experience in order to close the distance between himself and the people he seeks to please. Appeals always involve such acts of transformation and substitution. The politician becomes a farmer for the moment; or he substitutes an image of the farm boy from days past for the present image of the politician that stands before the eyes of the farmers. The identification depends upon the power of the appeal to close the distance.

Another tack would call for the politician to appeal not to the present condition of the farmers but to what they lack—power, that is. The politician thus aligns himself with the powers of the state capital and appeals to the audience by virtue of his association not with them but with what they need or desire. The farmers live out their yearning for power by allowing the politician to substitute for (or represent) them.

The metaphor of triangulation made its way into the methodology of the social sciences and came back to rhetoric and composition via ethnography. The methodology is nearly as popular in recent composition studies as it is in anthropology. The ethnographer who goes into the native village (or a composition class in an inner-city university) must find ways to corroborate testimony. What one villager says must be triangulated against what others say in the same site or in similar sites reported in the professional literature. To make a valid argument, the researcher must create dozens of appeals, all of which involve such triangulation. The whole activity roughly corresponds to the work of a sailor who plots a series of courses that leads the ship into the desired port.

Equally important in this navigational metaphor is the idea of motion. In some ways, the author, the person making the appeal, must move toward the audience, whether in identifying with what the audience is (farmers, as in our previous example) or with what the audience desires (power, in the same example). In navigating by way of common ground or desire, the author moves towards the audience; but this motion must be reciprocal. The audience must recognize and respond to the appeal, the point of triangulation. What is rhetoric, after all, but an attempt to move someone (in the Ciceronian sense of *movere*), either to incite people to action or to inspire a shift in attitude or position?

Also implied in the navigational metaphor is the notion of moving through something and the idea of resistance. Authors and audiences occupy stances or positions and must be set into motion against the resistance of inertia. The very medium of movement—the sea that must be navigated—increases resistance. In our metaphor, the place of the sea is taken by the medium of communication. We appeal through a medium.

We can think of the medium in all the ways made possible by contemporary theory. There is language, for example, the medium of communication that must be smoothed for easy passage or energized to motivate (in the literal sense of "motivate"—to set in motion).

Medium also implies contexts of various kinds—textual, social, historical, cultural—a virtual sea of channels, genres, forms, manners, mores, expectations, typologies, myths, habits, and patterns of all kinds that must be negotiated. Our farm-going politician may not be able to use the language of the political specialist or the lawyer to make his appeal as a farmer among farmers but must immerse himself in the colloquial, though he does so at the risk of appearing fake. He must appeal through the stereotype of the politician that the farmers in the audience surely apply to him. The old farm boy must shine through the current mask of the politician with his white-toothed smile and tailored suit. If the farmers cannot see that star through the fog of the political climate, they will not venture onto the sea.

One more point about the medium bears mentioning. What I am calling a medium is often modeled as a boundary or an obstacle. According to this view, linguistic and cultural differences are problems that must be overcome. An advertiser, for example, might appeal to some general bio-logical or human need in an effort to sway the broadest possible audience. So it is that Marshall McLuhan says advertising is the science of man em-bracing woman: the appeal to the widest possible experience (most people experience sexual desire and hunger, after all, since everyone lives in a body) is the best way to sell products because it casts the widest net. But the advertiser employing such appeals must either count on failing with a portion of the audience—the segment of the Christian or Islamic popula-tion, for example, who might find appeals to sex offensive—or count on the power of the appeal to break through such resistance. Unlike the con-cept of boundaries, the idea of media is grounded in the notion that lin-guistic and cultural differences are persistent and pervasive. They are never overcome so much as they are worked through.

An Example from Cultural Criticism

What have we got so far? Our etymological and metaphorical analysis sug-gests that appeals follow a triadic path. They are directed from an author to an audience by way of a position of value. The aim is to align the three positions—author, audience, and value. The success of the appeal depends upon the approach of the author to the audience (guided by common val-ues) and the reciprocal movement of the audience toward the author. Such a movement always takes place through a medium—language certainly but also contextual elements that include a wide range of social, cultural, and historical factors.

Consider an example: a paragraph from a chapter called "The Ecologi-cal Crisis as a Crisis of Character" from Wendell Berry's book *The Unset-tling of America: Culture and Agriculture* (1977). We can guess from the title that Berry is arguing that we can trace what's wrong with the envi-ronment to some qualities of human character that modern people tend to accept without question. One of these is professional specialization:

> The disease of the modern character is specialization. Looked at from the standpoint of the social *system*, the aim of specialization may seem desirable enough. The aim is to see that the responsibilities of government, law, medicine, engineering, agriculture, education, etc., are given into the hands of the most skilled, best prepared people. The difficulties do not appear until we look at specialization from the opposite standpoint—that of individual persons. We then begin to see the grotesquery—indeed, the impossibility—of an idea of com-munity wholeness that divorces itself from any idea of personal wholeness. (19)

Berry is appealing to our sense of ourselves as total individuals in an effort to shake us out of our identities as specialists, professionals, experts in one narrow field of human endeavor. He is writing from the position of the individual defined as a whole person to the position of a person defined by a function served within the system of modern life: doctor, lawyer, college professor, engineer, or computer scientist. When Americans are asked what they do, they give their profession. Berry is arguing that this professionalist view of life is damaging to our sense of ourselves and our sense of community.

So the paragraph defines two clear positions: the holistic community with its representative, the author; and the fragmenting system with its presumed representative, the reader. Now the author must appeal to a third position of value. It must be something whose value is accepted by both the author and reader, despite their differences.

The third position of value that Berry appeals to is health—physical health and emotional health. The word *health* comes from the same Old English root as the words *well* and *whole*. To be healthy is to be whole. Wellness is wholeness. In the King James Version of the Christian Bible, a person who experiences miraculous healing is said to be "made whole."

Berry appeals to the reader's desire for health by playing on the related idea of wholeness. The appeal ideally draws the reader away from the fragmenting system and toward the holistic community. The promise is that you can be a whole person and not just a partial system function if you join the community. The system on the other hand makes you sick by making you specialized: "The disease of the modern character is specialization." It makes one part of you swell with importance—the part of you that is a doctor, or a neurosurgeon; a professor, or an expert on the literature of male writers from 1880–1895—while the rest of you shrinks and atrophies. Swelling indicates illness, as does shrinking and atrophy. The system also separates you from other people, as if you needed to be quarantined because of your sickness; that's the suggestion of the last sentence with its reference to divorce, which everybody knows is rampant in modern life. Sickness and divorce—both of which are characteristic troubles (if not evils) of modern life—beset people in the system. Perhaps the alternative community has a chance to make them well, to make them whole—whole persons in whole communities. The author charts his course toward the audience, sailing by the star of personal health, and if the appeal works, the audience rows out to meet him.

While the author is the prophet or advocate of the holistic community, he nevertheless retains his identity as a separate individual. Theoretically we can find his view of the world appealing even if we don't find the author a particularly appealing person. Many readers find Wendell Berry himself a little too cranky; others question his attitudes about gender and race. He uses risky language that sometimes shocks the reader and may offend some audiences. He writes, for example, "If we began by making niggers of people, we have ended by making a nigger of the world" (12). The very use of the word *nigger* (instead of something like *slave*) will likely seem offensive, especially coming from the pen of a white Southern writer like Berry. Along the same lines, we might be inclined to agree with Berry's points about the value of small farming communities until we learn that he grows tobacco; or we might admire his refusal to use computers in his writing until we learn that his wife does all his typing for him (a sort of human computer).

But Berry is not speaking to us as a perfect embodiment of the community, only a representative. Likewise, we as readers are not perfect embodiments of the fragmenting system he attacks but representatives of it, as much victims as beneficiaries. If the appeal succeeds, our position will be aligned with the author's by the time we finish reading. We will join him under the banner of the holistic community. Taking up that position does not mean we will move to Kentucky, quit our jobs to become tobacco farmers, sell our computers and make our spouses type our papers. We will not become Wendell Berry. But we will begin to reinterpret our own lives according to new ways of seeing that share something with Wendell Berry's worldview.

An Example from Popular Cinema

Consider a related example: the popular science fiction film *The Matrix*. The film shares with Berry's essay the sense of conflict between community and system. It dramatizes the conflict by having machines rule the system—the matrix, that is—and having human beings in charge of the underground community, known as Zion. A similar pattern, people versus machines, appears in the *Terminator* films and in many other examples in the sci-fi genre.[3]

The images of modern life that appear in *The Matrix*, the scenes in a corporate office building or on the streets of the big city, the images that viewers can relate directly to their own lives, turn out to be generated by the matrix and its machine masters. Human beings have these images fed into their brains. They dream them in effect while in real life they are kept alive in glass tubes and made to generate the energy that keeps the machines running. They have been reduced from whole people to energy slaves. The film's hero, named Neo, is rescued from the matrix by the Zion people and made to see the plight of humanity as it really is.

An interesting thing about the film—and about imaginative fiction in general, whether in cinematic or print form—is that it both dramatizes rhetorical events and creates them. In other words, it works on two levels. On one level, the Zion people appeal to Neo; the characters engage in rhetoric. On another level, the film's creators appeal to the audience. Usually the two levels work in parallel. That is, the audience members gradually come to a new understanding of their world as the characters learn to see and act differently. So Neo at first resists the idea that his office job and his apartment and everything about his life except his lowest bodily functions, his breathing and metabolism, take place within a computer-generated illusion. As we watch Neo come to accept the truth, we may awaken to a truth of our own: we live in what amounts to a computer-generated world, we're always "plugged in," our lives are "governed" by machines, and so on. As Neo comes to find the fleshy, funky, earthy world of the Zion people preferable to living a clean, bright lie within the matrix, so we might too begin to look around for alternatives in our own world.

Of course, we the viewers would be justified in feeling a surge of irony when we notice that we are sitting in a dark theatre watching a media event as we come to this realization. We are plugged in, mediated, under the spell of the film. The recognition of irony might make us question the intent of the filmmakers. While the Zion people appeal to a position of value that favors flesh-and-blood immediacy and communities of whole people, perhaps we are being guided toward a different Zion under a different set of values. The movie theatre itself may be our Zion, our way of escaping the pressures of the life outside in the matrix of professional life. The community we escape to becomes the companions who join us in the dark theatre and the fictional characters on the screen who do what we cannot do— escape the matrix to perform heroic deeds. The value that guides us, to which the filmmakers appeal, is the sense of release, the relief that art and entertainment promise to the overworked, stressed-out denizens of the modern world.

Art always works on multiple levels in this way. In the next chapter, we will consider how appeals tend to multiply and become complex even in nonfiction and seemingly straightforward writing.

Advertising and Rhetorical Risk

Before going on to complexity, though, let's take a quick look at texts that work—or fail to work—using relatively simple appeals. The best examples come from advertising. In fact, one of the first times I ever remember hearing the word *appeal* as I am using it now was as a young boy watching TV.

An ad campaign for a certain toothpaste in those days promised that the product would enhance buyers' "sex appeal." The ads definitely got my attention. I can still remember them these many years later. I can't remember the brand name, perhaps because so many companies followed the lead

of the first one and used an appeal to sex in their ads. Cigarette companies certainly did so, as well as auto makers and just about everybody else.

The structure of this appeal is very simple and clear, but the direction
of the appeal is anything but straightforward. The toothpaste company
occupies the author position; the TV viewer, the audience position. The
company has toothpaste to sell; viewers need to care for their teeth but
are faced with many choices about which brand to buy. All brands con-
tain more or less the same ingredients and have the same claims to effectiveness. Dental health would seem to occupy the third position of value,
and indeed some companies do appeal in that direction. Nine of out ten
dentists recommend Product X, we are told; or Product Y performed better than other products in extensive tests. Other companies distinguish
themselves by virtue of slightly varying ingredients: some fancy scientific
name for an additive—something like "xonathiamine"—may distinguish
Product X from the run of the mill; baking soda in Product Y nostalgically
appeals to old-fashioned home remedies. But Product Z decides to bypass
the whole health issue. It creates an appeal to an altogether different position of value: sex.

It is fair to ask whether toothpaste has anything to do with sex at all.
On the one hand, it hardly seems sexy to think about cleaning food from
between your teeth and polishing off plaque and coffee stains. On the other
hand, sweet breath and shiny teeth have traditionally been associated with
physical beauty (at least in a Euro-American culture). Shiny, healthy teeth
also suggest youth and prosperity. Old people lose their teeth or have sour
breath; so do poor people who suffer from disease and bad nutrition.

To capitalize (literally) on these associations, the toothpaste ads show
lovely, young, prosperous-looking men and women whose gleaming teeth
occupy the central focus of my television screen. I'm looking at them,
without the least hint of doubt that these people have sex appeal. Some-
where in the back of my mind, the voice of reason is saying that no matter what toothpaste I use, I will never be as sexy as these people. But by
the time reason has whispered, the ad has already done its work. It has
insinuated itself into my mental life and perhaps left a mark on my unconscious mind, so that the next time I go to the store, I will reach for the
"sex appeal" brand without quite knowing why I am doing it.

The act of substituting a new position of value for a more obvious one
works like a metaphor. Instead of saying "love is an emotion pleasant but
sometimes painful," for example, we might use a metaphor: "love is a rose;
it brings beauty into our lives, but also thorny troubles." Instead of saying
"Product Z promotes dental health," we can say, "Product Z gives you sex
appeal." It is not lying to make this kind of substitution even though love

is not a rose in the strictest sense and toothpaste has precious little to do with your sex appeal. The rose does share some attributes with love, and clean teeth can help with your personal relationships on a superficial level. The rose metaphor creates appeal by substituting something sensual and concrete for something abstract and vague ("an emotion pleasant but sometimes painful") while the "sex appeal" angle in the ad capitalizes on the slight claim that clean teeth have on sexual attraction while setting aside the question of dental health. Most people would rather not think too much about dental health anyway. It has painful associations with the dentist's office, all that drilling and bloody cotton.

The idea of having "an angle" is an important one. "What's the angle?" people ask about both advertising and feature stories in the newspaper. A journalist, for example, might approach a story about a new scientific discovery by talking about its impact on cancer patients or by focusing on the scientists' personalities or by looking at the history of science. Each angle, each shift of perspective, will create a different kind of appeal. The angle amounts to the same thing that political commentators call "spin."

"Angle" and "spin" are popular terms for interpretation. You create a certain interpretation of events or concepts that will create the most positive associations in the mind of your public—or the most negative associations if you are trying to undermine an enemy's position. The terms are highly suggestive for a theory of appeals because they hint toward the idea of direction.

Appeals always involve direction and usually indirection. They say, "Don't look there; look here," or "Look here but also look there." They tend to focus and limit an audience's attention or direct it in some new way. The toothpaste ad says, "Don't think about the dentist; think about your sex life." *The Matrix* says, "Don't worry about the pressures of your life out in the real world; lose yourself in the dark fantasy world of the theatre." Wendell Berry says, "The environmental crisis is not so much (or not only) a problem of bad air and big machines; it is a problem of modern character. We might not be able to fix the air and water alone, but we can work on ourselves."

What the concept of direction adds to our model is this: When an author appeals to a position of value, it is always one among many possible appeals. Choosing one possibility over another creates risk, and rhetoric is always risky. One reason that authors develop complex appeals involves an attempt to minimize risk, as we shall see in the next chapter.

2 ► Appeals to Authority and Evidence

The best appeals are never simple. The more complex they become, the more "academic" they seem. I mean "academic" in the good sense—they are more likely to be accepted among experts and specialists in the university community; and "academic" in the bad sense—they begin to lose their effectiveness among audiences of educated nonspecialists, the general public, the traditional audience of rhetoric. Complex appeals tend to make a case "air tight" and intellectually rigorous, but they can also overwhelm or simply bore the audience. In making choices about how complex to make appeals, the writer always run risks.

The question is, what kind of risk can the writer afford to run? Academic authors generally accept the risk of boring or even alienating the general public in an attempt to increase the chance that a special audience—an audience of insiders—will accept the argument. They do so both by increasing the number of appeals and by appealing to authorities recognized as carrying weight with the insider audience. The way insider audiences communicate with each other and then reach outward to external audiences has engaged the attention of modern rhetorical scholars who have extended the limits of the traditional range of rhetoric with works on the rhetoric of science, engineering, economics, and other academic disciplines.[1]

Also known as "discourse communities" in modern rhetoric, insider audiences are not always academic. Religious communities, special interest groups, regional affiliations, and lifestyle enclaves of all kinds have their special ways of communicating. Much of the difference between appeals to academic audiences and nonacademic audiences comes down to questions about authority and evidence.

Authorities—Absolute and Otherwise

Consider religious discourse. One of the reasons that teachers of first-year composition and public speaking courses groan inwardly (if not outwardly) every time a student proposes to discuss religion has to do with the problem of authority. If a Christian preacher, for example, wants to convince his congregation of a point—let's make it controversial and say the preacher is a man who wants to argue that women should submit to their husbands in marriage—he cites the authority of the Bible. As an author, he takes the position of the unrelenting Christian confronting an audience of slightly more worldly believers. The position of value to which he appeals is represented by the Bible, which he and his audience accept as the Word of God even if the audience has been somewhat swayed by the tendency of the general culture to accept equality between the sexes. If he wants to make his case air tight, he increases the number of references to the position of women, drawing on Old Testament and New Testament and ranging over many different books within the holy text, and then asserts his confidence by challenging the audience to find contrary examples.

The congregation certainly qualifies as an insider audience. The distance between the position of the author and the position of the audience remains fairly small. The preacher worries that his congregation is drifting out of alignment, becoming worldly, so his sermon is directed to bringing the people back into line. It is all about realignment. It is easy to find a position of value to which to appeal. Insiders agree in advance about what counts as an authority. In Christianity, it's the Bible; in Islam, the Koran; in Buddhism, the sutras; and so on. In secular communities, absolute authorities would include the king (in feudal societies) or the law (in republics).

But outside the given community, the agreed-upon authority must compete with other authorities. The Bible is one book among many, or at best, one holy book among many. When students in a college rhetoric class try to argue that wives should submit to their husbands, they better base their arguments on something more than the Bible. They better develop appeals that work for people who are not committed Christians, who may even despise the Bible and what it stands for. If they don't, they will be dismissed as members of a closed circle of insiders, perhaps even religious fanatics. One key to the public view of the Bible is how it gets used metaphorically—as when somebody says of an instruction manual, "That's the mechanic's bible"—or how it gets used ironically, as when somebody says of a friend who's obsessed with a favorite novel, "That book is her bible, I swear." The metaphors suggest the possibility of many bibles, the multiplication of authorities in modern society; the ironic use suggests the association of holy books with fanaticism, the weakening of authorities in the public view.

In attending to how authorities multiply, weaken, and compete in modern cultures, with all the diversity and special interests, modern rhetoric differs from classical and medieval rhetoric. The question of how to make appeals becomes much more situational; that is, it depends upon which group an author is trying to reach. Audience and situation must be constantly reviewed (see chapter 3). Any single authority will not necessarily carry the weight it carries for an inside audience.

One mistake modern advocates of Christianity often make is to argue as if some secular authority, such as the ever-controversial Charles Darwin, has replaced the Bible. The problem is that Darwin is not an abso-lute authority among scientifically minded people. Darwinian theory is under constant review and adjustment. The late Mr. Darwin himself would hardly recognize what has become of his theory. Moreover, if a better theory comes along, one that more completely explains the facts, scien-tists may well abandon even the much-revised and rewritten theory of evolution. A scientific argument by definition is "falsifiable." The author must be willing to state the terms that would show his claims to be wrong and accept defeat if an opponent can meet those terms by producing the contrary evidence.[2]

Modern rhetoric does not so much replace one authority with another; rather it attacks the very idea of absolute authority. People who use rhetoric don't have to be atheists or moral relativists, but they must realize that the constraints on how we discuss issues are different as we move from com-munity to community, audience to audience. I may well be a Christian, but I can't hope to sway unbelievers by quoting the Bible. The one exception has to do with belief itself. St. Augustine, among other great preachers, recognized that preaching often succeeds by proclamation rather than by persuasion. If the hearts of the listeners are prepared, a mere telling of the Gospel will bring them to belief. If their hearts are hard, no amount of persuasion will work.[3] In this light, broadcasting the Bible makes good sense; it brings in new believers hungry for revelation. But using the Bible as an absolute authority for the purposes of drawing an audience to a position that the audience has already categorized as secular—the posi-tion of women in society, for example—is pointless.

Rhetoric does not always ask you to convert, to transform your entire being. Sometimes it is only about adjusting your position to find common ground with someone who is different from you. It is about working through differences rather than making another person into someone just like you. It is about softening the hearts of listeners and turning them to new ways of seeing, opening them to new ideas. In a world beset by con-flicting attitudes, sometimes maintained with great violence and aggres-sion, rhetoric can open a window of hope for a more peaceful commun-ion—or it can join the fray and engage opponents in verbal combat.

Evidence as a Substitute for Authority

Not only books and people have authority; facts do, too. If I say that I think my department head has betrayed me by giving a bad report of my work to the Dean, and then I'm shown a letter that the department head sent to the Dean praising me, then I ought to acknowledge that I was wrong and behaving with unwarranted suspicion. The letter has authority as evi-dence. If someone tells me that our friend Joe is selfish and has no social conscience, and I reply that I saw him working the soup line at the local mission, my observation has enough authority to make the other person reconsider that position (even if that person doesn't abandon it and remain skeptical, arguing for example that Joe hypocritically expands his own ego by working at the soup kitchen).

Evidence works best in quantity. Say I'm on a hike one day with my scientifically educated wife, and she shows me a male lizard bobbing its head in the presence of a female and tells me that this act is part of a mating ritual. As a nonscientist, I might be satisfied with the explanation. I accept her as an authority. But the insider audience of other scientists would want much more evidence—more field observations, references to the observations of other scientists reported in the literature, and perhaps even laboratory reenactments of the mating scene. They want data, evidence in quantity, arranged in tables and charts. Each data point in a scientific argument is a point of appeal. With each replication of the first observation, we get a new triangulation. Numbers matter in modern rhetoric.

Evidence developed in this way serves a function for scientific audiences similar to the function that absolute authorities like the Bible or the Koran serve in religious communities. One thing that absolute authority and evidence compiled as data have in common is that they tend to lose power when used with outsiders. For an audience of nonspecialists, data can seem overly abstract, distant from ordinary experience. Depending on the audience, the fact that the number of alcohol-related deaths on county roads rose from twenty-two to thirty-three last year might have less impact than the story of a high-school couple killed on the way to their senior prom by a drunk driver. In this particular case, we could give both the number and the story and increase the effectiveness among different members of the general audience. But the more complex the numerical facts and the analysis of data become, the less likely it will be that the general audience will stay with the argument.

Appeals to absolute authority and appeals to data have a common interest in creating air-tight cases. The doubt of inside audiences fades with the careful application of a method—the appeal to absolute authorities or to evidence; and with quantity—multiple references to the authority or overwhelming evidence. We say the case is air-tight or incontrovertible when the ability of the audience to cite conflicting authorities or produce equally convincing evidence gets taken away.

In classical times, such cases were generally considered to be outside the range of rhetoric. Rhetoric was said to simplify discourse for an audience of nonspecialists. Aristotle, for example, taught that arguments for academic audiences involved the systematic logic of deduction (reasoning from general principles to specific cases) and induction (reasoning from specific data to general conclusions), which followed highly elaborate rules and conditions. In the public forum, according to Aristotle, simplified versions would work: a kind of informal deduction (called "enthymeme") based on assumptions rather than formal deduction, and the use of examples rather than huge mounds of data for induction. If I wanted to convince an audience that a female colleague of mine should have been promoted when she was in fact denied promotion, for example, I might argue that if she had been a man, things would have been different. The assumption contained in my thesis (an enthymeme) is that men are typically favored over women in our society. Instead of proving my point by compiling all the data about promotions and men and women in the university, I might cite only one example of another colleague, a man, who was promoted with a similar record as the woman who was denied promotion. The argument would probably not hold up in court, and it certainly would not work in an sociological study of discrimination, but it might make university officials stop and reconsider their position.

In the classical view, rhetoric applies only to cases that cannot be solved authoritatively or scientifically. Rhetoric by definition has to do with things we argue about, not with cases that can be made air-tight. Modern rhetoric objects to this view, however, by rejecting the implication that decisions reached by science and systematic logic are necessarily different from decisions made more informally. What happens in court when we have conflicting positions taken by expert witnesses, for example, both of whom claim to have air-tight cases based on scientifically generated data? Modern rhetoric has ventured into specialized discourse communities and has found that the pull and push of appeals takes place there as well as in public forums. Theologians and scientists argue over the interpretation of authorities and data constantly. And wherever we have interpretation, we have rhetoric and its characteristic action of appealing.

One problem with the study of rhetoric in academic science and other insider communities is that, like the fields it studies, it grows technical and specialized rather rapidly. For that reason, this book, the purpose of which is to open an introductory path into rhetoric, will steer clear of advanced work in such areas as rhetoric of science and technical communication. We will mainly follow the trend of classical rhetoric in looking at examples intended primarily for a general audience, educated citizens considering topics outside their own fields of expertise. Almost every educated person in modern life is some kind of specialist or a member of some insider community. Even so, everybody must also communicate externally to people without the same background, a diverse and sometimes global population of readers. The aim of general rhetoric is to open the access to communication as widely as possible without compromising the message. Even when the writer works within a specialized discourse community, aiming for the widest access is a good idea. Like everybody else, specialized readers appreciate a lucid and fluent style and a navigable text that motivates as well as it informs.

Expert Writing that Reaches Beyond an Insider Audience

A good example of an expert essay that seeks an outside audience while still appealing to the kinds of authority and evidence approved within the discourse community is "Bowling Alone: America's Declining Social Capital," a study in political sociology. Written by Harvard professor Robert D. Putnam and published in the January 1995 issue of *Journal of Democracy*, it is a review article; that is, like the research papers undergraduates are often required to write in English classes, it doesn't report original research but surveys the published literature on a specific topic and offers an original interpretation of the evidence reported by others—a new slant, an angle, a "spin" on the evidence.

The topic of the article is "civic engagement," the participation of citizens in American democracy. Putnam begins by establishing the historical validity and currency of the idea that effective democracy and economic well-being depend upon citizen participation in such activities as voting, attendance at public meetings, and membership in clubs and organizations. For historical validity, Putnam appeals to the long-standing authority of Alexis de Tocqueville, whose famous book *Democracy in America* presented the observations of an insightful European commentator visiting the United States in the 1830s, when the young nation was seen as an early experiment in modern democracy. Tocqueville, whose influential work set an agenda for studies in history and the social sciences over several generations, argued that the American propensity to form and join organizations undergirded the social structure and provided a key outlet for democratic participation. To suggest the currency of the idea, Putnam shows how modern research continues to confirm Tocqueville's insight:

> Recently, American social scientists of a neo-Tocquevillean bent have unearthed a wide range of empirical evidence that the quality of public life and the performance of social institutions (and not only in America) are indeed powerfully influenced by norms and networks of social engagement. Researchers in such fields as education, urban poverty, unemployment, the control of crime and drug abuse, and even health have discovered that successful outcomes are more likely

in civically engaged communities. Similarly, research on the varying economic attainments of different ethnic groups in the United States has demonstrated the importance of social bonds within each group. These results are consistent with research in a wide range of settings that demonstrates the vital importance of social networks for job placement and many other economic outcomes. (199)

Putnam thus goes well beyond the authority of Tocqueville in building his case, adding authority with the mention of each study that confirms the main point. In the passage just quoted and in what follows, Putnam arranges the new authorities by subtopic and research specialization ("Researchers in such fields as education," "the sociology of economic development," the study of government, and so on). Part of his work is to step back a little, and while still maintaining his identity as a specialized researcher in the social sciences (an identity he establishes by footnoting his earlier, more specialized work), he takes a broader-than-usual look at related fields, expanding his field of vision beyond his own specialization of political science. He supports his general summaries with footnotes that list representative sources. One footnote cites nine different expert sources, most of which summarize even smaller studies that, taken together, include thousands of data points supporting their arguments. Again, numbers are important in modern rhetoric. Tocqueville still carries weight, but he must be updated and confirmed by recent studies carried out according to the norms of modern professional researchers. Authorities must be marshaled like armies.

Facts must also be marshaled. Putnam cites specific data from his sources, particularly information developed in surveys and polls, and presents it selectively but engagingly in such passages as the following:

- Among the college-educated, the average number of group memberships per person fell from 2.8 to 2.0 (a 26-percent decline); among high-school graduates, the number fell from 1.8 to 1.2 (32 percent); and among those with fewer than 12 years of education, the number fell from 1.4 to 1.1 (25 percent). In other words, at *all* educational (and hence social) levels of American society, and counting *all* groups memberships, *the average number of associational memberships has fallen by about a fourth over the last quarter-century.* (207–8; his italics)

- The proportion of Americans who socialize with their neighbors more than once a year has slowly but steadily declined over the last two decades, from 72 percent in 1974 to 61 percent in 1993. (208)

- The proportion of Americans saying that most people can be trusted fell by more than a third between 1960, when 58 percent chose that alternative, and 1993, when only 37 percent did. (209)

- [M]embership in . . . "women's" organizations . . . has been virtually halved since the late 1960s. By contrast, most of the decline in men's organizations occurred about ten years later; the total decline to date has been approximately 25 percent for the typical organization. (210)

But the appeal doesn't stop with updating and multiplying authorities or with marshaling evidence. Putnam also appeals to clear positions of value. The central concept of "social capital" represents one point of appeal. Drawing theory from several fields (the range of which is specified in a footnote citing six articles, one by himself), Putnam explains the concept: "By analogy with notions of physical capital and human capital—tools and training that enhance individual productivity—'social capital' refers to features of social organization such as networks, norms, and social trust that facilitate coordination and cooperation for mutual benefit" (200). "For a variety of reasons," he continues, "life is easier in a community blessed with a substantial stock of social capital" (200). By creating the analogy—as money (physical capital) is to individual well-being, so cooperative organization (social capital) is to community well-being—Putnam offers a rhetorical enhancement of his "neo-Tocquevillean" claim that cooperative organizations advance the good of democracy, and he sets up his thesis that "American social capital in the form of civic associations has significantly eroded over the last generation" (208), placing the future of democracy in question. In their spare time—which appears to be shrinking, with both adult members of the household working more and more hours outside the home—Americans seem to prefer to watch TV, attend self-help meetings with like-minded people, and stick close to home rather than voting, going to public meetings, socializing with the neighbors, or joining the P.T.A., the union, and grassroots political organizations. The replacement activities, according to Putnam, fail to replenish the "stock" of "social capital."

This appeal represents a particularly strong example of a position of value because it associates the position with a recognized concept of value—capital, stock, money. Where your treasure is, there will your heart be also. Likewise, the attempt to bring the audience into alignment with the position appeals to a sense of community, something lost or "eroded" in modern life (the metaphor of erosion also appealing to the sense of environmental loss, the erosion of good land and the pollution of water and air, another problem in modern life).

Putnam strongly communicates the sense that the private individual has grown isolated from the communal whole with the odd but memorable treatment of bowling, which unlike baseball or basketball can be played either as a team sport or an individual sport. In a single brief passage, Putnam expands the suggestion of his title that Americans these days prefer to "bowl alone":

> The most whimsical yet discomfiting bit of evidence of social disengagement in contemporary America that I have discovered is this: more Americans are bowling today than ever before, but bowling in organized leagues has plummeted in the last decade or so. Between 1980 and 1993 the total number of bowlers in America increased by 10 percent, while league bowling decreased by 40 percent. (Lest this be thought a wholly trivial example, I should note that nearly 80 million Americans went bowling at least once during 1993, *nearly a third more than voted in the 1994 congressional elections* and roughly the same number as claim to attend church regularly. . . .) The rise of solo bowling threatens the livelihood of bowling-lane proprietors because those who bowl as members of leagues consume three times as much beer and pizza as solo bowlers, and the money in bowling is in the beer and pizza, not the balls and shoes. The broader social significance, however, lies in the social interaction and even occasionally civic conversations over beer and pizza that solo bowlers forgo. Whether or not bowling beats balloting in the eyes of most Americans, bowling teams illustrate yet another vanishing form of social capital. (204–5)

Questioning Authority and Evidence: An Insider Responds

Putnam's article was appealing enough to catch the attention of President Clinton, who invited Putnam to Camp David to discuss the article after it appeared. The president drew upon the professor's ideas for the State of the Union Address in January 1996, in spirit if not in letter. He urged parents to join in the effort to educate their children, for example, by turning off the TV and getting involved in helping with homework and visiting the schools. The entire speech is shot through with appeals to the spirit of community and democratic participation. Big government, Clinton suggests, should yield to broad-based, energetic citizen action.

In accepting Putnam's authority and responding favorably to the appeal to communal values, President Clinton also seems to have accepted the implied position of the audience that "Bowling Alone" addresses—namely, a generation of Americans who cultivate an increasingly isolated private life centered around the nuclear family or tight circles of friends (at most) and who tend to leave the business of government to professionals, to politicians in office and the specialists who fill the offices of schools and other public services. The aim of both the essay and the State of the Union Address is to realign Americans with the old values of broad public participation and community responsibility.

The argument enjoyed a wide appeal but also stirred controversy. Putnam's opponents engaged him at the rhetorical level; that is, they noted the popularity of the argument and then addressed the audience that had likely been drawn to his communitarian position. In a frequently cited essay in the journal the *American Prospect*, "Unsolved Mysteries: The Tocqueville Files," Theda Skocpol undermines the authority of Putnam's essay by several tactics:

- She draws upon historical research to place Tocqueville's authority in question, arguing that he had a "Romantic" outlook on American life that was questioned and widely rejected as early as the end of the nineteenth century.

- She draws upon social science research to question the evidence and methods of Putnam's sources, arguing, for example, that he relies too heavily on one data source with questionable authority— the General Social Survey.

- Finally, she uses her rhetorical and interpretive skills to resist Putnam' appeal. She suggests that Putnam's position rests too heavily on the values of individualism with his choice of organizational memberships and social activities. "Ironically for a scholar who calls for attention to social interconnectedness," she writes, "Putnam works with atomistic concepts and data" and "largely ignores the cross-class and organizational dynamics by which civic associations actually form and persist—or decay and come unraveled" (3–4). She finds a particularly weak place in his treatment of women (and subtly engages her own "natural" authority over her male counterpart). "Consider what happens when better-educated women shift from family and community endeavors into the paid work force," she writes. "As capable women who once devoted energies to the PTA (and similar locally rooted federations) have switched their allegiances to workplaces and national professional groups, PTAs may have become less attractive for other potential members, including housewives" (4).

Skocpol thus suggests that it is not watching too much TV or staying at home that has altered the level of participation in such organizations as the PTA and Lion's Club; rather the way we work and live has altered our values and time commitments in such a way that some groups have become obsolete. Not only the quantity but the quality of participation has altered. While Skocpol accepts Putnam's "broad finding of a generational disjuncture in the associational loyalties of many American adults" (3), she disagrees with the causes and the interpretation of the data.

Skocpol's critique was appealing enough that Putnam and his publishers recruited her as a consultant when he published the book version of his article in 2000. Many of her objections rest on technical claims about the rules of using evidence and data, and her language (as you can see from the samples above: "atomistic concepts," "cross-class and organizational dynamics," "generational disjuncture") likewise reveals her position as a competing specialist—like Putnam, a Harvard political scientist. But she also questions the position of value to which he appeals—the ideal of the person defined as primarily as an individual, relatively free of class and gender identity, who voluntarily joins into the life of the democracy, or doesn't. Skocpol argues that many of the organizations Putnam studies did not thrive only from grassroots support but received strong institutional incentives—"top-down" incentives, such as company sponsorship of bowling teams—which have weakened along with individual participation. Skocpol worries that Putnam's argument enjoys wide appeal because it fits with the conservative trend of the times to remove government support of social services and leave the care of the poor and the sick to individuals, families, private organizations, and competitive business. And indeed, President Clinton's suggestion that "big government" can only do so much bears out Skocpol's warning.

Questioning Authority and Evidence: An Outsider Responds

A less "academic" and more intemperate version of this argument appears in an article published in the *Nation* on April 15, 1996, by the journalist and social critic Katha Pollitt. This article, titled satirically "For Whom the Ball Rolls," begins by explaining Putnam's appeal. "It's the sort of thesis academics and pundits adore," Pollitt writes, "a big wooly argument that's been pre-reduced to a soundbite of genius. Bowling alone—it's wistful, comical, nostalgic, a tiny haiku of post-industrial loneliness" (214). Citing Skocpol's rejoinder, Pollitt immediately begins to tug at the audience won over to Putnam's position, saying in effect to look around and see whom you've been aligned with: "Right-wingers" who like the thesis because "it can be twisted to support their absurd contention that philanthropy has been strangled by big government" and "Clintonians and communitarians" who like it "because it moralizes a middle-class, apolitical civic-mindedness that recognizes no hard class or race inequalities shaping individual choice: We are all equally able to volunteer for the Red Cross, as we are all equally able to vote" (215).

Pollitt attacks Putnam's position as a member of the elite class of "academics and pundits" with devastating irony: "Tenured professors may be too busy to sing in a choir (Putnam's former avocation): the rest of us are just couch potatoes" (215). Next comes the appeal to gender, which Pollitt invokes with gusto:

> Although Putnam is careful to disclaim nostalgia for the fifties, his picture of healthy civic life is remarkably, well, square. I've been a woman all my life, but I've never heard of the Federation of Women's Clubs. And what politically minded female, in 1996, would join the bland and matronly League of Women Voters, when she could volunteer with Planned Parenthood or NOW or Concerned Women of America, and shape the debate instead of merely keeping it polite? (215)

Pollitt's implication is partly methodological—that Putnam's sources focus on dying organizations rather than newer and more vibrant groups—but the cutting edge of her argument is rhetorical: Putnam's position is out of touch with what's going on right now; his outlook *is* nostalgic, in spite of his objections, and favors a social structure that has been eroded by the women's movement and by the entrance of women into the workplace. His argument neglects the poor and racially diverse and the working people of America who fail to join civic organizations not because they are busy watching TV but because every member of the household has to work, sometimes several jobs, to make ends meet or because the organizations are basically elitist, racist, and sexist. Even if most people had the time, they wouldn't join the worn-out organizations that Putnam studies; they would probably have more use for therapeutic groups like the "self-help" and twelve-step programs that, according to Pollitt, Putnam is too quick to dismiss.

While Skocpol engages Putnam politely as a member of the insider audience of political scientists (even while writing in a journal that allows her to court a wider audience), Pollitt takes him on as an outsider contemptuous of his supposed expertise. She goes for the rhetorical heart of his essay, the image of "bowling alone" with her title that parodies the famous saying of the English Renaissance poet John Donne: "Any man's death diminishes me, because I am involved in mankind; and therefore never send to know for whom the bell tolls; it tolls for thee" (316). The parody of Donne's elegiac phrasing—with its mournful rhetoric and its theme of human solidarity—allows her to deal ironically in "For Whom the Ball Rolls" with the suggestion that league bowling is good for the whole democracy:

> Putnam treats [the bowling leagues] as if they arose merely from the appetite of individuals for fellowship and tenpins. But in fact they

came out of specific forms of working-class and lower-middle-class life: stable blue-collar or office employment (businesses and unions often started and sponsored teams) that fostered group solidarity, a marital ethos that permitted husbands plenty of boys' nights out, a lack of cultural and entertainment alternatives. It would be amazing if league bowling survived the passing of the way of life that brought it into being, nor am I so sure we need to mourn it. People still bowl, after all. In fact they bowl more than ever, although they consume less beer and pizza, which is why league decline bothers the owners of bowling alleys. And despite Putnam's title, they don't bowl alone. They bowl with friends, on dates, with their kids, with other families. The bowling story could be told as one of happy progress: from a drink-sodden night of spouse avoidance with the same old faces from work to temperate and spontaneous fun with one's intimate friends and relations. (215–16)

"Love your neighbor if you can," Pollitt concludes, "but forget civic trust. What we need is more civic skepticism. Especially about people who want you to do their bowling for them" (216). She speaks with the temper of modern rhetoric. She has the confidence of a citizen who has claimed the right to speak regardless of her pedigree and credentials. She is confident and educated—see the reference to the great poet (Donne) and the assertion of her freedom to choose among the purveyors of expert discourse (in this case choosing Skocpol over Putnam). She is skeptical about evidence and other people's interpretations, and she is caustically suspicious of authority, an attitude that comes through in a remark about religion: "If church membership is down (good news in my book), it's hardly because people are staying home to watch TV. More likely, organized religion doesn't speak to their spiritual needs the way (for example) self-help programs do" (216).

Whatever you may think about this kind of contempt for authority, it is a force to deal with in modern rhetoric. Nothing is sacred. No authority is absolute, no evidence free from questions and counterexamples. Interpretation is the way of the world, and crafting effective appeals is the way you bring people to your side and stimulate cooperative action.

3 ▸ Rhetorical Situations

Chapter 2 noted that the emphasis of modern rhetoric differs from classical rhetoric in attending to how authorities multiply and compete and how appeals become much more situational. We need to qualify that statement a bit. Rhetoric has been situational from the start. It is always deeply contextual in its references to people, time, place, and action. The difference has to do with the degree of change from situation to situation and the consequent need for adjustment.

Because of the diversity of modern life—the number of different kinds of people who share our world, the wide variation of the educational background and experience of these people, the ethnic and cultural variety of life within any good-sized town nearly anywhere on earth, the rights of all people in democratic societies to have their views taken seriously by decision-makers, and the distance over which communications might travel because of the range of printed and electronic discourse—modern rhetoric necessarily differs from rhetoric as practiced in the classical Athens of Plato, Isocrates, and Aristotle, where authors mostly spoke directly to audiences that tended to be of the same class, race, gender, and nationality. Modern rhetoric must take greater pains with how to model and analyze rhetorical situations. The need for situational sensitivity is, in fact, one thing that makes rhetoric relevant as a course of study in the university right now.

To take the case of my own university, a recent study of how graduates fare in the workplace showed that employers rated our students high in the areas of specialized knowledge and technical competence but low in the areas of communication skills and ability to relate to people different from themselves. Modern rhetoric suggests that the two weaknesses are related. Good communication depends upon sensitivity to diverse populations within a wide range of rhetorical situations. The findings of the study hint that we have failed to give our students the rhetorical education they need.

As a first step in understanding how rhetoric can be used in the service of communicating in conditions of cultural, social, and geographical diversity, this chapter connects the model of appeals introduced in chapters 1 and 2 to modern theories about rhetorical situations.

Classical Roots and Modern Branches

The roots of rhetorical situation theory—and hence our model of appeals, which is strongly situational—go back to classical rhetoric, especially the works of Aristotle. Perhaps the two most famous contributions that Aristotle made to the rhetorical tradition were his classification of speech genres—which he called forensic, deliberative, and epideictic speeches—and his distinction among the different kinds of "artistic proofs": ethos, pathos, and logos.[1] Both triads of terms have to do with rhetorical situations.

The triad of speech genres is the most obviously situational. Each type of speech suggests a generic situation:

- Forensic speeches take place in the courts. The author is an advocate trying to sway a judge or jury with a narrative of events that appeals to the value of justice and the authority of the law.

- Deliberative speeches take place in the assembly. The author is a citizen trying to sway fellow citizens with a proposal for future action by appealing to such values as survival (in the case of war) and general prosperity (in the case of civic projects).

- Epideictic speeches take place on special occasions. The author celebrates the event (past or present) for an audience of contest judges or fellow citizens by appealing to communal values and cultural traditions.

One thing we learn from this categorization is that *genre*—meaning any recognizable kind of speech or written text, whether a forensic speech, an epic poem, an inaugural address, a news report, a sports broadcast, a technical proposal, or a promotional website—always works within a conventionally defined rhetorical situation.

The second Aristotelian triad—ethos, pathos, and logos—also has to do with rhetorical situations, though not so obviously. These are the elements most frequently referred to as "appeals" by scholars in classical rhetoric. In one of the most confusing uses of language in the rhetorical tradition, ethos is called an appeal to character; pathos, an appeal to emotion; logos, an appeal to logic or reasoning (the use of the simplified deductions and inductions that Aristotle calls enthymemes and examples—see chapter 2). The problem is that authors demonstrate their character (good or bad) in every utterance; likewise, the emotions of the audience might attach to just about anything in a text; and without reasoning, nothing would make sense. Thus, if we depend upon the concepts of ethos, pathos, and logos as our theory of appeals, we are left with a rather narrow and vaguely defined set of appeals. The three appeals are also difficult to distinguish from each other. An audience's emotions might be stirred, for example, by the good character of the author (which might inspire admiration, love, or jealousy) or by the author's bad character (which could cause irritation, anger, or fear). As well, the audience's emotions might be stimulated by an effective proof (which might cause them to feel satisfaction or admiration) or by ineffective proof (which could provoke contempt).

The real usefulness of ethos, pathos, and logos appears when we think about them as elements in a model of the rhetorical situation, such as the model outlined in the work of the modern rhetorical theorist James Kinneavy. Kinneavy noticed that in Aristotle

- ethos focuses on the author, the attractiveness of the character and the authority the author inspires,

- pathos involves the audience, especially the emotions of the audience, and

- logos involves references to the world shared by the author and audience.

Kinneavy suggests that the three elements constitute the three points of a "communication triangle"—which, following information theory, he calls the *encoder* (author), *decoder* (audience), and *reality* (the world), with the *signal* (text) filling the middle of the triangle, as if to hold the other elements together. Kinneavy uses his model, among other things, to generate a theory of communication genres or modes. Every element (author, audience, world, and text) is engaged in every communication, he argues, but an emphasis on one element will produce a different kind of discourse. Author-oriented discourse is expressive, audience-focused discourse is persuasive, reality-oriented discourse is objective, and text-oriented discourse is artistic.

For our purposes, the most important contribution that Kinneavy made was to suggest that ethos, pathos, and logos are something other than what we think of as appeals. They are more like positions with a spatial relationship to one other. Their relationship is triangular, hinting at the concept of triangulation. In the appeals model, they correspond not to the actions of appealing but to the position of the author (ethos), the position of the audience (pathos), and the position of value (logos).

What's missing in this neo-Aristotelian model is any sense of movement. It is a static picture, a snapshot instead of a movie. But modern rhetoric also suggests ways to set it in motion. Kinneavy himself points to the classical concept of *kairos* for this purpose. Kairos means something like timeliness, an awareness of the present situation of the audience and the need to act or change.

An even clearer version of timeliness and rhetorical movement appears in an influential article by the modern scholar Lloyd Bitzer entitled "The Rhetorical Situation." Bitzer identifies three elements that every author must consider: audience (the people who are being addressed), constraints (the limits upon what the speaker can say), and exigence. Exigence has to do with what prompts the author to write in the first place, a sense of urgency, a problem that requires attention right now, a need that must be met, a concept that must be understood before the audience can move to a next step. In classroom terms, an exigence is like the "prompt" that the composition teacher gives in a writing assignment. It is what moves a person to write and what defines the topic. Beyond the classroom, an author may be moved to write, for example,

- by something another writer has said, an incorrect interpretation or an outrageous claim;

- by a discovery, such as a new method for doing experiments or conducting business, that will help others to solve problems or meet needs they could not solve or meet before;

- by an event that requires interpretation and reflection, such as a terrorist attack, a proposal for war, or a big oil spill; or

- by an attitude that the author would like to change, such as sexism in TV ads, vocationalism in university education, or consumer naiveté in the automobile market.

Bitzer's theory is most important to the model of appeals for the idea of movement that comes across in his concepts of exigence and audience. An author is moved, or prompted, to take a position, to make a stand, by the exigence. The author's goal is to move the audience toward that position. The overall picture gives us an author and audience moving toward common ground. What brings them together is the shared position of value, the need for change or growth.

What the model of appeals takes from classical and modern rhetoric may be summarized this way:

- The position of the author draws upon Aristotle's concept of ethos, or character, as well as the modern understanding of ethos as a cultural outlook or worldview that characterizes a community. The author's position is not simply a personal account of himself or herself. The author is a complex individual who selectively reveals (or creates—or conceals) aspects of character pertinent to the rhetorical work required at the moment. The author's position represents a particular communal outlook that points toward the position of value and invites the audience to join (or return to) the community.

- The position of the audience (Aristotelian pathos, according to Kinneavy) differs from that of the author, even if only slightly (as in the case of the congregation that the preacher feels has slipped toward worldliness) or temporarily (as in the case of a community of scholars that has fallen under the influence of a faulty theory or has been swayed by bad evidence). Bitzer's concept of exigence suggests that something has divided the author from the audience and thus moved the author to create an appeal for alignment.

- The position of value is the triangulating point that defines (or reestablishes) the relationship, the common ground, of the other two positions. The author may merely refer to an already existing point (reminding the audience of an authoritative concept) or may actively construct a new image or idea that attracts the audience, using new evidence or recognized authorities (whether people, texts, or abstract concepts such as love, justice, and community). In this way, the position of value is like the neo-Aristotelian logos. We have been thinking of it as a star that guides the audience into the port of common interest with the author, but if we turn the model upside down, in the manner of Kinneavy's communication triangle, the position of value is the *ground* of the appeal, like the control tower of an airport, toward which the author moves and directs the flight of the audience by relaying signals.

Remember that the three positions do not exhaust the rhetorical situation but only model it. There are other elements that must always be considered. There is the *medium* of exchange, the language and form of communication as well as the cultural context that includes obstacles that must be worked through or avoided. There is also the former position of the author and audience, the *background* of this appeal. And there is the personal position of the author and audience members, the individual quirks and traits that get left out when the appeal is constructed but that might still influence its success or failure. There are always more elements than either an analyst of rhetoric or a user of rhetoric can focus on in any given moment.

Examples: Using Introductions to Set Up Situations

Successful authors usually show their awareness of the rhetorical situation early in their communications, in the introductions to essays or speeches, for example. Here authors reveal not only "where they're coming from" but also the implied position of the audience and the position of value to which they will appeal. The following examples give insights into the nature of the author and audience positions, suggesting that the difference between the author and audience *as persons* and *as positions* may be very important.

Example 1

By the end of the very first sentence in "Claiming an Education," we know that the poet and teacher Adrienne Rich is giving a convocation speech at a college for women:

> For this convocation, I planned to separate my remarks into two parts: some thoughts about you, the women students here, and some thoughts about us who teach in a women's college. But ultimately, those two parts are indivisible. If university education means anything beyond the processing of human beings into expected roles, through credit hours, tests, and grades (and I believe in a women's college especially it *might* mean much more), it implies an ethical and intellectual contract between teacher and student. This contract must remain intuitive, dynamic, unwritten; but we must return to it again and again if learning is to be reclaimed from the depersonalizing and cheapening pressures of the present-day academic scene. (27)

Beyond the superficial exigence of being invited to speak for this occasion (a classic epideictic situation, to use Aristotle's terms), Rich is driven by her experience as a former student and current teacher and her observations of academic life to take a position against the cheapening of education in which students are "processed" rather than taught. She appeals across the conventional divide between student and teacher, and no doubt she worries that some students have bought into the very system that she wants them to resist. The ground of her appeal, the position of value, is the common experience of womanhood.

This appeal to gender hints at the possibility that women might conceive a world different from the high-pressure and depersonalized world made by men. She uses the language of the marketplace—of processing (as in meat processing), grading (as in U.S. Grade A pork), banking ("credit hours"), and pricing ("cheapening")—to describe the world she rejects. But she also borrows a term from that world to suggest the alternative, or competing, world—"an ethical and intellectual contract"—though the idea of the legal contract at least suggests mutual agreement between equal human subjects, unlike the actions of grading, processing, and pricing, which involve human masters and objectified beings (animals domesticated for meat).

So she writes as a teacher to students, but she also writes as a woman to women, suggesting that they come together under the banner of feminine values to redefine the purpose and meaning of education.

Example 2

In "Hearing Voices," the Chickasaw writer Linda Hogan addresses an audience primarily composed of non-Indian readers. While retaining her identity, her Native American ethos, she appeals to the common treasure of folk wisdom, which affirms the view that the earth is not a dead thing to be exploited and abused but a living being with which human beings share a life:

As an Indian woman, I come from a long history of people who have listened to the language of this continent, people who have known that corn grows with the songs and prayers of the people, that it has a story to tell, that the world is alive. Both in oral traditions and mythology—the true language of inner life—account after account tells of the stones giving guidance, the trees singing, the corn telling of inner earth, the dragonfly offering up a tongue. This is true in the European traditions as well: Psyche received direction from the reeds and ants, Orpheus knew the languages of earth, animals, and birds. (78)

Example 3

By contrast, Frederick Douglass concentrates on his difference from his main readers in opening the famous narrative of his life as a black slave in the American South, his escape, and his resettling in the North. "I do not remember to have ever met a slave who could tell his birthday," he says in the first paragraph. "All the white children could tell their ages. I could not tell why I ought to be deprived of the same privilege" (13).

Driven by the need to win people to the cause of abolition, he appeals to the humanity of his primarily white, northern audience by stressing the inhumanity of slavery. In escaping, in learning to read and write, and in telling his story, he can assume the erect posture of a human being, but unlike the audience of free citizens, he bears the physical and psychological scars of slavery and will never know, for example, some of the things that his audience might include among the most basic of human experiences: the love of a mother, for example. He invokes in his readers the memory of having a mother as he tells of his own lack, with the hope of moving people toward him, away from their indifference to, or sympathy with, the slave-holding South:

> I never saw my mother, to know her as such, more than four or five times in my life; and each of these was very short in duration, and at night. . . . She died when I was about seven years old, on one of my Master's farms, near Lee's Mill. I was not allowed to be present during her illness, at her death, or burial. She was gone long before I knew any thing about it. Never having enjoyed, to any considerable extent, her soothing presence, her tender and watchful care, I received the tidings of her death with much the same emotions I should have probably felt at the death of a stranger. (13–14)

In an age in which the sentimental portrayal of motherhood took hold as never before, the institution of slavery, which destroyed motherhood and family life, also prospered. With great pathos and powerful irony, Douglass uses his lack of emotion—reinforced by his straightforward, unadorned style—to stir the horror of the audience.

The importance of values in Douglass's urgent response to the exigence of slavery is evident in the reaction of readers to his position over the years, from the early northeastern abolitionists who joined him in the cause to recent commentators on the African American experience. The modern African American feminist bell hooks, for example, writing for a very different audience, objects to Douglass's complaints about his mother. She shows first her understanding of the constraints under which Douglass wrote and the demands of the audience upon his writing: "Douglass surely intended to impress upon the consciousness of white readers the cruelty of that system of racial domination which separated black families, black mothers from their children" ("Homeplace" 385–86). But then she turns to the problem of value, arguing that Douglass appeals to his audience at a great cost, "devaluing black womanhood, by not registering the degree of care that made his black mother travel those twelve miles to hold him in her arms." Notice her repetition of the word *value:* "In the midst of a brutal racist system, which did not value black life, she valued the life of her child enough to resist that system, to come to him in the night, just to hold him" (386).

Example 4

The Latino essayist Richard Rodriguez almost appears to be answering a letter from his mother as he begins the chapter entitled "Mr. Secrets" from his memoir *Hunger of Memory:*

> I am writing about those very things my mother has asked me not to reveal. Shortly after I published my first autobiographical essay seven years ago, my mother wrote me a letter pleading with me never again to write about our family life. "Write about something else in the future. Our family life is private." And besides: "Why do you need to tell the gringos about how 'divided' you feel from the family?" (124)

Rodriguez defines his position as different from that of his family, as existing in a kind of lonely no man's land between his Mexican immigrant heritage and "the gringos." The audience to which he appeals is not one defined by ethnicity, but by literacy. By his fourth paragraph, his topic evolves into "a writer's loneliness." The problem he addresses is how to reconcile his affection for the old family—the very exigence for the essay is, after all, his worry over a letter he gets from his mother—with his decision to take up the ways of a different culture, one defined by its educational values and particularly by literacy.

The position of value to which he appeals is one he learned from his family—the communal ideal—but he offers a new interpretation that both separates him from his mother and father and ultimately honors them, not in the way they would want to be honored, but in a way consistent with his membership in the community of writers and readers to which he belongs as an adult. He reconciles the world of childhood and the world of the adult by celebrating his family in print and in public, and he appeals to other lonely literates to accept this reconciliation that he knows his family would reject.

Example 5

Finally, consider the first paragraph of George Orwell's famous essay from 1946, "Politics and the English Language":

> Most people who bother with the matter at all would admit that the English language is in a bad way, but it is generally assumed that we cannot by conscious action do anything about it. Our civilization is decadent and our language—so the argument runs—must inevitably share in the general collapse. It follows that any struggle against the abuse of language is a sentimental archaism, like preferring candles to electric light or hansom cabs to aeroplanes. Underneath this lies the half-conscious belief that language is a natural growth and not an instrument which we shape for our own purposes. (156)

Most of the rhetorical work in this paragraph goes to establishing the position against which Orwell will argue: the idea that it's no use fooling with the improvement of language because bad language is caused by a corrupt society. The paragraph suggests the identity of the implied audience in the first sentence, namely "Most people who bother with the matter at all," people who think about language and would thus be inclined to read a magazine article with a title like "Politics and the English Language." The position of the audience is also identified with progressive politics and modernity, as people who recognize the advantages of electric light and airplanes over candles and horse-drawn cabs and who understand how politics touches every part of modern life (largely because of the technological advances Orwell hints toward so adroitly: the centralized networks that provide such conveniences as electric light and the global transportation and communication made possible by air travel). He seems to say that modern people are the very ones who would be least likely to concern themselves with matters of language. Even if they do, they would probably see corrupt language merely as another sign of corrupt society. Short of revolution, how can we improve the language?

Once he establishes this position for the audience and the position of value associated with progress, Orwell attempts to divide the dismissive attitude toward language issues from the position of value, essentially arguing that you don't have to be old-fashioned to be concerned with the state of the language. You can keep the position that language is socially corrupted, he seems to say, but please consider a modified version:

> Now, it is clear that the decline of a language must ultimately have political and economic causes: it is not due simply to the bad influence of this or that individual writer. But an effect can become a cause, reinforcing the original cause and producing the same effect in intensified form, and so on indefinitely. A man may take to drink because he feels himself to be a failure, and then fail all the more completely because he drinks. It is rather the same thing that is happening to the English language. It becomes ugly and inaccurate because our thoughts are foolish, but the slovenliness of our language makes it easier for us to have foolish thoughts. The point is that the process is reversible. Modern English, especially written English, is full of bad habits which spread by imitation and which can be avoided if one is willing to take the necessary trouble. If one gets rid of these habits one can think more clearly, and to think more clearly is a necessary first step towards political regeneration: so that the fight against bad English is not frivolous and is not the exclusive concern of professional writers. (157)

Here Orwell appeals to the modern taste for reform and improvement by invoking the image of alcoholism—a bad habit that tends to feed on itself and lead to complete failure. The habit of bad language use, like the habit of drunkenness, is reversible; and good language, like sobriety, clears the mind. Clear thinking leads to "political regeneration"—a term that offers an alternative to the sickness and death connoted in such terms as "in a bad way," "decadent" (with its root word "decay"), and "collapse."

Thus Orwell argues that if we improve the language, we can heal society, make it well, regenerate it. He appeals to the value of health by a subtle analogy that links society to the human body and that thus appeals to an audience who might subscribe to the idea that "language is a natural growth and not an instrument which we shape for our own purposes." He then continues to appeal to the organic view by analyzing what he calls "specimens" of modern prose—like medical specimens a doctor would view under a microscope. Orwell invites the audience to join him under the banner of good health, sobriety, and progress—values associated more with social good than with good writing. Even if you aren't a writer, he seems to say, you might take an interest in language if you realize how it can contribute to the general health of society.

Situations—Social and Rhetorical

In all of these examples, the position that the author rhetorically assumes for herself or himself and the audience position to which the essays are addressed differ somewhat from the social roles assigned to the author and audience for the occasion:

- Adrienne Rich acknowledges her social role as a teacher and her audience's social role as students, but she refuses to rest there, addressing her audience woman-to-woman.

- Linda Hogan claims her identity as a Native American writing for a primarily Euro-American audience but refuses to accept the implied role of the quaint superstitious native who differs from her modern, educated, sophisticated, curious-in-an-anthropological-kind-of-way, Judeo-Christian readership. She reminds us that Europeans have a folklore, too, one that shares an animist perspective with Native American lore—the idea that the earth is alive.

- Frederick Douglass likewise refuses to accept the role of the ignorant ex-slave before an audience of educated whites. He emphasizes his difference from his readers even as he addresses them human to human. The difference is that he has had to fight to be recognized as human, a status they have assumed since birth.

- Richard Rodriguez starts off as an educated Mexican American son ostensibly addressing the complaints of his traditional mother but transforms his story into the appeal of a lonely writer seeking community with readers from all ethnic backgrounds who have been, in one way or another, alienated from their home identities.

- George Orwell comes forward in the role of professional writer addressing people in other professions but insists that good writing should be the concern of all politically conscious citizens, an identity he shares with the readership of political magazines.

These observations suggest that rhetorical situations involve imagined, fictionalized, constructed versions of the author and the audience. The authors create a narrator or "speaker" for their texts, sometimes called "the persona"—literally the "mask" of the authors, the faces they put forward to their audiences. But modern rhetoric suggests that the author makes a mask for the audience as well. Both Wayne Booth and Walter Ong have suggested that the author's audience is always a fiction. And Edwin Black refers to the rhetorical concept of audience as "the second persona." Reader-response theory speaks of "implied" and "ideal" audiences. The point is that the author has already begun to craft the appeal as the audience is envisioned and assigned to a position. Indeed, that is why I have been using the term "position" along with audience, author, and value—to emphasize the rhetorical, invented nature of these "characters."[2]

The success of the rhetoric depends partly upon whether the members of the audience are willing to accept the mask offered to them. They may cling to a different position or a more complex view of themselves. Among educated people these days, few enjoy being "positioned" or "manipulated." We like to think we can choose our own positions, make our own decisions. We might even grow mistrustful when a speaker refers to us together as "we" (as I have just done!).

The willingness of the audience to accept the position, to say "yes, I have behaved the way you say" or "yes, I do think that way sometimes" often depends upon the author's tone. "Tone" means simply the attitude of the author toward the audience and subject matter. Does the audience feel attacked, condescended to, confused, cajoled, humored, imposed upon, invited, pampered, pandered to, or seduced? To go back to our key term, rhetorical appeals (the pleading of cases) must appeal to (please) the audience.

There is no formula for how to achieve a certain tone. Tone is context-dependent. If a mother says to her son, "You have worked so hard!" the tone will be complimentary if she is admiring the work he has done in the backyard, but sarcastic if she is coming in from having done the work herself while he's been playing video games with his friends. As with so much else in rhetoric, it depends upon the situation.

The Situation—Simple and Complex

There is no end to any rhetorical situation. It has a receding horizon. The medium across which Adrienne Rich addresses her students is filled with cultural obstacles that make her students resistant to the idea that their teacher can talk to them woman-to-woman. There is the likely age difference, the idea of professional distance, the admiration they may feel for her as a famous poet, and the challenge or threat some of them may feel from her radical feminism.

On all sides of the simple version of the appeal—the positions of author, audience, and value—appear competing claims. Rich's students may be tempted, for example, to stick with the "masculine" model of graded, credited education. It has served them well, after all; they have made it to college and likely have good prospects for the future. Or they may see Rich's complaints against the educational system as a "straw man." It's really not all that bad, they may think; she has constructed a false image of education just to argue her radical points. Or, they may think, she's just rehashing the old vocational versus humanist argument about "liberal education." Currying that old workhorse with a new feminist brush may not make it run any faster in the modern world of specialized competitive learning.

For the appeal to work, it must focus the audience's attention, push the counterarguments into the background, and encourage the audience members to play along for a while even if they do not adopt the mask that the author has crafted for them. Or they may participate more as observers, standing back and watching the struggle that Rich or Rodriguez or Orwell works out with the imaginary audience, waiting until the outcome to choose sides or just forget the whole thing. The observer position is that of the rhetorical critic, the position that I have adopted in this chapter, which has many similarities with the position of the reader of a novel or the viewer of a film. We watch the characters struggle with appeals and decisions and reflect upon the meaning of the drama for our own lives.

The position of observer thus complicates the model much as the idea of a double audience and double author does—the author as a writing person and a constructed persona, the audience as a reading person and a "second persona," the author's fiction. If we think of rhetoric in this way, the work of reading and writing becomes both more complex and more creative.

Thus simple appeals within the text—the three positions interacting with each other—are merely a starting place for exploring possible interpretations. By focusing on the text, by reading closely, we hone our skills of attention. The root of the word *attention*—"to attend"—literally means to listen. Everyone has probably heard the truism that people these days lack "listening skills." The grain of truth in the observation is that if I am ever going to understand someone different from myself, I have to begin by listening. I could jump to conclusions based on what I know about Adrienne Rich—that she's a feminist, an "impractical" poet, a dreamer, a radical—or I could look more closely at how she positions herself and how she makes her appeals to me. By publishing her convocation speech and agreeing to have it included in a college reader, she now includes me within the range of her audience. Should I not listen because she was originally talking woman-to-woman to a group of college graduates? As a male reader who graduated from college over thirty years ago, should I accept the mask of the female listener and play along, or should I observe the game as an outsider and form my judgment from the possible interactions of the two positions? Both could be productive approaches to close reading, listening across the barriers of difference.

My contention is that this practice and other forms of the rhetorical enterprise are needed for effective communication in a culture that respects difference and diversity but still values community.

4 ▸ Appeals to Time

Sensitivity to time is crucial in both classical and modern rhetoric. For example, time plays an important role in Aristotle's classification of speech genres mentioned in chapter 3:

- *forensic speeches* narrate *past* events with a view to influencing present decisions and judgments;
- *epideictic* speeches focus on an event or occasion in the *present* time;
- *deliberative* speeches propose *future* actions based on current trends.

In modern times, the genres of technical and business writing follow a similar pattern:

- *reports* narrate the past;
- *instructions* deal with actions in the present time of the reader;
- *proposals* make arguments for future actions.[1]

But time-orientation in rhetoric involves more than just an awareness of the temporal context. It usually communicates a sense of timeliness or urgency. It focuses an audience's attention by concentrating on a particular moment in time. Two of the most important concepts in the rhetorical tradition—classical *kairos* and modern *exigence*—involve this special attention to the time of communication. Kairos has to do with finding the right argument for the right moment. Exigence suggests that topics emerge as urgent considerations at a particular historical time. The power of both concepts depends upon the author and audience coming to an agreement that the moment has arrived for a certain topic to receive close attention. Right now is the time.

The sense of urgency may have become associated with rhetoric when it first emerged as a response to social and political crisis in classical Greece, a time when democracy was knocking at the door of the old class system.[2] "There is usually a resurgence of rhetoric during periods of violent social upheaval," argues Edward P. J. Corbett in *Classical Rhetoric for the Modern Student* (32). The implication is that rhetoric, having been born in time of great change, takes on a new relevance again in a time of crisis. Corbett was introducing ancient rhetoric during an era that included the Vietnam War, the civil rights movement, environmental crises of various kinds, the so-called sexual revolution, and the advent of feminism. The watchword of students in those years was "relevance." An increasingly radical student population wanted to know what their education had to do with the changes that beset society on every side. Corbett's own rhetoric accommodates this demand. It builds upon an appeal to the times; he writes about classical rhetoric but he does so *for the modern student*.

The very word *modern* implies "right now"—at least in its ordinary usage, leaving aside (for the moment) academic concepts like "modernity" and "postmodernity," which suggest that "the modern" was itself a particular moment in time or a particular outlook associated with the history of the West, beginning in the European Renaissance and culminating in the mid-twentieth century. Despite this scholarly usage, the general public still uses the word *modern* to mean "current" or "attuned to the present moment." Modern technology, modern music, modern attitudes, modern conveniences all have to do with what is new or up to date. Modern rhetoric, in this sense, means a form of communication suitable for modern times, for right now.

The use of the word *modern* implies that time has a special value. It implies that it is good to be up to date and that modern things are better than old-fashioned, outmoded, old things. This attitude ties into an entire worldview or way of thinking, namely the concept of progress. Progress becomes an ideology for people in modern times. A modern person thinks that the world, or at least the human understanding of it, is generally improving. Because of advancing technology, accumulating knowledge, and increasing information, North Americans and western Europeans are inclined to see our world as better than that of our ancestors.

If we think about things this way, then modern rhetoric involves not just the recognition of timeliness but an *appeal to time*. Time becomes a position of value that authors use to draw audiences to their own positions. Authors may appeal to the past, present, or future, but the focus tends to fall on the need for change, the pursuit of something new, in the present.

Simple and Complex Appeals to Time

The news media and advertising industry often use a simple version of the appeal to time, with newness occupying the position of value. The very idea of "news" implies such an appeal. Consumers of news reports want to know what is different from yesterday, what has changed. The implication is that what remains the same is not worth reporting. The result, according to at least one media critic, is that news stories build upon the four D's: drama, disaster, debate, and dichotomy (Schneider 206). News favors the volatile and dramatic but has trouble sustaining interest in topics over the long haul. Issues "decay," as media critics like to say, meaning that an audience groomed on the four D's loses interest in stories rather quickly.

Advertising has an even stronger interest in promoting the "new and improved." The aim is to move consumers to buy new products. The idea of progress, with the suggestion that technology and research constantly and continuously improve the conditions of human life, offers a perfect underpinning for advertising. The latest car is faster, more powerful, safer, and more beautiful than last year's model. The latest computer allows you to do more things faster and with less effort.

Products that save time are particularly valuable, for as we hear again and again, *time is money.* Most people work for an hourly wage, so society's leading indicator of value—money, that is—becomes equated with time. We speak of needing more time in the same way we speak of needing more money. Time is a resource; time must be managed; time can be wasted. Time becomes not merely a rather abstract measure of our lives slipping by but a substance to be spent or hoarded as the occasion demands. We can spend time or save it or invest it.

The idea that time has an almost material value and that the new is more valuable than the old comes together in the concept of *modern. Modern* implies not just new and recent but a kind of culmination, a long-term investment of time that culminates in the present. Modern life is the result of eons of evolution and development. This assumption of progress provides the main energy for simple appeals to time.

But our most thoughtful authors rarely take a simple approach to such appeals. Rather than making time the position of value to which they appeal, they associate the valuing of time with the audience position they seek to change. They assume that the audience thinks of time as money, values newness over oldness, and thinks of the present as the culmination of progressive forces working over the ages. Then they offer a variation of this position or an alternative.

Think about the examples we have already considered in earlier chapters. We saw in chapter 3 how George Orwell begins his essay "Politics and the English Language" by arguing against the notion that "any struggle against the abuse of language is a sentimental archaism, like preferring candles to electric light or hansom cabs to aeroplanes" (156). As a modern author, Orwell feels he must justify his interest in language first by claiming that it is up to date, relevant for the present inquiry into political corruption. Similarly, even as Robert Putnam claims that American "social capital" has declined in recent years, he argues that Tocqueville's nineteenth-century observation about participation in social organizations remains a good measure of the health of a democracy. But Katha Pollitt disagrees. Putnam's vision, she says, is "nostalgic" and "square" (214, 215). In her view, the professor is out of touch with contemporary women's social motives in particular. In this argument, she combines an appeal to time with an appeal to gender (a topic we will consider closely in chapter 7).

Authors occasionally reverse the idea that the new is superior to the old while still retaining some of the characteristic rhetoric of modern times. In chapter 1, for example, we saw how Wendell Berry argues that "specialization" is a "disease of the modern character" (19). Though Berry clearly thinks that before the days of rampant specialization, things were better, he still appeals to time as a modern author. He claims something like newsvalue for his observation. I've got news for you, he seems to say: Modern life isn't as good as it appears to be. This move is conservative in the deepest political sense, but thoroughly modern in the rhetorical sense. Beginning with the Romantic writers in the late eighteenth and early nineteenth centuries, a common rhetorical strategy was to criticize features of the contemporary scene by referring to a lost past. A deep sense of loss and alienation pervades modern life in many of its moods and characteristic expressions.

The appeal to oldness is in many ways merely the flipside of the appeal to newness. Both impose a time limit on value. One says something is good if it is fresh and new. The other says something is good if it has stood the test of time. Modernism does not so much mean that we accept the new over the old but that we recognize a conflict between the two. Historical preservation, protection of old-growth forests and endangered species, collection of antiques, purchases of everything from vintage wines to vintage clothes, and all kinds of "retro" movements are just as much a part of modern life as wearing the latest fashions, keeping up with the information explosion, and obsessing over the nightly news. News and advertising may give the impression that modern audiences prefer the fresh and original over the old-fashioned and stale, but they may just as likely respond favorably to arguments for the mature and time-tested over the untested and merely fashionable. Who has not learned to look suspiciously at advertising slogans like "new and improved"?

Thus time appeals can generate several lines of argument:

- We can say that it's best to be up to date (as Pollitt does), valuing a break with the past.

- We can say that something that appears to be old has a new relevance (as Orwell does), suggesting a pattern of reemerging value.

- We can say that old ideas (or things or people) continue to have value (as Putnam does), suggesting a pattern of smooth continuity that may have gone unrecognized because of the modern trend toward dismissing the old.

- Or we can say outright that the new ways are inferior to the old ways (as Berry does), suggesting an ideal past corrupted by modern times.

All of these approaches are rhetorically modernist in the sense that modernism assumes the audience senses a discontinuity, a break with the past, which authors must acknowledge even if they are going to argue against the reality of the discontinuity. Appeals to time in modern rhetoric attempt to move the audience by engaging the sensitivity to time that characterizes modern life.

The Rhetoric of Crisis

One approach is to see a particular moment in time as a crisis point, a crossroads. A decision needs to be made; decisive action is required. Two roads open before us—the scene of Robert Frost's "The Road Not Taken," a familiar and frequently quoted poem in modern America, which begins with the line "Two roads diverged in a yellow wood" and ends with the lines "I took the one less traveled by, / And that has made all the difference."

The appeal to the present time as a crisis plays a key role in American political rhetoric. Consider an early example, Thomas Paine's aptly titled pamphlet *The American Crisis*. Paine was writing during the American Revolution, at a particularly dark time for the colonists, when Washington's troops had been defeated time and again by the superior force of the British. Paine begins by saying, "These are the times that try men's souls. The summer soldier and the sunshine patriot will, in this crisis, shrink from the service of their country; but he that stands it now, deserves the love and thanks of man and woman." Paine achieves a "right now" urgency by reference to the wintry context of his pamphlet. Paine was encamped with Washington's army during the famous winter at Valley Forge when the struggle became a matter not so much of defeating the British as keeping up the spirits of the American patriots. Legend has it that the great propagandist, who signed himself "Common Sense," used the head of a drum as his writing table.

The exigence is clear: Paine must write to drum up support for the war effort. The kairos of his argument—the timely force of it—he gathers by using the seasons as a metaphor. It is winter now. The "summer soldier and the sunshine patriot" will "shrink" from the harsh demands of a winter defeat. The nation needs people who can face the challenge of the cold, who can "stand it now." Using winter as a metaphor for times in which resources are depleted and spirits are low, Paine appeals to native heartiness and sturdy bravery, the will to survive that characterizes a nation of farmers who know what it means to endure the winter and brave the bad season.

An equally famous example, Abraham Lincoln's Gettysburg Address, also appears during a wartime crisis. The ostensible purpose of the address is to dedicate the union cemetery at Gettysburg. The battle that had been fought at Gettysburg proved to be the turning point of the American Civil War, the war that has been called the Second American Revolution, largely because of the connection between the two wars that Lincoln makes in this very speech.[3] He begins this way:

> Four score and seven years ago our fathers brought forth upon this continent, a new nation, conceived in Liberty, and dedicated to the proposition that all men are created equal.
> Now we are engaged in a great civil war, testing whether that nation, or any nation so conceived and so dedicated, can long endure.

Like Paine's arguments, Lincoln's speech addresses the special needs of the moment, especially the need to stay the course and win the war. And he uses the natural divisions of time to reinforce his rhetoric. As Paine uses the seasons of summer and winter metaphorically, Lincoln uses the divisions of a person's life, with a special emphasis on the time of birth. At eighty-seven years old, the nation has yet to be fully born, he suggests. It has been conceived ("in Liberty," the allegorical mother) and dedicated (to the proposition of universal equality), but can it survive long enough to be born? Lincoln makes the metaphor clear in the ending to his short speech by saying that those who remain alive must make sure that those who have died will be compensated by a "new birth"; we need to persevere, he says, so "that these dead shall not have died in vain—that this nation, under God, shall have a new birth of freedom—and that government of the people, by the people, for the people, shall not perish from the earth." Lincoln intensifies the argument by claiming that not just the nation but everything the nation stands for—liberty, equality, and union—risks death if the nation cannot endure. The very principles of modern democracy hinge on the actions of this moment.

The now-focus and crisis rhetoric we see in these passages become even more important as we move into the twentieth century and people's sense of their own power increases with the growth of technology and with globalization. The difference between present and past comes to seem stronger than ever in the years following the great changes brought about by the World Wars of the twentieth century. With the development of the atom bomb, people became particularly aware of the break with the past. The power to destroy the world with a single decision—the kind of power that had before been the prerogative of the gods—now fell into human hands.

Witness the concern of the novelist William Faulkner in his Nobel Prize acceptance speech of 1949:

> Our tragedy today is a general and universal fear so long sustained
> by now that we can even bear it. There are no longer problems of
> the spirit. There is only the question: When will I be blown up? Be-
> cause of this, the young man or woman writing today has forgotten
> the problems of the human heart in conflict with itself which alone
> can make good writing because only that is worth writing about,
> worth the agony and the sweat. (319)

In arguing that "problems of the spirit" have been overshadowed by the
nuclear threat, Faulkner sets up the position of the audience against which
he will take his stand. He stands as the kind of author for whom "the heart
in conflict with itself" is the only thing worth writing about. He urges the
aspiring writer to join him, letting go of the fear that separates modern
people from their ancestors, "leaving no room in [the] workshop for anything but the old verities and truths of the heart, the old universal truths
lacking which any story is ephemeral and doomed—love and honor and
pity and pride and compassion and sacrifice" (319). Ultimately Faulkner
appeals to values that he considers universal, "the old verities." Like Wendell
Berry, he sees a crisis in the modern character that must be overcome if
humanity is "not merely to endure" but also "prevail" (320). He invokes the
nuclear threat only to dismiss it as unworthy of our fear.

Paine, Lincoln, and Faulkner all develop their appeals in this way. They
define their audiences by associating them with a present problem, a moment of crisis, and then urge them to transform themselves by choosing
wisely. Something good—for Paine, American independence; for Lincoln,
the principles of equality and democratic governance; for Faulkner, literature based on universal truths rather than the fear of universal death—is
threatened by the crisis of modern times. Don't let America pass away with
the changing of the seasons, Paine seems to say. Don't let it die before it's
really born, Lincoln implies. Don't let fear destroy the human will and its
cultural expression in literature, Faulkner says. The authors appeal to a
brighter future in which the good can be sustained or recovered. They urge
the audience to let go of anchors in the present, a hurtful and troubling
time, and journey toward higher values.

Time as a Journey: A Rhetoric of Forward Motion

The forward motion of time, the movement from birth to maturity, thus
gets built into the ideology of progress, which authors frequently express
in the metaphor of time as a journey. The belief that death itself does not
end the journey but only takes it to the next transcendental stage—the
Christian heaven or some other version of the afterlife, rebirth according
to the doctrine of reincarnation, or simply the idea that a person contin-

ues to live on in the memory or genetic legacy of one's offspring—allows for a projection of the progressive ideal into the future. Such a belief gives force to Lincoln's appeal to realize the ideals to which so many lives have been sacrificed in the Civil War. Those who have given their lives continue to live in the principles for which they stood.

This line of argument appears strongly in the famous "I Have a Dream" speech delivered by Martin Luther King Jr. on August 28, 1963, in front of the Lincoln Memorial during a demonstration for civil rights in Washington, D.C. With the use of the old formula of "scores" for counting twenty years, King alludes to the Gettysburg address in his appeal to the past, a time he associates with the molding of the American character—the audience position to which he appeals:

> Five score years ago, a great American, in whose symbolic shadow we stand today, signed the Emancipation Proclamation. This momentous decree came as a great beacon light of hope to millions of Negro slaves, who had been seared in the flames of withering injustice. It came as a joyous daybreak to end the long night of their captivity.

As in Lincoln's speech, metaphors of time prevail. The people have come from the night of slavery into the dawn of freedom. And like Lincoln, King goes on to say that the movement is incomplete, stuck at a point of painful crisis:

> But one hundred years later, the Negro still is not free. One hundred years later, the life of the Negro is still sadly crippled by the manacles of segregation and the chains of discrimination. One hundred years later, the Negro lives on a lonely island of poverty in the midst of a vast ocean of material prosperity. One hundred years later, the Negro is still languished in the corners of American society and finds himself an exile in his own land. And so we've come here today to dramatize a shameful condition.

The use of the words "one hundred years later" repeated in the beginning of several sentences—a figure of speech called *anaphora*, one of King's favorite devices—not only intensifies the awareness of time in the audience but also reinforces the sense of stuckness, like a scratched record that will not advance to the next groove. It sets up the crisis rhetoric of the following passage with its anaphoric drumming on the phrase "now is the time":

> We have also come to this hallowed spot to remind America of the fierce urgency of Now. This is no time to engage in the luxury of cooling off or to take the tranquilizing drug of gradualism. Now is the time to make real the promises of democracy. Now is the time to rise

from the dark and desolate valley of segregation to the sunlit path of racial justice. Now is the time to lift our nation from the quicksands of racial injustice to the solid rock of brotherhood. Now is the time to make justice a reality for all of God's children.

Finally, like Paine, King invokes the seasonal context of the speech's moment—this time a sweltering summer day:

It would be fatal for the nation to overlook the urgency of the moment. This sweltering summer of the Negro's legitimate discontent will not pass until there is an invigorating autumn of freedom and equality. Nineteen sixty-three is not an end but a beginning. Those who hope that the Negro needed to blow off steam and will now be content will have a rude awakening if the nation returns to business as usual. There will be neither rest nor tranquility in America until the Negro is granted his citizenship rights. The whirlwinds of revolt will continue to shake the foundations of our nation until the bright day of justice emerges.

It is time to move forward from the dawn into the "bright day of justice," out of the cool darkness of the "valley of segregation" onto "the sunlit path of racial justice." From this point, King can declare his mountaintop vision of the promised land of racial equality. As naturally as the sun moves in the sky from dawn to high noon, his rhetoric suggests, let us complete the journey.

The time-as-a-journey appeal is not always associated with crisis rhetoric. The idea that we are stuck and need to move to the next stage can be communicated with less urgency than we find in Paine, Lincoln, and King. For a more reflective version, consider Aldo Leopold's influential essay "The Land Ethic." Since it first appeared in the 1940s, the essay has become something of an environmentalist manifesto. But in its original context, it was part of a collection of reflections on nature by a seasoned naturalist and forest ranger, written after he retired to his farm in Sand County, Wisconsin—a circumstance that partly explains its more measured approach and mellow tone.

Now a classic in the genre of nature writing, the book's very title, *Sand County Almanac,* suggests its concern with time. Traditionally, an almanac, such as the old *Farmer's Almanac,* is a day-to-day listing of times for sunrise and sunset and other valuable information for a particular year, along with sayings or bits of entertaining prose. One of the first Americans to make use of the Almanac genre for more literary purposes was the statesman and satirist Benjamin Franklin in the writings he signed "Poor Richard."

For all of the mellowness of a nature writer in retirement, Leopold begins "The Land Ethic" on a shocking note that emphasizes the difference between then and now:

> When god-like Odysseus returned from the wars in Troy, he hanged all on one rope a dozen slave-girls of his household whom he suspected of misbehavior during his absence.
>
> This hanging involved no question of propriety. The girls were property. The disposal of property was then, as now, a matter of expediency, not of right and wrong.
>
> Concepts of right and wrong were not lacking from Odysseus' Greece: witness the fidelity of his wife through the long years before at last his black-prowed galleys clove the wine-dark seas for home. The ethical structure of that day covered wives, but had not extended to human chattels. During the three thousand years which have since elapsed, ethical criteria have been extended to many fields of conduct, with corresponding shrinkages in those judged by expediency only. (201–2)

Leopold conveys the difference between our own time and Homer's Greece, which allowed the hero to murder his slaves, not just by the time reference but by reminding the audience of the mode of travel then and by using the Homeric language of "black-prowed galleys" and "wine-dark seas" to describe the ships of Odysseus.

The epic travels of the Homeric hero parallel the ethical travels of western civilization over three thousand years, which brings us to the current time in which, at least in theory, all human individuals receive ethical consideration. Now is the time, Leopold argues, to take the next step:

> The first ethics dealt with the relation between individuals; the Mosaic Decalogue is an example. Later accretions dealt with the relation between the individual and society. The Golden Rule tries to integrate the individual to society; democracy to integrate social organization to the individual.
>
> There is as yet no ethic dealing with man's relation to land and to the animals and plants which grow upon it. Land, like Odysseus' slave-girls, is still property. The land-relation is still strictly economic, entailing privileges but not obligations.
>
> The extension of ethics to this third element in human environment is, if I read the evidence correctly, an evolutionary possibility and an ecological necessity. It is the third step in a sequence. The first two have already been taken. Individual thinkers since the days of

> Ezekiel and Isaiah have asserted that the despoliation of land is not
> only inexpedient but wrong. Society, however, has not yet affirmed
> their belief. I regard the present conservation movement as the em-
> bryo of such an affirmation. (202–3)

The elements of Leopold's appeal to time should by now be familiar. We
have arrived at a decision point in a long journey. So far, so good—we have
made ethical consideration of people universal; people can never be treated
as property—but it is time to make a move—"the third step in a sequence"
in which the "first two" (the ethical accommodation of individuals to each
other first and second to society) "have already been taken." The idea of
journeying (stepping) gains intensity when the metaphor of a new birth
is suggested: "the present conservation movement" appears as "the embryo
of such an affirmation." It is time to say yes ("affirmation"), to take the next
"step" in the journey, to bring the "movement" to fruition, to extend ethical considerations to the land and thus give birth to the land ethic that
exists now in the embryonic state of conservationism.

When Rhetoric Resists Progress: Do We Go Backwards?

In the progressive rhetoric of writers like Paine, Lincoln, King, and Leopold,
going forward is always good. But as Albert Hirschman has shown in an
important contribution to modern rhetoric entitled *The Rhetoric of Reac-*
tion, the appeal has not been universally successful. From the eighteenth
century on, a reactive rhetoric has evolved in competition with the progressive trend of democratic politics and culture. Hirschman identifies
three lines of argument, or theses, associated with the reactive view—perversity, futility, and jeopardy—all of which turn on the idea of unintended
consequences:

> According to the *perversity* thesis, any purposive action to improve
> some feature of the political, social or economic order only serves
> to exacerbate the condition one wishes to remedy. The *futility* thesis
> holds that attempts at social transformation will be unavailing, that
> they will simply fail to "make a dent." Finally, the *jeopardy* thesis ar-
> gues that the cost of the proposed change or reform is too high as it
> endangers some previous, precious accomplishment. (Hirschman 7)

As an illustration, imagine an opponent of continuing the Civil War happens to be in the audience when Lincoln gives the Gettysburg Address.
This opponent might use the theses of perversity, futility, and jeopardy to
question the president's main points in this way:

- Perversity: By forcing the South to join the Union, aren't we violat-
  ing the principles of liberty that we are supposed to be fighting for?

- Futility: By emancipating the slaves, aren't we really giving them their freedom only to push them into another system of oppression—the "wage slavery" that plagues northern immigrants and workers?

- Jeopardy: By continuing the war, aren't we weakening our defenses against foreign powers, risking the very freedom we fought so hard to gain from England?

"One step forward, two steps back" is the cliché that best applies to these reactionary arguments. Many such arguments were in fact made against Lincoln and his Unionist supporters, but history has not been kind to them. Most people have decided that progress was a good thing as it applies to the emancipation of the slaves and the preservation of the Union.

Hirschman's aim is not to favor progressive over reactionary arguments, or vice-versa, however, but to reveal the kinds of patterns that have prevailed in modern political discourse since the French Revolution. The tendency in modern democratic states is to favor the progressive arguments. The idea of progress is so dominant that few people will accept the idea of "going backwards" or "turning the clock back." As Hirschman points out, however, progressive rhetoric often generates counterparts to the reactionary theses that, stripped down to their barest essentials, hardly seem more appealing in and of themselves:

Reactionary:	The contemplated action will bring disastrous consequences.
Progressive:	Not to take the contemplated action will bring disastrous consequences.
Reactionary:	The new reform will jeopardize the older one.
Progressive:	The new reform and the old reforms will mutually reinforce each other.
Reactionary:	The contemplated action attempts to change permanent structural characteristics ("laws") of the social order; it is therefore bound to be wholly ineffective, futile.
Progressive:	The contemplated action is backed up by powerful historical forces that are already "on the march"; opposing them would be utterly futile. (Hirschman 167)

Seen this way, as "extreme statements in a series of imaginary, highly polarized debates," the two sides both appear "badly in need, under most circumstances, of being qualified, mitigated, or otherwise amended" (Hirschman 167).

Hirschman's study offers a way of using rhetorical analysis to demystify appeals to values we take too much for granted. In general our analysis of appeals works this way: it does not so much offer a fool-proof machine for generating effective appeals; rather it increases our awareness of the possibilities and raises our suspicion about lines of argument that we might otherwise accept without question (in our own discourse as well as in that of others).

Time as Place

The appeal to time as a crisis or time as a journey involves a metaphorical connection of time with place. The past becomes a place we have been; the present, the spot where we stand now; the future, the land to which we go. Consider, for example, a few sentences from King's "I Have a Dream" speech to see how thoroughly he connects time to metaphors of place.

- "One hundred years later, the Negro is still languishing in the corners of American society and finds himself an exile in his own land." The implication is that African Americans have not moved since their emancipation; they remain in the corners of American life, cornered; they are exiles who ironically stay at home.

- "We have also come to this hallowed spot to remind America of the fierce urgency of Now." We return to the Lincoln memorial to memorialize emancipation and take up where that work left off.

- "Now is the time to lift our nation from the quicksands of racial injustice to the solid rock of brotherhood." Again, we are stuck— but to stay still is to die, like a person caught in quicksand.

- "[My] people . . . stand on the warm threshold which leads into the palace of justice." African Americans stand at the doorway like beggars who cannot move forward to claim the rights of ownership in the palace of justice.

Beyond its use in progressive politics, the identification of time with place has broad cultural implications worth mentioning as we shift our focus from time appeals to place appeals in the next chapter. The place-time metaphor is a characteristically modern rhetorical form. In the modern era, it works as it always has—to make the abstract concept of time more concrete, more manageable, easier to comprehend and talk about— but it also becomes an expression of a certain ethos of modernity, of a people marked by geographical mobility (to put it positively) and alienation from the land (to put it negatively). Modern political speeches urge us to journey through time. Modern science fiction tells of adventures in time travel. Modern physics explains the "space-time continuum." We seem to identify with "our times" more completely than we identify with our place.

As we turn to the next chapter, we will see that appeals to place—in competition with appeals to time—often signal discontent with the processes of modernization and its companion concept, globalization.

5 ▶ Appeals to Place

One of the most important contributions to modern rhetoric is Kenneth Burke's multivolume treatment of human motives. Writing in the aftermath of World War II, with the confounding behaviors of the Nazis, the imperial Japanese, and the inventors of the atomic bomb still fresh on his mind, Burke's focus fell upon his own specialty: human language, which he considered a form of symbolic action. Burke's ambitious goal in his books *A Grammar of Motives* and *A Rhetoric of Motives*, and in the various essays toward the proposed but never completed *Symbolic of Motives*, was no less than to understand the way people talk about how they make decisions, undertake new actions, or change their attitudes under the influence of propaganda and other forms of social speech and writing. No one has ever taken a harder look at how people use language to justify their behavior and motivate others (and themselves) into purposeful action.

In the first book in the series, *A Grammar of Motives*, Burke devised an approach to the analysis of everything from single sentences to complex literary texts and even life philosophies. He called his method "dramatism." In the simplest possible account I can give in ordinary language, dramatism amounts to an elaboration of the journalist's classic questions in reporting on news events: who, what, when, where, how, and why?[1]

In any human action:

- The question *who?* has to do with the *agent* of the action.
- *What?* deals with the *act*.
- *When and where?* deal with the *scene*.
- *How?* deals with the *means*.
- *Why?* deals with the *purpose*.

In analyzing the way people talk about their actions, Burke saw patterns that he called *ratios*, in which one dramatistic element—agent, act, scene, means, or purpose—is habitually explained in terms of another one. The ratios indicate certain philosophical outlooks. The ratio of agent and purpose, for example—the habitual connection of a person's actions with some rationale or purposeful aim—is characteristic of *idealism*. An idealist might explain the choice to study nursing by a love for humanity. By contrast, the ratio of agent and scene, or act and scene, is characteristic of *material-*

ism, a particularly modern way of looking at things. A materialist might explain the choice to study nursing by some experience in childhood (the influence, perhaps, of the life-saving help of a nurse after an accident) or because of family background (everybody in the family works in health care), which might suggest even a genetic predisposition: the person felt compelled to the choice by his or her very physical make-up.

Burke's ideas—greatly oversimplified in this brief summary—have left a strong mark on my approach to modern rhetoric through the study of appeals. I share with Burke an interest in

- what moves people to action,
- how habitual patterns of thinking and language-use characterize different world views, and
- how writers bring different elements of an argument into alignment— for him, the different elements in the ratios; for me, the different positions involved in an appeal.

But the appeals model also departs from Burke. One big difference is that it demands a closer look at the question of *scene*.

Burke appears to conflate the elements of time and place in his thinking in the modernist manner noted at the end of the last chapter. But a close look at the ways people make appeals indicates that, unless we want to overlook the rhetoric of certain discontented groups in modern times, we need to separate the questions of *when?* and *where?* Appeals to time and appeals to place make very different kinds of arguments and may even be characteristic of totally different outlooks on the world. Burke's treatment of time and place as parts of the same dramatistic element of scene— a kind of automatic ratio, an identification that goes unanalyzed in his work—may well suggest his own cultural bias as a modernist and Eurocentric thinker.

Thoroughly modernized cultures and individuals, some would say, suffer from a devaluation of place. Think of the simplest possible appeals, the kind that gel into sound bites and slogans. Just as clichés such as "time is money" hint at the value we put on time, so there are clichés that suggest our value of place, but none quite so pervasive and unambiguous as "time is money." We speak of "finding your niche"—an ecological metaphor—to talk about discovering your purpose in life and a place to work it out. We ask people, "Where are you coming from?" when we're having trouble understanding what they're thinking, as if their point of origin, some land of personal meaning, could explain a difficult or troubling idea. But both of these expressions hint at a loss of place as much as a grounding in place. Your "niche" is something you have to search for; "where you're coming" from is not where you are right now. Even a rather outmoded maxim like "Home is where the heart is" suggests a wandering heart that makes its home in several different places.

Mobility is a crucial value in modern life. Social and economic mobility—moving up in the world—is often tied to geographic mobility, the willingness and ability to travel around to find the best opportunities. The downside is a feeling of being uprooted and alienated from the land. The great majority of people in the United States, arguably the most modernized nation on earth, have a family connection to this continent of only a few generations. Most people move to a new town some time during their lives. Fewer and fewer people are rooted to the land by profession. Over 70 percent of American citizens worked in agriculture at the end of the nineteenth century; by the end of the twentieth, the number was fewer than 3 percent of the total population.

No wonder, then, that appeals to place in modern life often feel like a compensation for loss of the connection with the land. People play "virtual reality" games in fictional lands while they sit in small, air-conditioned enclosures that offer little contact with the outer elements of life. Environmentalists and other activists appeal to what seems to them a fading sense of connection with the land. Producers of children's television programs feel the need to explain where food comes from.

This chapter suggests that, emerging from this kind of life, special ways of dealing with the question of scene have evolved in modern rhetoric. One effect is that appeals to place rarely work unless they combine with some other kind of appeal. As we shall see, appeals to *race* and appeals to the *body*—introduced here and discussed in more detail in later chapters—often work together with appeals to place. As a point of departure, I want to ask, in a revised version of Kenneth Burke's scheme, how agents of action (who?) are connected with place (where?) and how questions of time (when?) compete with considerations of place in modern rhetoric.[2]

A Native American Perspective on Time and Place

In invocations of earthly places, modern writers are drawn to words with the prefix *re-*; they want to re-discover, re-veal, re-turn to the lost land. *Re-inhabitation* is the term the poet Gary Snyder has suggested as the watchword for political and cultural environmentalists (*Place in Space* 236–51; see also Buell). Only the Native Americans, whose myths and texts Snyder draws heavily upon, have a strong claim on original inhabitation in North America (though anthropologists suggest that even they came from Asia originally).

The Sioux activist and philosopher Vine Deloria Jr. appeals to this privileged position in his book *God Is Red*. He claims that Native spirituality differs from the imported Christianity of European Americans precisely in rejecting linear and time-based doctrines such as progress and development in favor of a cyclical, place-centered world view that honors sacred sites and timeless myths. Somewhat ironically, Deloria also claims a stronger sense of history for the Native outlook. The white world's sense of time is abstract, much like its sense of space. But Indian history, connected strongly with place, has heft and substance.

Old World religion went wrong, Deloria suggests, by pulling loose from its moorings in the Mediterranean region and imposing itself on the New World. As the tribal connection to place faded for the uprooted Europeans, the historical sense of mission intensified as if in compensation. Through such doctrines as "manifest destiny"—the claim that divine will guided white explorers, pioneers, and colonists—religion was first enlisted and ultimately engulfed by the secular ideology of progress. The advent of monotheism itself appears in Deloria's scheme as an allegory for the destruction of diversity by a single race, an imperial people driven by an imperial god, a local deity that expands and devours all the competition.

Indian religion takes a very different view of time and history, one conditioned by the sense of place. Deloria claims that "it is exceedingly difficult for a religion, once bound to history, to incorporate sacred places into its doctrine," but "religions that are spatially determined can create a sense of sacred time that originates in a specific location" (71). The forthrightly mythic narratives of tribal people occur within sacred time, "a long time ago" or "once upon a time." As the Pueblo novelist Leslie Marmon Silko explains, the old stories may be vague about their time frame largely because the stories are always still working themselves out in the present. Yet they are usually very specific about where they take place. "Even now," Silko writes in her essay "Landscape, History, and the Pueblo Imagination,"

> the people at Laguna Pueblo spend the greater portion of social occasions recounting recent incidents or events which have occurred in the Laguna area. Nearly always, the discussion will precipitate the retelling of older stories about similar incidents or other stories connected with a specific place. (40)

She writes, for example,

> [Since] the stories about boulders, springs, and hills are actually remnants from a ritual that retraces the creation and emergence of the Laguna Pueblo people as a culture, as the people they became, then continued use of that route creates a unique relationship between

the ritual-mystic world and the actual, everyday world. A journey from Paguate to Laguna down the long incline of Paguate Hill retraces the original journey from the Emergence Place, which is slightly north of the Paguate village. Thus the landscape between Paguate and Laguna takes on a deeper significance; the landscape resonates the spiritual or mythic dimension of the Pueblo world. (38)

From the perspective of rhetorical study, we can think of the Native American claim on the land as an identification of race with place, of ethos with homeland, or in the terms of Kenneth Burke's dramatism, a ratio between agent and scene, *who* and *where*. Along the same lines, Deloria argues that the white man's ethos connects race with history, also a ratio of agent and scene, but substituting *when* for *where*. The terms of the ratio inevitably affect one another. Just as in Indian spirituality place is rendered sacred by the repeated parallel actions of the people over time, so in progressive ideology history becomes mythic by its association with God's chosen people. In Deloria's view, concepts such as manifest destiny and progress do not partake of real history, the material conditions under which people live and work, but are merely propagandistic narratives that share with history a chronological structure.

If the place-centered narratives of the Indians are vague about time, the white man's time stories are similarly vague about place. The validity of progress is not place-dependent; progress is equally good wherever it is applied. And as Deloria argues, the narrative of progress is also vague about any people, such as Indians or Mexicans, who might be associated with the places where the narrative gets worked out. (The "wide open spaces" into which the pioneers and cowboys moved had in fact been inhabited by Native tribes for thousands of years.) Indians rarely get represented as flesh and blood realities in the narratives of progress; rather they appear as ghosts from the past, remnants of a story that progress has left behind, the gothic underside of modernist discourse (see Bergland). The present and the future become the exclusive domain of the people that progress favors. That domain, if it must be named, can be no less than the whole earth.

In this way, the narrative flows into the story of globalization and the modern concept of development. According to Deloria's interpretation, the concepts of "globalization" and "development" amount to a recent "variant of manifest destiny." Advocates of global technological development frequently "judge a society or civilization by its technology and . . . see in society's effort to subdue and control nature the fulfillment of [something like] divine intent" (69). They talk as if it is inevitable that people want to modernize their lives and live the way people live in the "developed countries." The sense of inevitability sounds to critics like Deloria very much as if they are saying that development is destiny, the will of God.

Deloria's writing takes on the character of an appeal as he examines the implications of the two perspectives for contemporary politics. What Indians have seen for a long time and what some whites have begun to realize, Deloria argues, is that technological development can succeed only at a great cost; it "falls flat" when confronted with the environmental record. "In less than two and a half centuries American whites have virtually destroyed a whole continent and large areas of the United States are now almost uninhabitable," Deloria writes (69):

> Ecology, the new left politics, self-determination of goals by local communities, and citizenship participation, all seem to be efforts to recapture a sense of place and a rejection of the traditional American dependence on progress—a temporal concept—as the measure of American identity. (74)

This passage shows that Deloria's argument is hardly devoid of temporally oriented rhetorical concepts like kairos and exigence. He is essentially arguing that the Indian worldview is a perspective whose time has come. But the appeal to place nevertheless prevails. The connections he makes and the authority he commands depend upon it. The audience position, or "second persona," to which he appeals becomes in this passage not other Indians like himself but certain outposts of Euro-Americans who now see the importance of place: environmentalists and communitarians, for example.

We can think of ideology, and perhaps even culture itself, as a set of habitual appeals so old and powerful that they have become the medium of public thinking and action. Any proposal for change must work through these encrusted appeals. Thus Vine Deloria can make his appeal to the discontents among the people of progress only by working through the appeal to history. He dismisses the ghostly image of the tribal peoples and appears on the historical scene as a real flesh-and-blood Indian who refuses to fade away. Originally published in the early 1970s as the environmentalist movement took root in the United States, his book was released in an expanded version in 1992 to coincide with the five-hundredth anniversary of Columbus's voyage.

But Deloria refuses to stop with kairos and exigence, which represent special versions of an appeal to time, treating time as if it were a place. Kairos and exigence say that we have arrived at a point in time as if we were time travelers. The point in time functions something like a sacred site. Deloria won't go that far; he insists that time is conditioned by place rather than the other way around. He appeals to the particular places that Indians hold sacred, where history crystallizes into myth—Wounded Knee and Little Big Horn, for example. The places are particular and real. The Place of Emergence where the People first entered into this world, says Leslie Marmon Silko, almost matter-of-factly, is "a little north of . . . Paguate." For me to say something equivalent from my cultural perspective, I would have to claim that the Garden of Eden is over by the shopping mall.

Speaking from the communal position of the Native American, Deloria nevertheless takes on the persona of a distinguished individual author in his appeal to readers in an individualist literate culture. His invocation of native place both identifies him with his community, a place-centered race of people, and appeals to disaffected Euro-Americans—people who have felt the tug of identification in specific places (in my own case, the sea islands and Appalachian foothills of South Carolina) but have seen the opportunity slip away as the places are transformed by forces travelling under the banner of progress, development, and growth, and as economic necessity has enforced geographic mobility.

The connection of race with place raises questions about the comprehensiveness of major concepts in rhetorical theory, notably kairos and exigence, which tend to be based in time and history. If Deloria's critique of temporality as a Eurocentric bias has any validity at all, then a rhetoric that takes these concepts as central to its mission may well embody that bias. Such are the stakes as we begin to think of rhetoric as a cross-cultural enterprise.

In this sense, the rhetorical appeal, as we have been developing it, becomes a good concept for anchoring a rhetoric of place because it strongly embodies the qualities of position, direction, and distance. The notion of an appeal to place is thus doubly interesting as a way to examine the largely unexplored tension between spatially oriented and temporally oriented rhetorical concepts, a tension that may be linked to cultural differences between tribal and modern, native and colonial, or local and global perspectives. Deloria's appeal could also activate another kind of racial longing—the vague feeling of dislocation and alienation that is the heritage of a people separated from their ancestral lands.

Local Versus Global: The Appeal of the Native American Perspective

We can use the appeals model to summarize our analysis of Deloria's critique:

- In the author position, Deloria stands for the indigenous population of the Americas, displaced by a European culture whose time-based religious practices favor material progress, technological development, and globalization, a culture that tends to impose itself globally without careful consideration of local people and places.

- The position of value to which he appeals is a spiritual tradition rooted in an awareness of sacred places.

- The audience position includes non-Indian readers discontented with the culture they have inherited from their ancestors, likely to identify with the Indian plight because of their sense of uprootedness.

The complex appeal to place in this Native American rhetoric competes with habitual appeals to time (progress, destiny, development, etc.) in the mainstream rhetoric of American life. In questioning the accepted view that large-scale technological developments (hydroelectric dams, complex systems of roadways, etc.) are appropriate and good no matter where they are applied, the appeal to place also highlights the conflict between ways of life that make claims to global fitness and ways of life associated with local practices and small communities.

The conflict between global and local perspectives becomes a focal point in Silko's appeals to place. In her phenomenally successful 1977 novel *Ceremony*, Silko gives us the memorable character of Tayo, a mixed-race Laguna Pueblo Indian from New Mexico (like Silko herself) who enlists with his cousin Rocky to fight in World War II. Though Rocky is a full-blooded Indian, he is much more concerned than Tayo with assimilating into the American mainstream culture. He is a good student in high school and a star football player. He goes to fight the war as a loyal American citizen. By contrast, Tayo goes out of clan loyalty to Rocky, urged by his family to take care of his cousin and come home safe. But Tayo comes unglued. When ordered to shoot a Japanese prisoner on the Pacific front, he sees the face of his Uncle Josiah superimposed on the man standing before the firing squad. Then Rocky dies on the Bataan Death March, and Tayo survives to come home alone. After treatment in an army mental ward for "battle fatigue," he arrives back in Laguna to find that his uncle has indeed died and that the land is beset by drought, for which Tayo blames himself: he had cursed the rain that hampered his efforts to carry the wounded Rocky on their march through the Philippine jungle. The bulk of the story is devoted to the process by which Tayo's healing accompanies a reinhabitation of his native land.

To the majority of novel readers in the late 1970s—highly literate, college-educated, modern people—Tayo could only have seemed an exotic character. His upbringing as a traditional Native American in an obscure spot in the New Mexican high plains must have seemed distant to readers in New York, Atlanta, and Los Angeles. What then was the appeal?

It's all about context, the rhetorical situation. For one thing, the theme of the returning soldier was a familiar one. The war in Vietnam had ended in 1975, and the images of Tayo's experience of jungle war would have resonated with the television images of war in Southeast Asia and the stories of post-traumatic stress that followed the soldiers home (or for returning soldiers themselves, it would have resonated with the actual memories).

For another thing, Tayo's uprootedness and the ensuing heartsickness would have appealed to a generation of young men and women who felt pulled here and there by the global forces beyond their control—if not global war, then the global economy. Social mobility has always been tied to geographic mobility in the U.S. economy. To move up, you have to move out. My own case was typical. I finished graduate school in 1979 and had to cut my ties to the place where my family lived, leave the South, and take a job in the Southwest—the only offer I got—teaching in a small college in central New Mexico, where among other new experiences, I found myself working with Pueblo Indians like Tayo. Ultimately the experience was enriching, but it definitely added new stresses to my life and gave me the uprooted feeling that cultural historians say is typical of modern life.

Finally, the non-Indian audience of modern readers (like me) could also connect with Tayo's realization that the evils of war eventually come home to roost even if their primary impact is felt halfway around the world. As Tayo discovers, the atom bombs that fell on Japanese cities were developed and tested in his own home state—at Los Alamos National Laboratory and Trinity Site—and the uranium was mined on his own reservation. The work of the atomic "witchery," as he sees it, continues even after the war is over. The atom bomb may have ended the war, but it left the world in a state of constant worry. That realization becomes part of the adjustment he must make to the postwar world. This literary depiction of a looming threat captures powerfully the sense of dread that characterized the Cold War experience of many of Silko's readers in the 1970s.

Silko's novel thus appeals to the reader's sense of war-weariness, uprootedness, and nuclear dread—the downside of economic prosperity and global technological development—to create sympathy for an alternative worldview based on the kind of local identities and place-centered rituals she celebrates in her novels and essays. She appeals not only as a traditionalist but also as a modern author. Her work is about the *return* to the land, the *re*inhabitation of place.

Reinhabitation: The Countercultural Perspective

This concept of reclaiming the land and the new rhetoric of place were also being worked out by non-Indian writers during 1970s, members of an increasingly articulate counterculture. The term "reinhabitation" was introduced into the debate by the poet and essayist Gary Snyder. No stranger to the counterculture, Snyder had gained some notoriety as a member of the Beat Generation in the 1950s, providing Jack Kerouac with the model for the character Japhy Ryder in his autobiographical novel *The Dharma Bums*. Having left his childhood home in the Oregon woods, where his family worked as loggers—first to study Asian literature and language at Berkeley, where he met Kerouac, and then to pursue his interest in Buddhism in Japan, China, and India—Snyder ultimately returned to live in the woods of northern California and began to produce writings that made a strong appeal to place. He won the 1975 Pulitzer Prize for his collection of poems *Turtle Island*.

In an introductory note, Snyder explained the title of *Turtle Island*, using the rhetorical act of renaming to develop a special appeal to place:

> Turtle Island—the old/new name for the continent, based on many creation myths of the people who have been living here for millennia, and reapplied by some of them to "North America" in recent years. Also, an idea found world-wide, of the earth, or cosmos even, sustained by a great turtle or serpent-of-eternity.
>
> A name: that we may see ourselves more accurately on this continent of watersheds and life-communities—plant zones, physiographic provinces, culture areas; following natural boundaries. The "U.S.A." and its states and counties are arbitrary and inaccurate impositions on what is really here.
>
> The poems speak of place, and the energy-pathways that sustain life. Each living being is a swirl in the flow, a formal turbulence, a "song." The land, the planet itself, is also a living being—at another pace. Anglos, Black people, Chicanos, and others beached up on these shores all share such views at the deepest levels of their old cultural traditions—African, Asian, or European. Hark again to those roots, to see our ancient solidarity, and then to the work of being together on Turtle Island.

Snyder is fully aware of the Indian critique of the imperialist "schemes" of Anglos like himself, as he makes clear in a comment from another essay:

> [Speak] of the United States and you are talking two centuries of basically English-speaking affairs; speak of 'America' and you invoke five centuries of Euro-American schemes in the Western Hemisphere; speak of 'Turtle Island' and a vast past, an open future, and all the life communities of plants, humans, and critters come into focus (*Place in Space* 248).

But he risks borrowing the Native name and the rhetoric implicit in the phrase "Turtle Island" to hold out hope for a new understanding of the New World. He takes the next step in the appeal to disaffected members of the mainstream culture, appealing to the "ancient solidarity" of tribal cultures. White and black people of the current generation did not arrive like their ancestors as conquerors or slaves but merely found themselves like sea turtles "beached up on these shores." Now begins the "work of being together on Turtle Island."

In the poems of *Turtle Island,* Snyder does his best to bring "a vast past, an open future, and all the life communities of plants, humans, and critters . . . into focus"—not by the kind of global pronouncements we see in the introductory note but by gritty depictions of life lived close to the earth. A good example is "The Dead by the Side of the Road," in which a countercultural speaker—a sort of shaman figure adrift in modern life—tells what he does when he finds animals killed by traffic along a California superhighway:

> How did a great Red-Tailed Hawk
> come to lie—all stiff and dry—
> on the shoulder of
> Interstate 5?
>
> Her wings for dance fans
> . . . .
>
> I never saw a Ringtail til I found one in the road:
> case-skinned it with the toenails
> footpads, nose, and whiskers on;
> it soaks in salt and water
> sulphuric acid pickle;
>
> she will be a pouch for magic tools.

(7)

So it goes for a "skunk with a crushed head," a fawn "hit by a truck on highway forty-nine," a doe "apparently shot" and left to die. Like the Indians before him, the speaker of the poem treats the dead animals with ritualistic respect ("offer cornmeal by the mouth"—a practice of Indian deer hunters, also mentioned in Silko's novels) and then puts them to use in the rituals of dance and magic—and poetry.

Notice how Snyder shows a kind of loving attention to the details of place—the identification of the local fauna as well as the numbering of the roads—which parallels the attention the speaker pays to the dead animals. The poem closes with a haunting image of how large-scale development—which goes under the name of progress—ignores the patterns of local life. The animals die because the great superhighways cut across their ancient pathways, the little trails that a person walking alongside the big highways, like the speaker of the poem, can still see:

> Pray to their spirits. Ask them to bless us:
> our ancient sisters' trails
> the roads were laid across and kill them:
> night-shining eyes
>
> The dead by the side of the road.

(8)

In this poem, roadkill becomes an image of every creature run down in the name of progress and development. The poem addresses the animals as "sisters" and then makes the most of their remains—in a rhetorical appeal as much as in pouches and fans.

Snyder's vision suggests a hybridized new breed of people who commit themselves to a "reinhabitory move" (*Place in Space* 236–51). It involves reconnecting with or returning to the sacred, the original, the crusted over, despoiled, or forgotten places where we find ourselves in the modern world.

A more recent example of a writer who develops this kind of appeal is Janisse Ray, whose 1999 book *Ecology of a Cracker Childhood* shows how living in the splendor of the California forests isn't the only way to find value in the place called home. Ray grew up, almost literally, in a south Georgia junkyard, the daughter of a mentally troubled father from a family of "Crackers," the usually derogatory name given poor whites of Scots-Irish descent who settled in the red-clay hills and sandy coastal plains of Georgia and South Carolina. Ray went off to college, spent time in the big city, but finally returned to settle on a farm in her old homeland. Her book explains why.

"My homeland is about as ugly as a place gets," Ray admits, anticipating the objections of an audience she knows will be suspicious of the people and places she celebrates:

> There's nothing in south Georgia, people will tell you, except straight, lonely roads, one-horse towns, sprawling farms, and tracts of planted pines. It's flat, monotonous, used-up, hotter than hell in summer and cold enough in winter that orange trees won't grow. No mountains, no canyons, no rocky streams, no waterfalls. The rivers are muddy,

> wide and flat, like somebody's feet. The coastal plain lacks the stark grace of the desert or the umber panache of the pampas. Unless you look close, there's little majesty. (13)

But, she goes on to say, "It wasn't always this way," and in remnants of protected land, "you can see how south Georgia used to be, before all the longleaf pine forests that were our sublimity and our majesty were cut. Nothing is more beautiful, nothing more mysterious, nothing more breathtaking, nothing more surreal" (13–14). Playing off the word "nothing" in this passage—beginning with "There's nothing in south Georgia" and finishing with the "Nothing . . . more beautiful" sentence—Ray teaches her audience how to "look close." Looking close means seeing not only what's there but also what has been lost:

> Longleaf pine is the tree that grows in the upland flatwoods of the coastal plains. Miles and miles of longleaf and wiregrass, the ground cover that coevolved with the pine, once covered the left hip of North America—from Virginia to the Florida peninsula, west past the Mississippi River: longleaf as far in any direction as you could see. In a longleaf forest, miles of trees forever fade into a brilliant salmon sunset and reappear the next dawn as a battalion marching out of the fog. The tip of each needle carries a single drop of silver. The trees are so well spaced that their limbs seldom touch and sunlight streams between and within them. Below their flattened branches, grasses arch their tall, richly dun heads of seeds, and orchids and lilies paint the ground orange and scarlet. Purple liatris gestures across the landscape. Our eyes seek the flowers like they seek the flashes of birds and the careful crossings of forest animals. (14)

This great forest is now gone across much of its range—from Virginia, from Louisiana, from Texas, from South Carolina—but good-sized remnants remain in Georgia and north Florida. "It is a loss," says Janisse Ray, that "shadows every step I take" (15). The remnants of the forest become a "shrunken . . . baby" she holds in her arms (15), a victim of her own Cracker ancestors, who were victims themselves:

> Passing through my homeland it was easy to see that Crackers, although fiercely rooted in the land and willing to defend it to death, hadn't had the means, the education, or the ease to care particularly about its natural communities. Our relationship with the land wasn't one of give and return. The land itself has been the victim of social dilemmas—racial injustice, lack of education, and dire poverty. It was overtilled; eroded; cut; littered; polluted; treated as a commodity,

sometimes the only one, and not as a living thing. Most people worried about getting by, and when getting by meant using the land, we used it. When getting by meant ignoring the land, we ignored it. (164–65)

The time has come to value the land in a new way, Ray argues. She appeals to a new generation of Crackers like herself. There is no need to be ashamed of our history, she suggests. Our ancestors behaved as they did for reasons we can understand. But we have to find different ways to "defend [the land] to death." We need to see it as a living being like ourselves, she suggests. As in Native American rhetoric, she combines place appeals to race appeals (insofar as Crackers can be considered a separate race).

She also combines her appeals to place with appeals to the body, personifying the forests and the landscape. "The rivers are muddy, wide and flat, like somebody's feet," she says (13). The pine forests once thrived on "the left hip of North America" (14); the grasses have "heads" and the flowers "paint the ground" (14). The land is not a "commodity" (165) but a "baby" (15) and a "victim" (165). Like Aldo Leopold before her, Ray wants people to value the land as much as they value human life, so she describes the land in terms normally associated with the human body. Ray professes to feel the story of the longleaf pines "scrawled on my bones" (4). In an effort to instill in her audience the high value she places on the perpetuation of the forests, she appeals to their experience of their own bodies as a source of identity with the "communities of life" she celebrates.

The complex appeal to place and body appears again in the work of recent African American writers. Surviving generations of the "African Diaspora," they find themselves doubly dislocated by the experience of modernism. Forced to leave Africa and dragged into slavery, displaced Africans later left the rural South to escape captivity or racism or rural poverty. Perhaps for this reason, argues the essayist bell hooks (who spells her name without capitals), "many contemporary black folks see no value in supporting ecological movements, or see ecology and the struggle to end racism as competing concerns" ("Touching the Earth" 56). Working in the opposite direction, hooks argues that "collective black self-recovery" can only take place "when we begin to renew our relationship to the earth, when we remember the way of our ancestors" (56).

"Living in modern society, without a sense of history," hooks contends, "it has been easy for folks to forget that black people were first and foremost a people of the land, farmers" (53): "African settlers in Florida taught the Creek Nation runaways, the 'Seminoles,' methods for rice cultivation. Native peoples taught recently arrived black folks all about the many uses of corn" (52).

The "psychological impact of the 'great migration' of black people from the agrarian south to the industrial north" has yet to be studied carefully, hooks notes, but it is clear enough that "it altered the communal practices so central to survival in the agrarian south" and "fundamentally altered black people's relationship to the body": "Working in conditions where the body was regarded solely as a tool (as in slavery), a profound estrangement occurred between mind and body" (54). In the industrialized north, black people could no longer "cultivate a spirit of wonder and reverence for life," could not grow "food to sustain life and flowers to please the soul," could not "make a connection with the earth that was on-going and life-affirming" (53).

"When the earth is sacred to us, our bodies can be sacred to us," hooks writes (56). The key point in this appeal—a point hooks shares with writers as different from her as Deloria, Silko, Snyder, and Ray—is that places, like bodies, have a history, and the connection of places with bodies reconnects individuals to the history of a people, to ancestors. Modern appeals to place, in this sense, always advocate what hooks calls "collective self-recovery" (56).[3]

Virtual Places, Empowerment, and the Promise of Utopia

Before turning to a more detailed account of appeals to the body in the next chapter, let's take a quick look at one more, altogether different kind of appeal to place. How many times a day do we hear the invitation to "visit us at www.whatever.com"? In what sense is the treatment of web "sites" and computer "environments" as if they were real places like the treatment of forests as if they were communities of people?

The short answer is that both involve the sort of substitution or swerve from the ordinary perception of things that is typical of rhetorical appeals. We want people to see things differently so that they will reconsider what is most valuable to them. This kind of rhetoric involves the risk of playing into our opponents' worst fears. Critics of "virtual reality" say that it undermines our sense of social responsibility to the local community. If we spend all our time visiting, shopping, even flirting online, we lose touch with local people and places. Likewise, critics of environmentalism argue that "tree-huggers" care more about the land than they do about people. Personifying the landscapes—treating forests as "babies" and "victims"— would seem to support the allegation.

But by adding the element of racial and regional ethos, writers like Deloria, Silko, Snyder, Ray, and hooks anticipate this objection and humanize their particular versions of environmentalism. They tie environmental health to issues of human health (physical or mental or both). If improper use of pesticides is killing the local pine trees and woodpeckers, it's probably killing the local people, too. If strip mining is changing the character of the local land, it's probably disturbing the identity of the local people as well.

The producers of virtual marketplaces make only limited efforts to show a similar consideration for the locales and real-life communities that they seem so eager to replace. The environmentalists studied here (though not all environmentalists by any means) have no desire to compete with programs of social improvement; they want to improve the land as a place of human inhabitation. Developers of virtual communities, by contrast, compete with local communities for the attention and business of shoppers and clients. The attention of key audiences is like a limited resource. With information accumulating on every side, what will appear so valuable that it cannot be ignored? One of the claims that virtual places like websites make on our attention is that they put at our fingertips the kinds of shopping opportunities and other activities that would require great physical effort to carry out in the real world, that would require us not only to go out to the store but perhaps to go to many stores in many cities to get what we want. The same is true of dating services, banking options, online gaming, and insurance sales.

What we have here is a claim to empower the individual in new and extraordinary ways, to make us the masters of worlds formerly inaccessible because of their diffusion in place and time and their distance from the places we call home. As we will learn in the next chapter, the claim to empower an audience is typical of certain appeals to the body, especially in the rhetoric of technology.

The point we need to make here, in closing, is that modern rhetorical practice often involves the promise to relieve audiences of the restrictions they feel from being tied to one place and being confined within a human body. Virtuality is one of several components in a utopian vision, according to which people assume positions formerly reserved for the gods. From the perspective of a place-conscious worldview, however, anything claiming to be utopian must arouse suspicion, for the literal meaning of the word *utopia* is "no place."

6 ▸ Appeals to the Body

In the last chapter, we saw how the "Cracker" ecologist Janisse Ray combines appeals to place with appeals to the human body, personifying the disappearing pine forest as an abused baby, a victim. This rhetoric follows a well-established tradition in nature writing.

In the 1962 environmentalist classic *Silent Spring*, for example, Rachel Carson argues that human health depends upon the "health of the landscape"; pesticides and industrial pollution produce, in her words, "scars of dead vegetation," leaving trees with a "weeping appearance" (69, 70, 71). And, just as the earth's "body" experiences health and illness like our own, so our bodies share cycles and chemical interactions with the earth: "There is also an ecology of the world within our own bodies" (170).[1]

Similar personifications appear in "Thinking Like a Mountain," a companion essay to Aldo Leopold's "The Land Ethic" in *A Sand County Almanac*. Leopold urges readers to resist the short-term thinking of ranchers who kill wolves to protect their herds and increase deer populations on their land. Ultimately such practices unbalance the ecology, leaving more deer than the land can support. The deer strip the mountainsides of vegetation, destroying their own food supplies and driving themselves into starvation. From the vantage point of the mountain—a personification of ecological awareness, the habit of "thinking like a mountain"—the big picture unfolds that deer and men ordinarily cannot see in their headlong pursuit of short-term goals (Leopold 129–33). The adoption of the personifying strategy in environmental rhetoric makes perfect sense according to the logic of Leopold's "Land Ethic." It extends to the land the rhetoric traditionally used to promote the rights of man and woman.

Throughout the history of rhetoric, appeals to the body have been associated with the ideals—and the shortcomings—of democracy. Democratic philosophers, poets, and politicians have appealed to the common experience of the body to argue for the fundamental kinship and equality of all people. This approach has often earned them the contempt of opponents. In ancient Greece, the politically conservative Plato portrayed the rhetoric of his democratic competitors in Athenian education as a low art, fit only for confusing the minds and firing the emotions of the rising masses. In modern times, the critic and historian Daniel Boorstin, in the same spirit, has belittled rhetoric by associating it with advertising and shallow image-oriented politics, which he calls the "rhetoric of democracy." This dismiss-

ive attitude recalls Marshall McLuhan's bemused commentary on advertising as the science of man embracing woman—which brings us back to
my starting place for thinking about modern rhetoric as an art of appeals:
the old ads for a brand of toothpaste that supposedly increases the user's
"sex appeal."

Without accepting the elitist position on the failings of rhetoric and
democracy—or for that matter, of advertising—this chapter is an invitation to take a closer look at this mainstay of mass rhetoric: appeals to the
body.[2] It's important to keep in mind two points about this category of
appeals that we will develop as we go:

1. Appeals to the body are contextually determined and are rarely as
   simple as they seem but usually work in combination with other
   appeals to suggest complex understandings of values.

2. Any approach to value may well begin with a valuation of the body
   so that appeals to the body are not merely a useful approach but
   an essential element in any effective communication.

In connection with appeals to the body, we will also consider two grand
themes of modern writing: the problem of human suffering and the near
obsession in modern times with power.

The Body Politic

Try this experiment: spend thirty minutes watching television or listening to commercial radio and make a list of the products advertised and the
basic approach of each ad—noting especially those that mention food, sex,
or health. You'll probably find that a significant number of ads have to do
with products dealing with eating, drinking, or digestion: restaurants, pizza,
cereal, snacks, coffee, beer, soda, antacids, laxatives, and so on. Most other
ads will appeal to your desire to be free from illness and well groomed or
otherwise attractive. Often these types combine: Drink our low-calorie
beer so you can feel good and look good while you quench your thirst and
have sex with beautiful partners.

It's all too easy to conclude from such an experiment that Americans
are materialistic and obsessed with their bodies. They eat too much, drink
unwisely, and then pay the price for indulgence in worrying about their
digestive health and their appearance. Am I too fat? Do I have bad breath?
Am I sick?

But think about the television audience—as objectively as you can, letting go of any tendency you may feel toward moral superiority or defensiveness about TV culture—the one certain thing we could say about viewers

on any given day is that they represent a very wide variety of people. Given this diversity, what are the advertisers' options for appealing to them, especially if they have only a minute or two to capture their quick-to-wander attention? One thing they can count on is that all these people have bodies to care for and worry about. They have to eat and perform vital functions, and they are likely beset by sex drives and the attendant anxieties.

If not morally commendable, the appeal to the body in advertising is at least understandable. Moreover, advertising is not the only branch of discourse to have solved the rhetorical problem of the mass audience by appealing to the body.

Consider, for example, the case of Walt Whitman, who has a stronger claim than perhaps any other nineteenth-century American poet on having anticipated the extreme modernism of the twentieth century. Whitman invented free verse, championed free speech, claimed to represent the common working people of his day, and tried to cut all ties to European high culture and become the New World poet of democracy. Writing in a new age of near-universal literacy in which innovative printing and paper technologies made possible the penny press and the dime novel, Whitman worked as a journalist and magazine story-writer before he settled into his vocation as a poet. He was intimately acquainted with the advertising, shameless self-promotion, sensationalism, and constant political scuffling that characterized the early efforts of the mass media to capture the attention of the great democratic masses—an audience wider and more varied than history had yet seen. No wonder that to the high-minded Ralph Waldo Emerson, who admired Whitman's power but worried about his taste, Whitman's poetry seemed to mix the mysticism of the *Bhagavad Gita* with the rowdyism of the New York *Tribune.*

Whitman was committed to democratic ideals and to the free expression of what he called "the poetry of the body." In "Song of Myself," a key poem in every edition of his famous compendium *Leaves of Grass,* the poet says he will "speak the pass-word primeval" and "give the sign of democracy" (48). And he makes the crucial connection between democracy and the body. He proclaims, "I am the poet of the body and I am the poet of the soul" (45), refusing to accept the traditional poetic hierarchy that would set spiritual matters on a higher plane than merely physical life. In lines designed to shock his Victorian readers out of their middle-class complacency, he said such things as "Divine am I inside and out, and I make holy whatever I touch or am touch'd from / The scent of these arm-pits aroma finer than prayer" (49). The poet of democracy can be no sentimentalist or prude, he insists:

I do not press my fingers across my mouth,
I keep as delicate around the bowels as around the head and
    heart,
Copulation is no more rank to me than death is.
I believe in the flesh and the appetites,
Seeing, hearing, feeling, are miracles, and each part and
    tag of me is a miracle.

(48–49)

    To see how Whitman enlists appeals to the body into the service of his political ideals, consider a passage from another poem composed before the Civil War and later titled "I Sing the Body Electric." The scene is a southern slave market: "A man's body at auction." The poet imagines taking the place of the auctioneer, disgusted because "the sloven does not half know his business":

Gentlemen look on this wonder,
Whatever the bids of the bidders they cannot be high enough
    for it,
For it the globe lay preparing quintillions of years without
    one animal or plant,
For it the revolving cycles truly and steadily roll'd.

In this head the all-baffling brain,
In it and below it the makings of heroes.

Examine these limbs, red, black, or white, they are cunning
    in tendon and nerve,
They shall be stript that you may see them.

Exquisite senses, life-lit eyes, pluck, volition,
    Flakes of breast-muscle, pliant backbone and neck, flesh not
flabby, good-sized arms and legs,
And wonders within there yet.

Within there runs blood,
The same old blood! the same red-running blood!
There swells and jets a heart, there all passions, desires,
    reachings, aspirations,
(Do you think they are not there because they are not
    express'd in parlors and lecture-rooms?)

> This is not only one man, this the father of those who shall
>   be fathers in their turns,
> In him the start of populous states and rich republics,
> Of him countless immortal lives with countless embodiments
>   and enjoyments.
>
>   (*Leaves* 85–86)

Whitman takes the reader of his day out of the "parlors and lecture-rooms," the comfortable abodes of the literate class where the "slave question" gets discussed, and urges them to look at slavery in the very places where it thrives—the auction block of the slave market. The man on the block has a body just like you, he says. Brain, blood, nerve, and tendon, the body is a real thing, not an abstraction—and it is beautiful. It is the product of long eons of evolution and holds the promise of future generations: "this [is] the father of those who shall be fathers in their turns." And regardless of what you may think about race, this is your human brother who shares the "same old blood" and feels the same "passions, desires, reachings, aspirations." Past and future coalesce in this present moment: the sale of a human body. The slave trader does not "know his business" in more senses than one. His business attempts to put a money value on a human being who is priceless.

Whitman thus combines an appeal to time—"the quintillions of years" and "revolving cycles" contained in the present moment, the future of "populous states and rich republics"—with appeals to place (come out of the lecture room, he says, and see the moral horror and the wasted beauty of the slave market) and the body—the beautiful means of human achievement, the focal point of human kinship. The slave is not an object or an animal, but a son and father.

Whitman was participating in what amounted to a new valuation of the body that followed the democratic revolutions of the late eighteenth and early nineteenth centuries in Europe and America.[3] The breaking down of the old human hierarchies of race and class required people to take a new look at the so-called Great Chain of Being, the concept that placed human beings on a scale a little below God and the angels but above the animals that were, in their turn, above the plants and simpler living things. In this system of values, inherited from the ancients, human beings had a claim to a higher position than animals because of the human soul, said to be lacking in the lower beings. Plato, for example, had represented the human condition in his dialogue *Phaedrus* as a chariot-driver struggling with two horses. The driver strives to let the soul take the lead, the noble horse that pulls him toward heaven, while restraining the troublesome horse that pulls him earthward—suggesting the body and the emotions. Within the broad category of human being, the tendency was to suggest that the class system replicated the Great Chain, with aristocrats, artists, and intellectuals lording over workers, peasants, and slaves, who were said to be "little better than the animals." Those who were fit only to work with their bodies in the Platonic scheme lost touch with the human soul that distinguished them from the animals.

By proclaiming himself the poet of the body as well as the poet of the soul, Whitman was leveling the traditional hierarchy. For Whitman, equality in human relations meant forgoing appeals to the soul in favor of a body-awareness that stressed the kinship of all human beings. Working people did not have the luxury of concentrating on their souls and pursuing the spiritual gifts of art, literature, and anything more than the roughest religious forms. But they shared with everyone else human feelings and the experience of joy and suffering that came from a conscious mind—the "all-baffling brain"—in a sensitive body.

Though no doubt Whitman would have kept intact the idea that humans are superior to animals, he obviously thought about that difference too. In some ways, the animals are superior to us, he suggested. "I think I could turn and live with animals," he says in *Leaves of Grass*, "they are so placid and self-contain'd": "They do not sweat and whine about their condition, / They do not lie awake in the dark and weep for their sins." The animals are perhaps the best democrats, after all: "Not one kneels to another, nor to his kind that lived thousands of years ago" (54).

In these whimsical thoughts, Whitman anticipated the animal rights movement of the late twentieth century. His words remind me of an experience I had with my daughter once in Santa Fe, New Mexico, when she was a little girl about ten years old. We went to a fast-food restaurant for breakfast and ran into a protest for animal rights. Years later, after she had decided to become a vegetarian, we remembered one of the posters the protesters carried. In an appeal to the body for the kinship of all animal beings, the sign said, "Never eat anything with a face."

The Body Impoverished

The appeals to the body and the democratic rhetoric we see in Whitman take on a special urgency in the literature of reform. The social realist writers of nineteenth- and twentieth-century novels such as Stephen Crane's *Maggie*, Upton Sinclair's *The Jungle*, and John Steinbeck's *The Grapes of Wrath* join investigative journalists in our own time in dramatizing the conditions of the poor for an audience of more affluent readers who are perhaps unaware of the nature and degree of suffering in the lives of the rural and inner-city poor. Appeals to the shared experience of the body often combine with appeals to place designed to raise the awareness of readers who enjoy good health and prosperity in the best neighborhoods of the city and suburbs.

A good example appears in the work of the contemporary journalist Jonathan Kozol, who has spent his entire career calling attention to the plight of poor children in the United States. Consider this passage describing life in a South Bronx neighborhood, from his book *Amazing Grace: The Lives of Children and the Conscience of a Nation:*

> Depression is common among children in Mott Haven. Many cry a great deal but cannot explain exactly why.
>
> Fear and anxiety are common. Many cannot sleep.
>
> Asthma is the most common illness among children here. Many have to struggle to take in a good deep breath. Some mothers keep oxygen tanks, which children describe as "breathing machines," next to their children's beds.
>
> The houses in which these children live, two thirds of which are owned by the City of New York, are often as squalid as the houses of the poorest children I have visited in rural Mississippi, but there is none of the greenness and the healing sweetness of the Mississippi countryside outside their windows, which are often barred and bolted as protection against thieves.
>
> Some of the houses are freezing in the winter. In dangerously cold weather, the city sometimes distributes electric blankets and space heaters to its tenants. In emergency conditions, if space heaters can't be used, because substandard wiring is overloaded, the city's practice is to pass out sleeping bags.
>
> "You just cover up . . . and hope you wake up the next morning," says a father of four children, one of them an infant one month old, as they prepare to climb into their sleeping bags in hats and coats on a December night. (4–5)

A sense of being trapped prevails in the passage and gives it rhetorical unity. It is too dangerous for the children to go outside and play the way their counterparts among the rural poor can do. Their windows are bolted and barred, imprisoning them in their own homes—which are not their own after all but merely a place the city provides (and to some extent, neglects). Even if they could go outside, there is only more squalor, none of "the greenness and healing sweetness" of a countryside home. The city is a trap, and so is the home. You can freeze to death in your own bed. Disease pursues you. Who can read the sentence about asthma without inhaling deeply and being thankful for the ability to take a "good deep breath"? The disease increases the sense of entrapment, the claustrophobia. When everything closes in, you can't get enough room to breathe. Shortness of breath can be a symptom of anxiety as well as asthma, and like anxiety, the disease reported here is not only physical but affects the mind as well. Who said that depression is the disease of privilege or that sleeplessness affects only the aged? There was a grim joke in the Great Depression that people were too poor to be mentally ill—but Kozol's investigations suggest otherwise. Moreover, the appeal to health strives to build identity. Even people who have not been poor have been sick and know what it means to suffer with illness.

One interesting rhetorical strategy in the passage is Kozol's restrained style. He invites us to feel the condition of the poor with our bodies—take that deep breath and imagine what it would be like to do without it; remember the prospect of freezing to death when you pull up the bed covers on a cold December night. But he does not overwhelm us with a sensationalistic account and a flurry of adjectives and adverbs, the conventional markers of judgment in English prose. For a descriptive passage, there are few adjectives and adverbs here—"squalid" and "dangerously"—but imagine the things he could have said: unconscionable, pathetic, egregiously neglectful, grim, sad, sorry, mind-boggling, intensely fearful, god-forsaken, inhuman. Instead, he tells us the story in language almost as plain as the children themselves might need to understand, he makes his observations, and for the most part, he leaves the judgments and the inferences to the reader.[4]

Kozol also avoids pious abstractions such as justice, honor, and dignity. The picture he gives is hard and concrete. To some extent it "speaks for itself." We can see the injustice, dishonor, and lack of dignity. He doesn't have to preach us a sermon. In this sense the appeal to the body urges us to come down from the heights of abstract thinking and feel the world we are trying to think about.

The existentialist philosophers and realist writers of modern times teach us to mistrust the easy abstraction or the quick judgment. We know the world best by experience, and the best writing urges us to experience the trouble of the people described vicariously, imagining their worries and their hurts with a visceral intensity, feeling it in our own bodies.

The Body Embattled

The novelist Ernest Hemingway, who developed his famous "telegraphic" version of the plain style as a war correspondent in Europe, pioneered this rhetorical approach in his writing about human suffering. Of the old abstract language used to describe feats of warriors, he writes

> I was always embarrassed by the words sacred, glorious, and sacrifice and the expression in vain. We had heard them, sometimes stand-

ing in the rain almost out of earshot, so that only the shouted words came through, and had read them, on proclamations that were slapped up by billposters over other proclamations, now for a long time, and I had seen nothing sacred, and the things that were glorious had no glory and the sacrifices were like the stockyards at Chicago if nothing was done with the meat except to bury it. There were many words you could not stand to hear and finally only the names of places had dignity. Certain numbers were the same way and certain dates and these with the names of places were all you could say and have them mean anything. Abstract words such as glory, honor, courage, or hallow were obscene beside the concrete names of villages, the numbers of roads, the names of rivers, the numbers of regiments and the dates.

The abstractions mean nothing to the men who stand to be treated like a herd of cattle on the way to the slaughterhouse—or worse: they will only be buried and not used for meat. They seem to be dying without purpose, and the purposelessness extends to the old language of war, once used to fire the emotions of warriors and still shouted at them as they stand in the rain. After the experience of war, the words seem hollow and meaningless— much more so than place names and the numbers of military units and dates, which at least are useful to the soldiers in finding their way in battle and orienting themselves in a chaotic world.

Hemingway's writing is typical of strong appeals to the body in its attempt to activate all the senses of the reader. His imagery, the word pictures he creates, involve not just memorable visual images, which engage the sense of sight—the soldiers milling around in the rain and listening glumly to speeches shouted at them—but also the senses of hearing (words shouted in the rain, the rain itself, the noise of posters "slapped up" over other posters), touch (the wetness of the rain, the slapping of the posters), and even, with some imagination on the part of the reader, smell: the stockyards at Chicago.

After the great slaughters of World War I, made only worse by the technology that was supposed to have saved mankind, the literature of war tended to emphasize the brutality of human conflict. All of humankind, not just the lower classes, came to be depicted as little better than the animals—or worse because human beings violated the high-minded promises of rationality and religion in order to engage in brutal acts or, as Hemingway suggests, used the very words of reason and religion to justify their acts.

The appeals to the body that animated this rhetoric were pioneered in the nineteenth century in accounts of the Civil War, often considered one of the first modern wars because of the use of more powerful rifles and automatic weapons and the tactics of total war, with attacks on civilian targets and campaigns of attrition. The poet of the body Walt Whitman, volunteering in the army hospitals in Washington, D.C., saw many of the effects of the war and wrote about them. He worried that "the real war will never get in the books" (*Specimen Days* 778). "It was not a quadrille in a ball-room," he said (779); it was "about nine hundred and ninety nine parts diarrhea to one part glory" (qtd. in Loving 274).

Whitman's war rhetoric combined strong appeals to the body with mythic references that would stir the fear and sympathy of his readers. He draws upon the imagery of eternal punishment in a passage titled "A Glimpse of War's Hell-Scenes" in his memoir *Specimen Days*, building upon the famous comment of General William Tecumseh Sherman, "War is hell":

> In one of the late movements of our troops in the valley, (near Upperville, I think,) a strong force of Moseby's mounted guerillas attack'd a train of wounded, and the guard of cavalry convoying them. The ambulances contain'd about 60 wounded, quite a number of them officers of rank. The rebels were in strength, and the capture of the train and its partial guard after a short snap was effectually accomplish'd. No sooner had our men surrender'd, the rebels instantly commenced robbing the train and murdering their prisoners, even the wounded. . . . Among the wounded officers in the ambulances were one, a lieutenant of regulars, and another of higher rank. These two were dragg'd out on the ground on their backs, and were now surrounded by the guerillas, a demoniac crowd, each member of which was stabbing them in different parts of their bodies. One of the officers had his feet pinn'd firmly to the ground by bayonets stuck through them and thrust into the ground. These two officers, as afterwards found on examination, had receiv'd about twenty such thrusts, some of them through the mouth, face, &c. The wounded had all been dragg'd (to give a better chance also for plunder,) out of their wagons; some had been effectually dispatch'd, and their bodies were lying there lifeless and bloody. Others, not yet dead, but horribly mutilated, were moaning or groaning. Of our men who surrender'd, most had been thus maim'd or slaughter'd. (748)

"Demonization"—representing enemies as inhuman and in fact superhuman in the evil of their actions and intentions (see chapter 8)—is a common rhetorical strategy in wartime propaganda. Make the people afraid, one of Adolf Hitler's chief propagandists is reputed to have said, and they will accept anything. In this passage, Whitman, a New Yorker and supporter of Lincoln and the Union, seems to be engaging in this kind of rhetoric. The rebel rangers appear as a "demoniac crowd." But he doesn't stop there.

He goes on to show how Union soldiers took their revenge with equal savagery. Demonization is not a rhetorical tactic for him so much as an effect of war on the human psyche. It turns people into demons and predatory animals:

> Multiply the above by scores, aye hundreds—verify it in all the forms that different circumstances, individuals, places, could afford—light it with every lurid passion, the wolf's, the lion's lapping thirst for blood—the passionate, boiling volcanoes of human revenge for comrades, brothers slain—with the light of burning farms, and heaps of smutting, smouldering black embers—and in the human heart everywhere black, worse embers—and you have an inkling of this war. (*Specimen Days* 749)

The implication is that you don't have to die to go to hell. War is a living hell, and there's a deeper hell in every human heart.

The Body Disabled—and Embraced

One particularly poignant rhetoric of the body comes from the field known as disability studies. A key figure in that movement is the essayist Nancy Mairs, a sufferer of multiple sclerosis. I almost wrote "a victim," but Mairs would never want to be called a victim—this woman who proudly accepts the label "cripple" as a way of raising awareness of the modern human being's unacknowledged dependency on the body. She uses her own crippling disability as a means of turning readers toward their own bodies as the source of identity itself.

In the essay "Carnal Acts," she writes,

> Research suggests that I was infected by this virus, which no one has ever seen and which therefore, technically, doesn't even "exist," between the ages of four and fifteen. In effect, living with this mysterious mechanism feels like having your present self, and the past selves it embodies, haunted by a capricious and meanspirited ghost, unseen except for its footprints, which trips you even when you're watching where you're going, knocks glassware out of your hand, squeezes the urine out of your bladder before you reach the bathroom, and weights your whole body with a weariness no amount of rest can relieve. An alien invader must be at work. But of course it's not. It's your own body. That is, it's you. (393)

She tugs the reader toward her condition with the switch to the second-person "you" early in this passage, and rightly so, for her condition, though it is an extreme example perhaps, is not different in kind from the human condition. We all have bodies that seem sometimes alien; they don't fit with the mental image we have of ourselves; they seem to let us down at crucial times. The alienation from the body is built into Western culture, Mairs argues: "The Western tradition of distinguishing the body from the mind and/or the soul is so ancient as to become part of our collective unconscious. . . . I *have* a body, you are likely to say if you talk about embodiment at all; you don't say, I *am* a body" (393).

One of Mairs's goals as a writer is to "write the body," to call attention forthrightly to the things that in her upbringing as a graceful young lady she was taught never to mention (such as "urine" in the passage just quoted). It was not so much her body, she suggests, as the education in grace and charm that let her down. It did not prepare her for life as a cripple; it only brought her shame. Her education taught her to write bodiless prose in "a voice that had shucked off its own body" (398), but when she became ill, she resolved to speak the "unspeakable," to bring the body into the foreground with her vivid imagery and blunt diction:

> No one is going to leave me speechless. To be silent is to comply with the standard of feminine grace. But my crippled body already violates all notions of feminine grace. What more have I got to lose. I've gone beyond shame. I'm shameless, you might say. You know, as in "shameless hussy"? A woman with her bare brace and her tongue hanging out. (399)

Until I read Mairs, I was always suspicious of the way we use the term "voice" when we talk about writing. We praise good writing by saying the author has a strong or distinctive "voice." We encourage novice writers by saying "Now you're finding your voice." I always thought of this usage as a weak metaphor that participates in a devaluation of writing in favor of speech. *Voice* has the advantage of suggesting something as uniquely individual as fingerprints, but *style* also suggests the particular ways of writing associated with an individual author. We often refer to the style of Hemingway or Dickinson, the special patterns of written English that characterize their works. So shouldn't we reserve "voice" for spoken language and say "style" when we talk about writing—a word derived from the instrument of writing, the *stylus*, or pen?

Mairs would say—or shout—no:

> I've found my voice . . . just where it ought to have been, in the body-warmed breath escaping my lungs and throat. Forced by the exigencies of physical disease to embrace my self in the flesh, I couldn't write bodiless prose. The voice is the creature of the body that produces it. (399)

The idea of voice in writing, as Mairs so dramatically hints, is a special appeal to the body. If you trace writing back to its source, there will always be a body present, a hand pushing the pen or tapping the keyboard, a throat vibrating with the "silent" words on the page or screen.[5]

The Body Empowered

The appeals to the body we have covered so far—presenting a relatively comfortable audience with images of life as the poor live it, the claustrophobic trapped feeling of being unable to breathe or so cold that you worry about freezing to death in your sleep; or the hellish scenes of war where all human reason and its abstract categories of honor, justice, and love get stripped away to reveal the brutish underside of life; or the struggles of the disabled person just to get up in the morning—may evoke emotions such as fear and disgust. The risk is that the audience will turn away from the message, repulsed by a kind of natural defensiveness. But the authors are counting on a different response, a sort of natural fascination, the kind of curiosity that causes people to look closely when they pass the scene of an automobile accident, often in spite of their conscious wishes.

Modern rhetoric fully acknowledges and occasionally invokes unconscious motives such as the human fascination with death and evil. Beginning in the nineteenth century, scientists like Darwin brought people face to face with their animal origins, and political thinkers like Marx and Engels took an interest in how people often acted contrary to their own best interests, driven by ideologies, or "false consciousness"—ideals that had little to do with their material existence but kept them enslaved to particular ways of working and living. The philosopher Nietzsche argued that all the seeming goodness of humanity was really directed toward the often unconscious drive to power; most people behaved like a herd of mindless cattle while a privileged few strove to grasp the means to take charge of the herd.

The interest in unconscious motives reached a new height with the invention of psychoanalysis by Sigmund Freud at the turn of the twentieth century. We need not go into Freud's famous theories of personality and development here, many of which have been discredited and have lost their claim to scientific validity. Even so, Freud remains one of the great mythologists of modern culture and a powerful resource for modern rhetoric. Above all, Freud taught that we are not always fully aware of why we do things and that our every success seems fraught with a sense of dissatisfaction, with guilt or incompleteness. The dissatisfaction may arise from some old experiences that still rumble around deep in our minds but never quite rise to consciousness—some real or imagined deprivation or failing from childhood, for example.

In his 1930 book *Civilization and Its Discontents*, Freud—who was himself suffering from the ravages of mouth cancer at the time and was forced to use an ill-fitting prosthetic jaw—directly addresses people's worries and fears about the inadequacies of the human body. In earlier times, according to Freud's account, people saw themselves as "feeble animal organism[s]" and "formed an ideal conception of omnipotence and omniscience" that, being denied to humanity, could be embodied in the gods. "Today," however, "[man] has come very close to the attainment of this ideal"—"he has almost become a god himself" by the power of his technology. He builds "auxiliary organs" to extend his powers—microscopes and telescopes to extend his vision, communication devices to send his voice around the globe, airplanes that allow him to fly, fortresses that add layers of protection to his tender skin:

> Man has, as it were, become a kind of prosthetic God. When he puts on all his auxiliary organs he is truly magnificent; but those organs have not grown on to him and they still give him much trouble at times. Nevertheless, he is entitled to console himself with the thought that his development will not come to an end precisely with the year 1930 A.D. Future ages will bring with them new and probably unimaginably great advances in this field of civilization and will increase man's likeness to God still more. But [for now] we will not forget that present-day man does not feel happy in his Godlike character. (44–45)

Freud reminds us that what makes modern people proud is their sense of power, the notion that they are living out their ancestors' dreams and fantasies about power. Notice the appeal to time that draws upon the modern concept of a break with the past.

But, as Freud makes clear, along with this new feeling of Godlike omnipotence comes a suspicion that things aren't what they seem to be. Underneath all our glory, we still have our weaknesses—perhaps we are even worse off than our ancestors because now we have come to depend upon our "prosthetic organs." It is our machines and inventions that have the power, not we ourselves, our own bodies. These devices have not grown to us, so they can be taken away, leaving us exposed and powerless.

Think about the controversies today over devices like the calculator and the computer. The calculator allows math students to work faster and more accurately than ever before, but the persistent worry is that students' ability to do simple math without the aid of the machines is getting lost. This line of argument is very old. In Plato's dialogue *Phaedrus*, Socrates expresses the same worry about writing. If we write everything down, will we ultimately lose our powers of memory?

Even a technology as seemingly simple as writing thus threatens the integrity of the mind as the philosopher understands it. With the change of technological scale in modern times, the worries intensify. We're reminded of our vulnerability when a large-scale electrical failure brings the computerized and air-conditioned society to its knees. Just as our "prosthetic organs" give us trouble, so our restructured environments fail us at times.

With this view in mind, go back to your experiment with TV and radio ads. Chances are, any of the ads that do not appeal directly to your desire to eat or have sex have to do with your desire for power or security. Think about car and truck ads in particular. The images suggest freedom and release—a sleek automobile speeding down the highway with no barriers in sight—or superhuman strength and power: a four-wheel-drive truck pulling a huge load up a gigantic incline. Even if you can't run a hundred yards or push the lawn mower up the hill in your own backyard, you can get the speed and power you need by buying a new car or truck. Power is what the advertisements promise, and this kind of promise rests upon an appeal to the body that sets the limitations of the actual body against the potential of the ideal body, the body extended by technology.

To take a more disturbing example, think about the rhetoric of terrorism, a uniquely modern form of symbolic action. Terrorism results from a conflict between the drive for power and the sense of powerlessness that both pervade the modern world. It turns large-scale technological systems against the people who usually most enjoy the benefits of these technologies. People usually ignored or despised by the powerful can use thus disrupt systems of transportation, communication, and commerce. In this way, they gain the attention of the world. With attention comes some measure of power.

In the September 11 attacks, for example, a small group of militants unassociated with the usual aggregations of world power (nation states and multinational corporations) hijacked commercial airliners—technologies that embody godlike speed, mobility, and energy in a modern society—and used these planes to attack symbolic places: the World Trade Center and the Pentagon, nerve centers of commercial and military power on the global scene. Having used violence on the grand scale to attract the attention of another global force—the news media—the militants locked into the power of mass communication. The once powerless militants had successfully, and tragically, co-opted the power of high technology and the great nations.

One lesson that arises from a rhetorical analysis of terrorism is ironically similar to the message of early democratic rhetoric. When life is confronted in its barest essentials, we all must live and die in our own bodies. All power is limited. To think otherwise—to believe the fantasies of power that get acted out in advertising and in acquisition—may allow us to forget those limitations, but terrorism confronts us with the truth in the old maxim of "live by the sword and die by the sword." The power we desire and court with such fervor can always be used against us.

We have seen how appeals to local places tend to question globalist values. In a similar way, appeals to the individual human body—the home place of the self—may be used to question the values implicit in high technology and the promise of godlike powers.

In Sum: From Identification to Difference

In appeals to the body, authors use language and imagery to stimulate the senses in the hope that audiences will feel a visceral tug toward various positions of value.

- Advertisers extol the value of products with the promise of speeding buyers along the path to personal power.

- Advocates of democratic politics communicate their traditional values of "life, liberty, and the pursuit of happiness," or "liberty, equality, and fraternity."

- Reformers and activists appeal to the audience's sense of kinship with the sick, oppressed, and suffering to foster the values of social service and responsibility.

- Essayists and novelists communicate the horrors of war, the thrill of street life, or the alternating feelings of liberation and panic associated with the experience of power.

Appeals to the body, like all appeals, vary minutely in their purposes, but the general aims can be summarized according to changes that authors seek to produce in an audience's awareness, attitudes, and action:

- Appeals can aim to open up readers' *awareness* (calling attention to the condition of poor children, for example).

- Appeals can aim to change readers' *attitudes* (debunking the idea that war is about honor and glory, for example, or that technology is the key to human power).

- Appeals can aim to move the reader into *action* (to buy a new product, vote a certain way, or go to work for a political cause).

Appeals to the body can help us work through our differences with other people by focusing on common ground. But even as they promote identification among diverse groups, appeals to the body can also contribute to a stronger sense of difference, sometimes even an aggravated and persistent sense of difference, as we have seen in the rhetorics of disability and terrorism. The differences between males and females, to which we turn in chapter 7, and the differences between the races, the topic of chapter 8, provide further cases in point.

7 ► Appeals to Gender

Much of the liveliness in human society—along with much of the tension—arises from differences between men and women. The division of the sexes certainly doesn't begin in modern times—it's as old as Eden—but shifting opportunities for women in modern cultures beget more and more frequent questions about how much is "instinctual" and how much is "learned"—how much "nature," how much "nurture"—in what people assume about the way men and women operate. Is motherhood, for example, an "instinct" or the result of "social conditioning"? Because such questions cannot be answered fully by biological science, they fall within the traditional purview of rhetoric. Again, rhetoric traditionally deals with things that we argue over, not things that can be settled by clear evidence.[1]

The physical differences between the sexes and their roles in reproduction, which are distinct, obvious, and striking to begin with, tend to become even more pronounced and more complicated when we consider the ways that societies apply the principles of *gender*, the categories of "masculinity" and "femininity." People immersed in any given society are likely to think that the traits and roles normally included in the gender categories are "natural": the man hunts, the woman cares for the children; men are straightforward and tend to be brutal; women are communal and tend to be devious; men are from Mars, women from Venus—and "that's just the way it is."

But in fact, the categories, traits, and roles shift, sometimes subtly and sometimes dramatically, as we look across different cultures. What's considered masculine behavior in some societies—farm work, for example—may be undertaken by both men and women in other societies, or perhaps only by women. An aspect of feminine beauty in one culture—smooth skin, for example—may appear as gender-neutral in a second culture, or may be a matter of something like social class and not a concern of gender at all in a third culture.

Because of the fluidity of gender, appeals that involve sexual differences can never be merely categorized as appeals to the body. The very distinction between sex and gender—sex defined as a bodily condition ("nature") and gender defined as the result of social conditioning and training ("nurture")—is not so easy to sort out as you may think. Investigative journalists have revealed, for example, that hermaphroditism is much more common among newborns than most people ever knew and that doctors, with and without permission of the parents, have been known to "correct" the condition, leaving only a nagging confusion to haunt the "male" or "female" patient in later years. Beyond the genitalia, "masculine" traits, such as broad shoulders, heavy musculature, and facial hair, and "feminine" traits, such as broader hips, pronounced breasts, and sparse body hair, vary widely among individuals and racial types. Still the categories persist, to be alternately bolstered and undermined by the practice of rhetoric.

Appeals to time and the questions of modernity also affect the rhetoric of gender. People living in modern democracies tend to feel superior when they regard the practices of cultures that closely monitor the division of the sexes and the control of the body. Tribal customs such as female circumcision and social rules involving women's clothing (veiling and long dresses that cover the legs) are judged on a scale ranging from unconscionably cruel to merely unfair. It is hard to see them otherwise once the values of liberty and equality come into play. The old patriarchal cultures, in which the power to make decisions and control the key processes of life belong exclusively to older men, are treated with contempt by most educated people in modern Western societies. Such social hierarchies appear as premodern and outmoded in cultures that pride themselves on allowing men and women to mingle more or less freely in public and make their own choices about how to display, care for, and share their bodies.

But feminists, along with gay, lesbian, and transsexual activists, often argue that a fundamental patriarchy still exists in modern cultures beneath the mask of social tolerance and individual liberty. And even if you don't subscribe to these political perspectives, it doesn't take much looking around to see that, no matter how modern the culture, practically everything in the social landscape remains heavily gendered. In the United States, choices at every stage of life are shaped by gender categories. The conditioning begins even before we're able to make our own choices. Parents are still urged to buy pink for girls and blue for boys in baby clothes. The togs for little boys have trucks, frogs, and bulldog puppies stitched into them; the girls get little pink flowers, hearts, and fairies. In the next stage of life, toys divide between beginner baking ovens and baseball bats, baby dolls and action figures, ballet slippers and BB guns. By adolescence the patterns are set, and the self-policing and peer pressure begin. Even the brightest and most self-aware high-school students seem to make choices that divide neatly along gender lines. Data from standardized tests, for example, reveal that young women favor and perform best in courses and on tests in the humanities and arts, while young men do best in math and science. This trend has been present from the beginning of such testing and continues to this day despite the women's movement and scholarship programs encouraging girls to cross over into the technical fields. And the division certainly doesn't end with the onset of adulthood. We have magazines for men with a heavy emphasis on sports and magazines for women that concentrate on fashion. Hollywood markets romantic comedies for women ("chick flicks") and "action-adventure" shows for men (chase scenes and big explosions linked together by the thinnest possible plots—"dick flicks"?). Entire television networks are devoted to audiences divided by gender.

Such heavy investment in the division of genders raises questions of personal and political power. Who gets to do what? And what measure of liberty and equality can you count on? Society has different expectations of men and women, and how to work within these expectations or slip free of them often becomes a matter of how you position yourself as a woman or a man, how you appeal to gender.

To come to terms with this kind of appeal, we might begin by asking who benefits most from any particular way of defining gender categories and who "pays the price"? A quick survey of modern rhetorical practices leads, not surprisingly, back to the advertisers.

Marketing Gender: Empowered or Exploited?

I remember an ad from the late 1970s or early 1980s. Like many other educated, middle-class, young professionals in the western world, I was trying in those days to make sense of gender relations under the influence of the women's movement and the consequent perception of changes in home and workplace roles. I happened to be writing a book about sexuality in literature at the time, but I wasn't just studying gender formally; I was also trying to figure out how to behave as a responsible human being.

The ad pictured a dressed-for-success working woman bursting into the family home and shouting out a brassy show tune to the accompaniment of an invisible orchestra. The bluesy style of the music strongly suggested the atmosphere in a stripper bar. I don't remember the product advertised and not much of the lyric the woman was belting out—only one line in fact: "I can bring home the bacon, / fry it up in the pan."

The ad had appeal for me, I confess. I realized its general corniness, but it seemed encouraging and empowering for women. It allowed them a position in the traditional world of men. The cliché of "bringing home the bacon" meant, as usual, making money to support the family, but with a slight twist. The superwoman in the ad could bring it home and fry it up, absorbing the roles of man and woman—breadwinner and bread-baker—without (and this is important) losing her sex appeal. Indeed, the implication was that she got even sexier when she got liberated. No longer the home-bound drudge, she gave the impression that her liberation brought with it the freedom to express a tantalizing sexual naughtiness. She combined the intellectual appeal of the smart businesswoman or lawyer, the comfort of wife and mother, and the raw attraction of the stripper. She could have it all for herself and still be everything her family and her man could ever need.

I eventually forgot about the ad, but I was jolted back into remembering it and somewhat embarrassed by its former appeal for me when, in 1989, I encountered a new book called *The Second Shift* by the Berkeley sociologist Arlie Russell Hochschild. The book reported on a long-term study of couples in which the husband and the wife both worked. The question was, with both partners working, who covered the housework and childcare, the "second shift" of work that every family must account for? The short answer was that the women did most of the work at home. Sure enough, they were bringing home the bacon and frying it up in the pan, but they didn't feel particularly sexy and empowered. They felt tired, and some felt exploited.

Hochschild introduces *The Second Shift* with a reference to the same kind of advertised image that caught my eye. Chapter 1 begins this way:

> She is not the same woman in each magazine advertisement but she is the same idea. She has that working-mother look as she strides forward, briefcase in one hand, smiling child in the other. Literally and figuratively, she is moving ahead. Her hair, if long, tosses behind her; if it is short, it sweeps back at the sides, suggesting mobility and progress. There is nothing shy or passive about her. She is confident, active, "liberated." She wears a dark tailored suit, but with a silk bow or colorful frill that says, "I'm really feminine underneath." She has made it in a man's world without sacrificing her femininity. And she has done this on her own. By some personal miracle, this image suggests, she has managed to combine what 150 years of industrialization have split wide apart—child and job, frill and suit, female culture and male.
>
> When I showed a photograph of a supermom like this to the working mothers I talked to in the course of researching this book, many responded with an outright laugh. One daycare worker and mother of two, ages three and five, threw back her head: "Ha! They've got to be *kidding* about her. Look at me, hair a mess, nails jagged, twenty pounds overweight. Mornings, I'm getting my kids dressed, the dog fed, the lunches made, the shopping list done. That lady's got a maid." Even working mothers who did have maids couldn't imagine combining work and family in such a carefree way. "Do you know what

a baby *does* to your life, the two o'clock feedings, the four o'clock feedings?" . . . They envied the apparent ease of the woman with the flying hair, but she didn't remind them of anyone they knew. (Hochschild 1–2)

The advertised image appeals to the desire for enough power to do it all, to be able to accomplish all that life sets before you—and to avoid the hard choices that life in a modern society puts before you, above all the choice of how to divide the labor in working families, a decision that has led to more than one divorce.

Even at the time I first saw the ad, I understood that the appeal was directed not only to the working woman who longed for sufficient power to succeed in a double role, but also to the "enlightened" man, the kind of person I understood myself to be in the late 1970s. The man wants his wife to "fulfill herself" by having a career, but he doesn't want to give up the wife and mother who takes care of everything at home, leaving him free to be the "principal breadwinner."

Professor Hochschild's rhetorical strategy involves an "unmasking" of the ad's appeal. As chapter 3 suggests, rhetorical situations always involve "personae," literally masks. The "first persona" is the author position, the "I," the face put forward to the world. The "second persona" is the audience position constructed by the author, the "you" to whom the performance is addressed. In the supermom ads, the producers put forward the image of the empowered woman, the "I" that sings, "I can bring home the bacon." I always supposed that the implied "you" of the ad would be the overworked housewife or working mother that longs to be like supermom. "Buy our product," the advertiser says indirectly through the agency of supermom, and you can be like "me."

But the working mothers whose stories appear in *The Second Shift* aren't buying the image: "They envied the apparent ease of the woman with the flying hair, but she didn't remind them of anyone they knew." They accept the mask of what I assumed to be the second persona, overworked and exploited, but they reject the image of supermom as unreal and unattainable. She is only an image, a fantasy figure.

The fantasy works in the service of educated men sensitive to the demands of the women's movement but worried about the challenge to their position. One of the most disturbing findings I remember from Hochschild's research was that the educated professional men in the study were more likely than the working-class men to proclaim the need of husbands to share the housework and childcare with their working wives; but, when it came to actually chipping in and doing the work, the professional men were, if anything, less likely to contribute than their working-class counterparts.

As the old saying goes, they talked the talk but didn't walk the walk. It was just the opposite with the working-class men.

The irony in this situation turns on the reversal of expectations revealed in this situation of inequality. This particular appeal depends upon the creation of not just a first and second persona, an "I" and "you," but also a third persona: "they." The author appeals to the audience by forming an inner circle of knowledge—what "you" and "I" can see but others are oblivious to: "They" don't get it. The force of the irony is directed against the third persona "them." In Hochschild's book, the position of the third persona is occupied by the professional men who don't hold up their part in the equal relationship they profess to believe—and by the advertisers who support them. Supermom appears as the advertisers' mask, or their puppet. Hochschild's research deflates the farce, revealing the true authors of the ad and their beneficiaries—"them." Her "I" appeals as a working mother—who tells her own story in the preface—reaching out to an audience of "you" other working mothers who are tired out from trying to live the life that supermom supposedly succeeds in, a life that "we" find too hard to manage.

The irony and unmasking led me to take another look at my mental image of the old "bring home the bacon" ad. With new eyes, I could see that the ad appealed to me by approaching me with a fantasy image. The sexy composite of working woman, housewife, and stripper said to me, in effect, "Don't you want a woman like me?" It could be that men like me were always the intended second persona, the "you" of this ad. The sad part is that the implied third persona was the overworked housewife working virtually two jobs, a first shift at the store or factory or office and the second shift at home. As I watched from the position of observer or distanced social critic, Professor Hochschild removed the mask of the second and third personae and exchanged the places, making the overworked housewife the "you" she addressed and treating the neglectful husbands and their accomplices the advertisers as the third persona. Now it became us against them, and I found, with some dismay, that the old "enlightened" version of myself of the 1970s belonged in the position of "them."

The short answer to our question about power, then, is that professional educated men stand to benefit most from the values and ideology implied in the appeal of such ads. Working women pay the price, as do homebound women who continue to perform heavy, sometimes unfulfilling labor in a low-prestige job (often these days receiving a share of contempt from women who do pursue careers outside the home).

But if men stand to get empowered and women exploited by such rhetoric, what do the marketers stand to gain? I see two possible explanations. First, by siding with men of the professional class, they appeal to the group most likely to control the greatest percentage of the society's capital resources, the guys with the money to buy the products. Second, and more subtly, they benefit by perpetuating gender divisions of any kind—the stronger, the better. It only stands to reason that if products can be divided by gender—if men are likely to make decisions about some products and women about others—you can more easily "target" the market for your ads. You know it's best to advertise cleaning products during "soap operas" (hence the name) and trucks and beer during football games. About the only time you ever see a man cleaning house in an ad, he appears like "Mr. Clean" as a fantasy figure who shows up to rescue the housewife in distress from the burden of her work. In the world projected by advertising rhetoric, housekeeping remains women's work.

Demystifying the Image: The Appeal to Fulfillment and Health

Many of the ideas and rhetorical strategies found in Hochschild's study were anticipated in the now classic book *The Feminine Mystique,* published by Betty Friedan in 1963. Friedan, who went on to found the National Organization of Women (NOW) and become a preeminent leader in the American women's movement, offers a powerful example of a technique favored by modern rhetoric and suggested in our analysis of *The Second Shift.* Call it image competition.[2]

Considering the reputation Friedan earned as a pioneering feminist in the 1960s, she uses a surprisingly subtle and unthreatening image to set up a rhetorical situation that turns out to have great power. In her first chapter, she slowly works her way toward the articulation of an unnamed problem that gradually comes first into focus in what was then a familiar, everyday image: a ladies' coffee group, which serves as not only the focal point of the problematic image but also a projection of the book's ideal audience. Instead of the expected small talk and gossip, or worries over children and husbands, these housewives and mothers are talking about themselves. Letting go for once of the ideal of selfless womanhood, the ethos of wife and mother who sacrifices personal needs for the family, they find that they share a sense of vague dissatisfaction. Friedan describes their problem with a famous phrase that Henry David Thoreau applied in *Walden* to the lives of "most men": "quiet desperation." Before the meeting, Friedan tells us, the women had been saying to themselves, "There isn't any problem":

> But on an April morning in 1959, I heard a mother of four, having coffee with four other mothers in a suburban development fifteen miles from New York, say in a tone of quiet desperation, "the problem." And the others knew, without words, that she was not talking about a problem with her husband, or her children, or her home. Suddenly they realized they all shared the same problem, the prob-

lem that has no name. They began, hesitantly, to talk about it. Later, after they had picked up their children at nursery school and taken them home to nap, two of the women cried, in sheer relief, just to know they were not alone. (19–20)

Women like these and the people who know them—their husbands and their children—may feel that Friedan is addressing them directly, I to you, by the end of the book. But the subtlety and much of the rhetorical power of *The Feminine Mystique* arise from a more indirect approach, tipped off by the author's use of pronouns. She does not write from the radicalized position of "we," inviting dissatisfied women to join together under the banner of feminism. Nor does she follow the practice of the advertisers who invite housewives to identify with images like supermom, saying in effect "You can be like me." Instead she borrows the rhetoric of objectivity from the magazine psychologists and doctors of the day; she steps back and invites the audience to join her as observers of the condition of women, treating the ladies of the coffee group and other cases in the third person: "*they* all shared the same problem," "*they* were not alone." To reinforce the audience in the observer's role, Friedan quotes authorities, such as (male) doctors reporting on "the housewife's syndrome" and "the housewife's blight" (20–21). But rather than becoming distant and cold, the rhetorical situation becomes highly dramatic as case after case appears. Author and audience assume the role of research observers watching an experiment in the process of going bad, or theatre-goers beholding a tragedy of human waste and sorrow, left to wonder, how do our own lives compare? The "problem" comes to seem more and more familiar.

In her second chapter, Friedan takes the image she has impressed upon the minds of the observing audience—the unhappy housewife with the vague malady that unfolds in chapter 1—and places it into competition with the image of the happy housewife and ultrafeminine helpmate that prevails in the advertisements and feature articles of a typical women's magazine of the day:

The image of woman that emerges from this big, pretty magazine is young and frivolous, almost childlike; fluffy and feminine, passive; gaily content in a world of bedroom and kitchen, sex, babies, and home. The magazine surely does not leave out sex; the only passion, the only pursuit, the only goal a woman is permitted is the pursuit of a man. It is crammed full of food, clothing, cosmetics, furniture, and the physical bodies of young women, but where is the world of thought and ideas, the life of the mind and spirit? In the magazine image, women do no work except housework and work to keep their bodies beautiful and to get and keep a man. (36)

The magazine woman is yet not augmented to the point of supernatural power, as the "lady with the flying hair" would be in the images of the 1980s. This woman is reduced. Like the specialist in Wendell Berry's critique of modern society (see chapter 1), one part of the woman is unhealthily distended—the life of the body and particularly the function of reproduction—but she is denied "thought and ideas, the life of the mind and spirit." Like the person reduced to slavery, her humanity is denied and she is treated like a lower being, at best a child, at worst an animal.

Friedan expands the image and traces its American history for the remainder of her book. She argues that, under the burden of this image, women's "wasted energy [is] destructive to their husbands, to their children, and to themselves" (377). The unfulfilled woman, striving to deny her wholeness to fit the image, opens herself to all kinds of resentments, neuroses, and physical ailments. The experiment is failing; the tragic waste continues. Women are not merely sad; they are sick, and their sickness is spreading to the whole culture.

The image of the thoughtful, awakening woman remains somewhat poorly defined in this early work by Friedan—realistically so, considering the argument that it is hard even to think outside of images so pervasively imposed upon us by the mass media, as Orwell ominously warned in his novel *1984*. But the awakening has begun in the coffee circles and in the pages of books like *The Feminine Mystique*. Friedan concludes that only "when women as well as men emerge from biological living to realize their human selves, those leftover halves of life may become their years of greater fulfillment":

> Then the split in the image will be healed, and daughters will not face that jumping-off point at twenty-one or forty-one. When their mothers' fulfillment makes girls sure they want to be women, they will not have to "beat themselves down" to be feminine; they can stretch and stretch until their own efforts will tell them who they are. They will not need the regard of boy or man to feel alive. And when women do not need to live through their husbands and children, men will not fear the love and strength of women, nor need another's weakness to prove their own masculinity. They can finally see each other as they are. And this may be the next step in human evolution. (377–78)

"Fulfillment" becomes aligned with "healing" in the constellation of values that guides Friedan's appeal to her audience. She appeals along the lines of traditional humanism. Wholeness (health) involves not just the body, but also the mind and spirit. When women are asked to remain in a state of childhood, or when their importance is limited to bodily functions such as sex and reproduction or animal functions such as physical labor, they are stuck in a biological world. In Friedan's time, women could vote and get an education, but they were asked to take on a kind of voluntary mindlessness. In a poignant appeal to time, Friedan calls for "the next step in human evolution."

Images of the Body and the Problem of Stereotyping

The mildness of Friedan's humanist rhetoric no doubt accounted for her wide appeal and sympathetic audience, but many writers in the women's movement felt the need early on to turn up the volume. One of these was Germaine Greer, whose book *The Female Eunuch* attracted a wide and more radical audience when it came out in the early 1970s. Like Friedan, Greer begins in the position of the observer, using passive-voice verbs and third-person pronouns to describe the plight of women, but at the very end of her book, in a kind of feminist manifesto entitled "Revolution," she switches abruptly to the first-person plural "we"—"We have but one life to live, and the first object is to find a way of salvaging that life from the disabilities already inflicted upon it in the service of our civilization" (326)—and then she ends by directly addressing the reader with the second person in her very last sentence: "What *will* you do?" (329).

Much of the edge that Greer achieves throughout her book comes from her focus on the female body and particularly female sexuality. In the introduction, she writes,

> female sexuality has been masked and deformed by most observers, and never more so than in our own time. . . . What happens is that the female is considered as a sexual object for the use and appreciation of other sexual beings, men. Her sexuality is both denied and misrepresented by being identified as passivity. The vagina is obliterated from the imagery of femininity in the same way that the signs of independence and vigor in the rest of her body are suppressed. The characteristics that are praised and rewarded are those of the castrate—timidity, plumpness, languor, delicacy and preciosity. . . . [F]emale reproduction is thought to influence the whole organism in the operations of the *Wicked Womb*, source of hysteria, menstrual depression, and unfitness for any sustained enterprise. (5)

Greer, a British woman who relocated to the United States, caught the spirit of the European women's movement of the late 1960s, particularly the French feminists who took to the streets with banners saying "WE ARE ALL HYSTERICS." The word "hysterical," which derives from the Greek word for "womb," has been used since ancient times to describe an illness that crosses the boundaries between mind and body but has also been used in association with a dismissive attitude toward the complaints of women. By claiming the word that had for centuries been used against them, the French feminists found a way of celebrating their difference from those who would oppress them. "Yes, we are different," they said in effect, "but now you must deal with our difference rather than using it as a stigma; you must work through it rather than around it."[3]

Greer uses a similar tactic, arguing that, in the prevailing imagery of the times, women's sexuality has been seen primarily as something lacking. Because woman lacks the male genitalia, she takes on the attributes of the eunuch. What has really happened is that the reality of her own sexuality has been denied, the image of the vagina removed from sight and made mysterious, an object of fear and loathing. The result is not only misrepresentation, but ultimately violence, an attempt to act out in real life what has happened in the social imagination: namely, the destruction of the woman. The penis becomes a sword or a gun in popular symbolism, and the cycle of violence is perpetuated.

Repetition, the motor for this kind of image-perpetuation, gains force in a culture where print and broadcasting media allow mass reproduction of imagery, where television and internet flood the home and saturate the mind with images designed for quick consumption and easy memory. So it is that the practice of stereotyping emerges and takes hold as a key problem in modern times. The very word derives from the print industry; it signifies the ability of the printing press to create master images and reproduce them with exact precision. Thus, as Greer writes, "the myth of the Eternal Feminine, nowadays called the *Stereotype*," becomes the "dominant image of femininity which rules our culture and to which all women aspire":

> Assuming that the goddess of consumer culture is an artifact, we embark on an examination of how she comes to be made, the manufacture of the *Soul*. The chief element in the process is like the castration that we saw practiced upon the body, the suppression and deflection of *Energy*. Following the same simple pattern, we begin at the beginning with *Baby*, showing how of the greater the less is made. The *Girl* struggles to reconcile her schooling along masculine lines with her feminine conditioning until *Puberty* resolves the ambiguity and anchors her safely in the feminine posture, if it works. When it doesn't she is given further conditioning as a corrective, especially by psychologists, whose assumptions and prescriptions [amount to] the *Psychological Sell*. (5)

In this passage from her introduction—with each italicized topic covered in later chapters—Greer hints at how the entire life of the stereotypic woman gets imprinted by the male-dominated institutions of social life: church, family, school, state, and health care establishments (particularly the mental health industry), all reinforced by advertising, mass communication, and the entertainment industry.

Anticipating that she will be criticized for not offering solid alternatives for the gender system she criticizes, Greer follows Friedan in suggesting that we cannot yet know what woman will become when she is fully liberated. But considering the spiraling violence against women, Greer argues, we must stop it at its root. The root of the violence, in her view, is the prevailing image of the woman's body as something either threatening or totally without value, something lacking. So—unlike Friedan who points ultimately to the humanistic values of mental and spiritual fulfillment, the things men and women ought to have in common—Greer hones in on the differences in an appeal to the body. Not until women's bodies are valued at the same level as men's will men, and women themselves, stop treating the female body as an object to be feared, loathed, punished, erased, and destroyed.

Breaking the Hold of Stereotypes: Shifting Perspectives

To get a stronger hold on the problem of stereotyping, consider an example from imaginative literature: *The Left Hand of Darkness*, a science fiction novel written just about the same time as *The Female Eunuch*. The author, Ursula K. Le Guin, invites the reader to join her in a story that involves a "thought experiment." An earthly envoy representing an interplanetary federation is sent to a planet inhabited by humanoids with no permanent sexual identities. These aliens are neither male nor female until they enter *kemmer*, their season of estrus. In kemmer, any individual may manifest as male or female and in the course of a lifetime may experience both states. From their viewpoint, the envoy—a normal male earthling—lives in a state of more or less permanent kemmer. Thus he is received as a curiosity by his hosts, who think of him as a "pervert." As an anthropologist as well as a diplomat on a sensitive mission, he finds that he must struggle with stereotypes that he has never given a second thought but that inform every habit of his thinking about other people. Here's a typical case, in which the envoy describes one of the planet's denizens:

> He was the superintendent of my island; I thought of him as my landlady, for he had fat buttocks that wagged as he walked, and a soft fat face, and a prying, spying, ignoble, kindly nature. He was good to me,

and also showed my room while I was out to thrill-seekers for a small fee: See the Mysterious Envoy's room! He was so feminine in looks and manner that I once asked him how many children he had. He looked glum. He had never borne any. He had, however, sired four. It was one of the little jolts I was always getting. (48)

Le Guin says in her introduction to the novel that science fiction usually comes closer to describing the present than predicting the future. The hint suggests that the envoy's struggle with stereotypes and the "jolts" he gets from time to time are typical experiences in modern life. The fact that he is a black man underlines Le Guin's point: It is painful and difficult to work through the encrusted stereotypes and assumptions we carry with us in an effort to understand, with the care of a professional diplomat and anthropologist, the reality of the Other. The envoy's race, a huge issue on his home planet, turns out to be of little consequence in this new setting, but his masculinity, his gender, figures powerfully in his relations with people from the host planet.

The suggestion is that such categories as race and gender are relatively arbitrary. They are socially constructed. They are like language in the sense that any word, such as "tree," bears an arbitrary relationship to the object it refers to in nature, the thing with leaves and bark. The meaning is attributed by language users, and the word changes from culture to culture. Though arbitrary, however, the attributions are no less real. They inspire violent emotions (pathos), determine the qualities of character (ethos), and even affect reasoning (logos). The connection between language and thinking has been a matter of great concern in modern rhetorical theory, linguistics, philosophy of language, and cognitive psychology. It would be extremely difficult to separate thought from language or some other kind of symbol system (such as numbers or the visual images and movements of dreams). We think in signs.

This cognitive dimension of symbolic activity suggests that when stereotypes predominate in language, they take root in the mind, place limits on what a person can think, and can only be dislodged by a jolting shift of perspectives. The jolt that Le Guin's envoy feels also comes from a rapid shift in perspective—a common experience of travelers in foreign countries. Their old habits of interpreting the world bump up against a new reality. Old positions must be reconfigured; old habits adjusted to new information. Rhetoric often serves as an accompaniment to, or a substitute for, the jolting experience of foreign travel and cultural exchange.

8 ▸ Appeals to Race

The study of rhetoric grows increasingly complex as you realize how appeals tend to build upon other appeals to create a kind of vast molecular structure. The process occurs in even the simplest texts, much less in the often difficult and complex communications we encounter daily in contemporary life.

With increasing complexity, the rhetoric of race—our topic in this chapter—builds upon many of the appeals we have already seen at work:

- Martin Luther King Jr. crafted *appeals to time* to give a sense of urgency to a problem that had gone untreated in American democracy for too long: the inequality of access to basic rights and privileges based on race alone (chapter 4).

- Unlike King—who argued that African Americans, long ago removed from their native place against their will, should now be able to enjoy the benefits of advanced modern civilization—the Native American activist Vine Deloria Jr. invoked *appeals to place*. He appealed to people disaffected by the feeling of displacement and alienation from the land that accompanies modernization. He held up the example of the American Indians who take their identity from the land instead of imposing their civilization upon the land. Not only should indigenous peoples be allowed to pursue their own version of place-centered civilization, he argued, but perhaps the displaced descendants of the old European pioneers should take a lesson from the Natives and consider "reinhabitation" as an alternative to economic and geographic mobility and expansion (chapter 5).

- Walt Whitman, in his antislavery poetry, used *appeals to the body* to shake up the racists among his fellow European Americans and argue for the essential unity of mankind in the stream of human evolution (chapter 6).

- Finally, in the last chapter, we saw how in negative *appeals to gender*, stereotypes can serve as a form of social control, leading one group to feel superior or inferior to another, or simply different. The practice is not limited to communicating differences of gender but also extends to ethnic, racial, and national differences.

This chapter takes a closer look at practices like stereotyping that empha-size the "otherness" of certain ethnic groups and considers how rhetoric can identify, resist, and defuse such practices.[1]

To add to the picture of complexity, the chapter considers the rhetoric of race alongside another topic central to the theory of modern rhetoric—namely *literacy*. Far from being just a question of whether a person can read or write, literacy has come to stand as one measure of a person's status in the modern world. We use the word *literate* as a synonym for "educated" or "competent" in such phrases as "scientifically literate," "computer liter-ate," or even "socially literate." In these instances, *literate*—competency in the medium of the written word—is extended to mean fit for life in some specialized area of knowledge or human action. Considering race and lit-eracy together allows us to complicate our theory of appeals by showing how issues of media and language are bound up with thematic concerns such as time, place, gender, and race.

Othering: Forms of Racial Rhetoric

As we saw in chapter 7, stereotyping serves to belittle the status, or the very being, of other people. Stereotypes reduce the complexity of individuals and cultural groups, focusing attention on a carefully limited set of char-acteristics—usually negative, as when Ursula K. Le Guin's character, the envoy to the genderless planet in *The Left Hand of Darkness*, treats his land-lord as feminine because he has wide wagging hips and enjoys gossip. In addition to an overgeneralization, what we get in such stereotypes is a cari-cature, a cartoon image that overemphasizes certain features. We see ste-reotypes of Asians with preposterously slanted eyes; Africans with thick lips and black (not various shades of brown) skin; Jews with big noses and beady eyes; Anglo-American tourists with fat bellies, big bankrolls, loudly colored shirts, and peering cameras.

Stereotyping and other kinds of racist rhetoric attempt to separate an inner circle of author and audience—"us"—from a group of others: "them." The word that has emerged in recent years to describe this general prac-tice is "othering." Related forms of othering include simple diminishment of character, full-scale dehumanization, and demonization:

- *Diminishment of character* involves the denial of key human quali-ties. A common stereotype used during the days of the Vietnam War, for example, was to say that Asian people, because they live in overpopulated conditions, do not feel the same value for life that westerners do. There is a devastatingly ironic scene in the award-winning documentary film *Hearts and Minds*, in which a well-known American general makes this claim in an interview. The scene then shifts abruptly to a group of Vietnamese women wailing in grief over their kinspeople who have died in an attack on their village. The shift of perspectives creates a mental jolt—in technical terms, "cognitive dissonance." The habitual pattern of thought suddenly doesn't fit the situation, and the viewer sees that the stereotype of the enemy—though perhaps useful for preparing soldiers to kill in the service of war—cannot account for the reality of human life in the war-torn country. The viewer's experience is somewhat like the "little jolts" that Le Guin's protagonist regularly experiences in *The Left Hand of Darkness*.

- *Dehumanization* takes diminishment to new heights in a kind of reverse personification. In personification, an author attributes human characteristics to nonhuman beings, objects, or abstractions. Aldo Leopold uses a personification in his essay "Thinking Like a Mountain"—"The mountain sees what men and deer cannot"—though mountains do not think and see in a literal sense. In dehumanization, by contrast, people are deprived of their humanity and made to appear as animals or objects. In ordinary language, we sometimes say, "She uses him for a doormat," or we refer to social conformity as "herd behavior." When Frederick Douglass tells his primarily Euro-American, sentimental, Christian audience that he was denied the experience of knowing and loving his mother in slavery (chapter 3), the force of the appeal arises from the reader's realization that slavery is a dehumanizing institution. Human beings are treated like domestic animals.

- *Demonization* goes the other way, attributing almost superhuman powers of evil to an enemy. President Reagan once called the Soviet Union "the evil empire," for example, and the Ayatollah Khomeini of Iran referred to the United States as "the Great Satan." Part of the strategy of Rachel Carson's attack on the chemical industry in the environmentalist classic *Silent Spring* is to associate the pesticide industry with black magic; the chemicals, in her language, are "brewed" like witch's broth and sprayed over the earth as a "chemical death rain" (17, 21). In Leslie Marmon Silko's *Ceremony*, the story of the Native American Tayo's reinhabitation of his native land after his traumatic experience in World War II (chapter 5), European Americans are likely to feel shocked to see a traditional story in which their own kind is demonized. The invasion of North America by white people is explained as the result of a terrible spell cast during a contest among powerful witches.

People can use the rhetoric of othering to single out any class of people for abuse. Common divisions include gender, social class, ethnicity, skin color, religious affiliation, sexual preference, age, national or regional citizenship, educational background, or political partisanship.

In the United States, race has been a persistent category of otherness. The predominantly white European founders of the nation brought with them a history of class consciousness, religious persecution, and regional identity. Even as they looked for freedom from such prejudices, race relations became a problem as the colonists came into conflict with the indigenous people of the Americas and as slavery took root in the South. In the experiment with American democracy, the treatment of Native and African Americans initiated a long and complex history with an equally complex rhetorical profile. Things have grown only more difficult with each successive wave of foreign immigration.

Literacy and Racial Identity

In the nineteenth century, as the prospect for universal literacy among citizens came to seem an attainable goal with the spread of inexpensive reading matter and public education, literacy became involved in race relations. The ability to read and write had always been used as a standard for civilized status in the Western world, at least since the invention of the printing press. The earliest use of the root word in English was probably the negative "illiterate" to mean unlettered or ignorant, lacking in education (Barton 20–22). The right to literacy and the personal and political empowerment of the once unlettered were central concerns in democratic education. But literacy educators faced some serious challenges related to race. Native Americans, who did not have written languages before contact with Europeans, were considered uncivilized and were taught in early missionary schools to abandon their own languages and learn English on the way to assimilation. This situation produced long-term resentment and resistance. African slaves were kept purposely uneducated, and after emancipation, literacy tests were sometimes required in the Southern states as a way of keeping blacks from voting, creating another stream of resentment and bad faith.

No wonder that the old racial tensions came to the surface when literacy theorists such as Marshall McLuhan and Walter Ong suggested in the 1960s and 1970s that reading and writing may form the psychological foundation for individuation—the process by which people come to think of themselves as selves and not as outgrowths of some family, community, or ethnic group. They argued that literacy and its consequent self-actualization may even be necessary for higher levels of thinking. Critics sensitive to race politics have dismissed the claims of the literacy theorists

as not only overstated but even racist, a scholarly way of reasserting the ideology of progress and making modern societies seem superior in every way
to premodern, preliterate cultures, many of which continue to exist and
even flourish in today's world.

To see how the intertwined themes of literacy and race work out as rhetorical appeals, we will analyze three examples from African American literature: the nineteenth-century autobiographical classic *Narrative of the Life
of Frederick Douglass: An American Slave*; a modern text that updates and
extends the tradition of the slave narrative, *The Autobiography of Malcolm
X*; and a contemporary novel, *A Lesson Before Dying*, by Ernest Gaines. To
explore rhetorical otherness in a very different form and to show how rhetorical analysis can use appeals theory to tease out the relationship among
many themes in a more extended analysis, we will also consider a final example, the science fiction story "Enemy Mine."

Diminishment in Narrative of the Life of Frederick Douglass

In the most famous of the many nineteenth-century slave narratives, the
great abolitionist and former slave Frederick Douglass devotes a good deal
of space to how he learned to read and write. He associates literacy with
liberation and dates his first desire to escape from slavery from the time
he realized that slaves were kept purposely ignorant:

> Very soon after I went to live with Mr. and Mrs. Auld, she very kindly
> commenced to teach me the A, B, C. After I had learned this, she
> assisted me in learning to spell words of three or four letters. Just at
> this point of my progress, Mr. Auld found out what was going on,
> and at once forbade Mrs. Auld to instruct me further, telling her,
> among other things, that it was unlawful, as well as unsafe, to teach
> a slave to read. To use his own words, further, he said, ". . . A nigger
> should know nothing but to obey his master—to do as he is told to
> do. Learning would *spoil* the best nigger in the world. Now," said
> he, "if you teach that nigger (speaking of myself) how to read, there
> would be no keeping him. . . . He would at once become unman-
> ageable, and of no value to his master. As to himself, it could do him
> no good, but a great deal of harm. It would make him discontented
> and unhappy." (31)

With a deep sense of ironic satisfaction, Douglass goes on to explain how
in fact the master was right. Having gained the rudiments of reading, Douglass only wanted more. The self within him began to stir, and a world of
possibility awakened. The master's words, he says, "sank deep into my heart,
stirred up sentiments within that lay slumbering, and called into existence an entirely new train of thought" (31):

It was a new and special revelation, explaining dark and mysterious things, with which my youthful understanding had struggled, but struggled in vain. I now understood what had been to me a most perplexing difficulty—to wit, the white man's power to enslave the black man. It was a grand achievement, and I prized it highly. From that moment, I understood the pathway from slavery to freedom. It was just what I wanted, and I got it at a time when I the least expected it. Whilst I was saddened by the thought of losing the aid of my kind mistress, I was gladdened by the invaluable instruction which, by the merest accident, I had gained from my master. Though conscious of the difficulty of learning without a teacher, I set out with high hope, and a fixed purpose, at whatever cost of trouble, to learn how to read. (31–32)

In associating literacy with liberty, Douglass appeals to several values that his contemporary audience would have shared and that still resonate for modern readers. Notice how he subtly appeals to the religious values of his predominantly Christian audience by comparing his experience to a religious awakening: a "special revelation . . . dark and mysterious." He also stands for individual determination and willingness to work hard even if it means working alone—a determination suggested by the repetition of a word that proved valuable throughout the history of the civil rights movement, namely "struggle." And he stands for the value of continuous personal improvement, captured in words like "achievement," which has proved serviceable throughout the history of American education. (Think of all the "achievement tests" and "achievement awards" given by public schools over the years.)

The ingenuity of Douglass's appeal depends partly on the particular medium in which he is working—namely the written autobiography, the narrative of selfhood. His audience is composed of readers silently perusing his story. By placing literacy at the center of his appeal, he reaches out to the audience engaged in the very act that he most desires to accomplish and to which he attaches an immense value.

Dehumanization and Demonization in The Autobiography of Malcolm X
Besides Martin Luther King Jr., no African American leader had more impact on the philosophy and politics of race in the formative years of the 1960s than the Muslim spokesman Malcolm X. Malcolm understood the crucial importance of media. As a dynamic speaker, he found ways to get his message into the newspapers and onto the airwaves. He learned how to manipulate interviewers and use shock techniques and overstatement to bring attention to his "Black Nationalist" message—the idea that black

people in the United States should define their values and social aspirations as separate from those of the dominant "white" culture. When the opportunity arose for him to work with the successful black journalist Alex Haley (author of *Roots*) to produce *The Autobiography*, Malcolm saw that he could use the literate medium to extend his voice even further and make his message lasting—an important consideration for a man who had prophetically foreseen his own death. He could also, like Frederick Douglass, use the traditional narrative of selfhood to appeal to a worldwide educated audience and to redeem himself from what he saw as the distorted images of the mass media and the vicious lies spread by his enemies about his character and his program. When the book appeared in print, following Malcolm's assassination in New York City, it quickly became a bestseller, then a classic in the literature of African American selfhood. It was eventually made into a popular film directed by Spike Lee and starring Denzel Washington.

The self that Malcolm shows to the world in this book emerges in three successive stages, each drawing upon characteristic themes and qualities of autobiographical rhetoric, and each adding a new layer of complexity and depth. The first stage recalls the confessional writings of other prominent religious leaders, such as St. Augustine, in its "confessional" quality. In showing what Malcolm ultimately rejects, it gives a detailed and highly engaging treatment of Malcolm's experience in the criminal underworld of the ghettoes in Boston and Harlem—the selfhood of "Detroit Red," as he was known in those days. The key position of value to which the narrative appeals in this section is success. As a high school student in Lancing, Michigan, Malcolm shows great promise of success, but when he tells one of his teachers that he wants to be a lawyer, the man advises him to pursue a trade such as carpentry, something more suitable to the reality of Negro opportunity. Malcolm grows bitter. He moves to Boston to live with his older sister and gradually drifts into the underworld associated with the jazz clubs of the day. He ends up in Harlem, where he achieves success as a hustler, using legitimate "Negro jobs" on the railroad and as a waiter to front for his activities as a numbers runner and drug peddler. At this point, the autobiography also recalls the "celebrity memoir" in the way it offers cameo glimpses of famous musicians, actors, and political leaders with whom Malcolm came into contact as a gangster and hipster in the urban world.

The great irony of the narrative becomes clear when we notice how Malcolm uses the theme of dehumanization. The persona of Detroit Red is successful in the way his high school teacher advised him to be and in the way he learned to be in the criminal world. But ultimately his craving for success, as defined by the white man or by the criminal underclass, makes him unsuccessful as a human being. As a child, he saw his mother enslaved by the welfare system. In the eyes of the welfare people, Malcolm reflects, "we were just *things*"; they "acted as if they owned us, as if we were their private property" (12, 13). Out of this virtual slavery, he emerges into the seeming freedom of the criminal life with its thrills and its big payoff, but in becoming a "full-time hustler" and leaving the "Negro jobs" behind, he ultimately realizes that the fully human world remains at a distance, beyond his reach: "When you become an animal, a vulture, in the ghetto, as I had become, you enter a world of animals and vultures. It becomes truly the survival of the fittest" (105). The hustler realizes that he is "uneducated, unskilled at anything honorable," but remains proud that he is the predator rather than the prey: "I considered myself nervy and cunning enough to live by my wits, exploiting any prey that presented itself" (111). There is little time or space to enjoy the fruits of success in this world, however:

> Full-time hustlers never can relax to appraise what they are doing and where they are bound. As is the case in any jungle, . . . if he ever relaxes, if he ever slows down, the other hungry, restless foxes, ferrets, wolves, and vultures out there with him won't hesitate to make him their prey. (112)

In this alternative world of the "ghetto jungle" (115), illiteracy is the norm. "I would bet that my working vocabulary wasn't two hundred words" (137), Malcolm says. Even so, there is a kind of shadow education, a sort of criminal literacy in which competence and knowledge are highly valued. Older hustlers "school" the younger ones who work with them (114). Many of the old-time hustlers are barely literate by the standards of the larger world but have remarkable memories and great aptitude for working with numbers. "If they had lived in another kind of society," Malcolm reflects sadly, "their exceptional mathematical talents might have been better used. But they were black" (120). As for his own intelligence, Malcolm concludes, "Through all this time of my life, I really *was* dead—mentally dead" (128).

The second stage of selfhood requires that the "dead" Malcolm be reborn, the "free" Malcolm, who is really enslaved to the predatory laws of the ghetto, be liberated. Ironically, this liberation occurs in prison. The section of the book that tells the story of his transformation as a prisoner draws upon the genres of prison memoirs and conversion narratives. From the prison memoir (works like *The Bird Man of Alcatraz*), Malcolm takes the experience of the person who must redefine a place in the world after everything has been taken away. From the conversion narrative (such as the story of St. Paul in the Christian Bible, which Malcolm specifically mentions), he takes the image of total transformation or "rebirth" of the person suddenly inspired by a vision of the truth.

The spark he needs comes from his family members who have joined the Nation of Islam and who visit him in prison and appeal to him to consider the teachings of the Reverend Elijah Muhammad. Muhammad's message appeals to Malcolm's anger and his inherent sense of his own worth. His simmering anger is aroused by Muhammad's forthright image of how society has been reconstructed and history rewritten for the sake of the white man's gain and the black people's degradation. His sense of self-worth is revitalized both by Muhammad's African-inflected history of the world and the subsequent recovery of his own powers of literacy and intellectual curiosity, which had been discouraged by his white teachers and then nearly obliterated by the jungle life of the hustler. Embarrassed by his spelling and penmanship when he begins to write letters to Mr. Muhammad himself, Malcolm teaches himself to write again by copying page after page from the dictionary, expanding his vocabulary and improving his speed at notation. With the help of the prison librarian, he reads to the point of exhaustion. "My homemade education gave me, with every additional book that I read," says Malcolm, using an appeal to the body, the metaphors of disability to dramatize both illiteracy and political brainwashing, "a little bit more sensitivity to the deafness, dumbness, and blindness that was afflicting the black race in America" (182). Inspired by Muhammad's vision, Malcolm devours world history, philosophy, and religion—nearly ruining his eyes reading in the bad light of the prison cell. He joins in the prison debates, honing his skills as an orator and expert in disputation.

The deep insight that Malcolm takes from Elijah Muhammad to work out his anger toward the white man incorporates a rhetoric of demonization. Having been defined all his life by otherness—as an object to be owned by the welfare people and as an animal to be left to his own wiles in the urban jungle or caged in a prison cell when he threatens the white world—Malcolm turns the tables on otherness. He argues that while "the black convict is the most perfectly preconditioned to hear the words, 'the white man is the devil,'" in fact demonization has a broader appeal:

> You tell that to any Negro. Except for those relatively few "integration"-mad so-called "intellectuals," and those black men who are otherwise fat, happy, and deaf, dumb, and blinded, with their crumbs from the white man's rich table, you have struck a nerve center in the American black man. He may take a day to react, a month, a year; he may never respond, openly; but of one thing you can be sure—

when he thinks about his own life, he is going to see where, to him, personally, the white man sure has acted like a devil. (186)

Malcolm is himself surprised at the rhetorical effect of saying "the white man is a devil": "That would shock many of [the prisoners]—until they started thinking about it" (186). But the appeal is undeniable.

Part of the strength comes from the power of this rhetoric to liberate the victims of racism from self-blame. What Malcolm comes to realize over the years is that he has internalized a value system that will always regard him as an object, an animal, or a threat. When success is denied to him in the dominant society, he seeks it in the underworld, but there he finds a success that can never fully succeed. It is an underworld in the truest sense—a hell. He is "dead" in that world. And the hellish place ultimately serves whom? Not the hustlers who feed on the illusion of success and freedom, but the economy of those who own the city and make the rules. The logic of the figure is undeniable. If the white man ultimately controls and allows the hellish place to exist, he must be the devil. The black person is victimized by the limiting of options. You can take a "Negro job" or you can prosper in the criminal world. Directly or indirectly, you remain in the service of the white man.

The third stage of selfhood as represented in the book comes when Malcolm slips free from the influence of Elijah Muhammad's rather narrow interpretation of Islam and develops his own view of life. Only then does he become a "self-actualized" human being. This section of the book finds its literary roots in the coming-of-age narrative. Having become a minister for the Nation of Islam after his term in prison, he experiences the disillusionment, jealousy, and betrayal that are all too common in the visionary leader's development. He discovers the limits of the institutional setting of the Nation of Islam and finds himself in need of a larger context for self-definition. Likewise, the Nation of Islam rejects him as a leader who is gaining too much power by his charismatic energy in the public world.

If literacy has provided the means of his first expansion of self—his reading taking him out of the limited vision of the world as constrained by a racist norm—world travel and the experience of a truly international religion allow his eyes to be opened further. In particular it is his pilgrimage to Mecca that helps him to realize that color racism is not universal and that the version of Islam he has embraced is, like everything else in North American society, limited by the very racism it deplores. When he sees Muslims of all colors hugging and greeting one another on the way to the pilgrimage, he says, "The feeling hit me that there really wasn't any color problem here. The effect was as though I had just stepped out of prison" (328). When he returns to the United States to form his own Black Nationalist group, the Organization of Afro-American Unity, he returns with a less exclusionary attitude. He still believes as he did before in the unification and self-definition of North American blacks, but he sees now the possibility of a more idealistic view: "True Islam taught me that it takes *all* of the religious, political, economic, psychological, and racial ingredients, or characteristics, to make the Human Family and Human Society complete" (382).

Along with this broader vision comes an appeal for broader understanding. He pleads for an objective readership:

> I think an objective reader may see how in the society to which I was exposed as a black youth here in America, for me to wind up in a prison was really just about inevitable. It happens to so many thousands of black youth.
>
> I think that an objective reader may see how when I heard "The white man is the devil," when I played back what had been my own experiences, it was inevitable that I would respond positively; then the next twelve years of my life were devoted and dedicated to propagating that phrase among the black people.
>
> I think, I hope, that the objective reader, in following my life—the life of only one ghetto-created Negro—may gain a better picture and understanding than he has previously had of the black ghettoes which are shaping the lives and the thinking of almost all of the 22 million Negroes who live in America. (386)

As we learn in Alex Haley's epilogue to *The Autobiography*, Malcolm X was assassinated at a relatively early point in this last stage of his development, perhaps before he could realize the fullest version of his new vision.[2] What we cannot doubt is the importance of education and open-mindedness to Malcolm in his last days. His pursuit of the truth led him to an ever-greater desire for knowledge and an ever-broadening context of understanding. He had already undertaken the study of Arabic and wanted to learn not only the African languages, he said, but also other languages, such as Chinese, "because it looks as if Chinese will be the most powerful political language of the future" (387). In one of the final paragraphs of the book, he says, "I would just like to study. I mean ranging study, because I have a wide-open mind" (388).

Rehumanization in A Lesson Before Dying

Writing nearly a century and a half after Douglass, and three decades after Malcolm X, Ernest Gaines crafts a similar appeal to the values of literacy and individual worth in his 1993 novel *A Lesson Before Dying*. As with Malcolm's, Gaines's outlook is more deeply ironic than Douglass's and more fully seasoned by the author's sense of tragedy in the history of American race relations after slavery. But the tone of gentle insistence in Gaines sets him apart from Malcolm. The change in tone may derive partly from a shift in place, from the urban North that forms the setting of Malcolm's narrative to the rural South of Gaines's story. Or it may have more to do with the shift in historical context. Whereas Malcolm felt the need to break the hold of a blindness enforced by long-term racial ideologies, Gaines needed only to build upon the work of predecessors like Douglass and Malcolm, creating a rhetoric remarkable less for its intellectual and emotional shock than for its sustained tug at the reader's sensibility. He needs to keep alive the audience's sense that racism continues in one form or another and requires constant vigilance, a strong sense of history, and the continuing education of a broad public.

From his vantage in the early 1990s, Gaines reflects back on the time just before the civil rights movement took hold in the 1960s, before King and Malcolm inspired a new generation, back to a time when in places like the rural Louisiana that the novel depicts, many of the old plantation values and practices of one hundred years earlier still prevailed. At the time of the novel's action, the African American descendants of slaves still live in a district called "the quarter" (far too reminiscent of the term "slave quarters") and work the land that belongs to other people in the practices known as tenant farming and sharecropping. As Dr. King said in his "I Have a Dream" speech, too much had gone unchanged. Freedom was a technical thing for black people, a legal state but not a real experience, and justice was too often denied them.

The narrator of the novel is an educated African American man, the community school teacher Grant Wiggins. His aspirations lie beyond the little village where he grew up, where he lives with his domineering aunt at the time of the story, and where he learns to belong again after he is transformed by the experience on which the story focuses. A young man of the community, named Jefferson, follows two tough friends into a liquor store and gazes in disbelief as a disagreement leads to a shoot-out between the white store owner and the other young men who, like Jefferson, were drunk when they came into the store. As he is leaving in confusion, two white men walk in and he is discovered to be the sole survivor of an armed robbery in which the white store owner was murdered.

At his trial, the public defender tells the all-white, all-male jury that Jefferson had nothing to do with the crime but was an innocent dupe of the other two. The store owner shot his two friends but left him to live, after all. Then, in a classic, if ironic, deployment of racist rhetoric, he appeals to the jury's sense of superiority by first diminishing Jefferson's character, calling him a boy and a fool, then fully dehumanizing him, dropping him to the level of a pathetic domestic animal, a farm machine, a thing. He calls him "this" again and again, using the demonstrative pronoun rather than the personal pronouns usually applied to human persons. Language appears to fail him, offering no word for this thing brought before the court:

> "Gentlemen of the jury, look at this—this—this boy. I almost said man, but I can't say man. Oh, sure, he has reached the age of twenty-one, when we, civilized men, consider the male species has reached manhood, but would you call this—this—this a man? No, not I. I would call it a boy and a fool. A fool is not aware of right and wrong. A fool does what others tell him to do. A fool got into that automobile. A man with a modicum of intelligence would have seen that those racketeers meant no good. But not a fool. A fool got into that automobile. A fool rode to the grocery store. A fool stood by and watched this happen, not having the sense to run.
>
> "Gentlemen of the jury, look at him—look at him—look at this. Do you see a man sitting here? . . . Look at the shape of this skull, this face as flat as the palm of my hand—look deeply into those eyes. Do you see a modicum of intelligence? Do you see anyone here who could plan a murder, a robbery, can plan—can plan—can plan anything? A cornered animal to strike quickly out of fear, a trait inherited from his ancestors in the deepest jungle of blackest Africa—yes, yes, that he can do—but to plan? . . . No gentlemen, this skull here holds no plans. What you see here is a thing that acts on command. A thing to hold the handle of a plow, a thing to load your bales of cotton, a thing to dig your ditches, to chop your wood, to pull your corn. That is what you see here, but you do not see anything capable of planning a robbery or a murder. He does not even know the size of his clothes or his shoes. Ask him to name the months of the year. Ask him does Christmas come before or after the Fourth of July? Mention the name of Keats, Byron, Scott, and see whether the eyes will show one moment of recognition. Ask him to describe a rose, to quote one passage from the Constitution or the Bill of Rights. Gentlemen of the jury, this man planned a robbery? Oh, pardon me, pardon me, I surely did not mean to insult your intelligence by saying 'man'— would you please forgive me for committing such an error?" (7–8)

After continuing a bit longer in this vein, the defender says, "I would as soon put a hog in the electric chair as this" (8). After this appeal to the jury's sense of the absurd, he makes a final plea to their personal moral sense: "Each and every one of us must live with his own conscience" (8). None of it works, of course, and Jefferson is condemned and sentenced to die by electrocution.

Grant Wiggins's aunt sits with her friend, the godmother of the accused, Miss Emma, whose mind attaches to the phrases of the defender's closing argument—the mention of literature and history and government—the mention of intelligent awareness that distinguishes people from animals, awareness captured in the ideal of education. A plan develops between the two women who insist that Jefferson must at least die with dignity, as a man and not a "hog."

That's where Grant comes in. Pressured by the two forceful women, Grant surrenders and agrees to visit Jefferson in his jail cell. The women insist that he can make a man out of Jefferson by teaching him what he failed to learn in the brief time he spent in school. Grant goes first out of obligation and has no idea how to proceed. He brings food from home and Jefferson mocks him by grunting like a hog as he roots his face into the gift. Far too complex to yield to a brief summary, the drama of the two men unfolds with little breakthroughs by which everyone is transformed. Grant brings Jefferson a radio, and the jailers allow the prisoner to play it after lights out. Grant breaks down in tears of frustration on one visit and confesses that he needs Jefferson and everyone like him. He is diminished by the social world in which he works in the same way that the defender diminished Jefferson. He is called "professor" by the local white people but with an undercurrent of mocking irony, set against the knowledge that he is really only the keeper of a one-room school house, hardly a professor. His learning has not made him free but only more aware of his "place" and his alienation. Without Jefferson and his students, he has no purpose in life.

When Grant explains the situation to Jefferson, recognition dawns. Jefferson understands Grant as a kind of fellow prisoner and is moved to submit to Grant's suggestion that he write down his thoughts and feelings. Once he begins, the writing flows out of him. The sheriff is in turn moved by Jefferson's commitment to the writing and allows the light to stay lit in his cell. The circle of humanity spreads as Grant brings news of Jefferson back to the school, then brings the children themselves to the jail to visit, and finally shares Jefferson's writings with the students.

We would call these jottings illiterate, but they are clearly the efforts of an awakening human being to communicate with his own kind. Jefferson's writing is dialogic, always concerned with his audience and with making a strong connection. Here are some samples, showing Jefferson's progression from living in a world of sense impressions, to wondering over his dreams and interior state of mind, to reconnecting with his community, and finally on to forming a deeply moral relationship with his mentor (and student) Mr. Wiggins:

- its evening an i done eat my rice an beans an i done had my cup of milk an the sun comin in the windo cause i can see it splashin on the flo and i can yer ned an them talking an thats bout all for now. (226)

- I jus cant sleep no mo cause evertime I shet my eyes I see that door an fore I git ther I wake up an I dont go back to sleep cause I dont want walk to that door no mo cause I dont know what back o ther if its wher they gon put that cher or if it spose to mean def or the grave or heven I don't know I wonder if boo went to heven cause I know he didn git religin firs. (228)

- mr wigin you say you like what i got here but you say you stil cant give me a a just a b cause you say i aint gone deep in me yet an you kno i can if I try hard an when i ax you what you mean deep in me you say jus say whats on my min so one day you can be save an you can save the chiren and i say i don't kno what you mean an you say i do kno what you mean an you look so tied sometime mr wigin i just feel like telling you i like you but i dont kno how to say this cause i aint never say it to nobody before an nobody aint never say it to me. (228)

- lord have merce sweet jesus mr wigin where all them peple come from when you ax me if some chiren can com up here an speak to me i didn kno you was meanin all them chiren in yo clas an just siting ther on the flo all quite in they clean close lookin at me an I coul see some was scared o me but mos was brave an spoke an my litle cosin estel even com up an kiss me on the jaw an I coudn hol it back no mo (230)

- sky blu blu mr wigin (234)

- good by mr wigin tell them im strong tell them im a man good by mr wigin im gon ax paul if he can bring you this (234)

The reader of the novel is invited to share the position of Grant Wiggins. Gaines crafts his story to create an identification with a broadly literate audience. At the beginning of the novel, it is hard to disagree with the public defender that Jefferson has acted the fool and been duped by his friends, even if we recognize the racism of the white lawyer's language. But the appeal to our sense of literacy, a seed first planted by the defender's words, gradually grows and ultimately erodes our sense of distance from the uneducated and dehumanized figure of Jefferson. His very desire for communication and communion makes him companionable. In accepting him as a fellow literate—locked away in the cell of his own individual fate but reaching to connect with the outer world, feeling limited and inadequate at every touch of the pen to paper (haven't we all known the feeling?)—we come to accept him also as a fellow human being. In such an identification, does our own humanity not expand and seek new levels? One of the key themes of modern rhetoric, especially as derived from Kenneth Burke, is that acts of identification among individuals often begin with such gestures as the rhetorical appeal.

Race, Place, and Literacy in "Enemy Mine"

Barry Longyear's science fiction story "Enemy Mine" is a kind of modern parable that shows how appeals to race, place, and the body come together in a complex portrait of how people differ from each other and how they can potentially reach common ground. Again, we see that the choice of medium for representing these issues—in this case, the differing media of literature and film—can have a profound effect on the direction the appeals ultimately take.

Science fiction authors treat alienation literally—the appearance in the future of unknown life forms—and refer indirectly to the present world of the audience where increasing globalization is the norm. The fictional aliens clearly represent ethnic, national, and cultural differences. Confronted with these fictional representations of the Other, readers are to some degree liberated from their usual habits of thinking about specific groups, creating a fresh perspective on the general problem of racism.

The alien in Barry Longyear's 1979 short story "Enemy Mine," the basis for the 1985 film with Dennis Quaid and Louis Gossett Jr., is the enemy that the human star warrior Willis Davidge, the story's white male protagonist and narrator, takes as his own, at least at the outset of the story. He is "my enemy" or "enemy mine." The hostility gets personal when the two characters are shot down, cut off from their comrades, and isolated on Fyrine IV, a desolate planet over which they had been engaged in an air battle.

The alien character, a role filled brilliantly in the film version by the black actor Louis Gossett Jr., is a crystallization of almost every state of otherness the white man could imagine. He, or it, is reptilian, hermaphroditic, and yellow in color. With its incomprehensible language and offensive odor, this Drac, as the race is known, only makes things worse by showing itself to be more competent as a survivor and a warrior. In the film version, the hungry Davidge first comes upon the Drac eating heartily beside a warming campfire. The man stages a surprise attack, but the Drac manages to subdue, disarm, and capture him. After forming an uneasy truce, the Drac is quick to learn the man's language and calls him by his rightful name, while the man struggles with Dracon and settles for the nickname Jerry when he is slow to grasp the Dracon name, Jerriba Shigan.

Though Davidge serves as our narrator, we quickly perceive through a filter of irony that the speaker is an older, wiser version of the protagonist we first encounter. For much of the story, he is an obtuse and dull-witted version of the stereotypical fly-boy, football jock, and superficial American. When at the height of a dispute he goads the Drac by insulting the revered Dracon philosopher Shizmaat, Jerry responds by insulting the only figure of any significance the Dracs have been able to discern after years of monitoring broadcasts from Earth—Mickey Mouse.

What becomes first a truce and ultimately a deep friendship is a rather typical case of adjustment to otherness in science fiction, a theme as prominent in the early pulp magazines as it was in other, better-known films of the 1980s, notably *ET* and *Close Encounters of the Third Kind*. While the short story sustains a stronger social critique, the film presents the adjustment in a more predictable and conventional manner. In the print version of the story, Davidge and the Drac's descendants must carve out the beginnings of a new civilization since the characters affected by contact with aliens cannot readjust to the still bigoted societies from which they came, while in the film, Davidge is instrumental in bringing his human cohorts to a new understanding of Dracs, and the Dracs themselves are presented as an alternative society. The friendship theme has been dismissed by one commentator on the film as the product of "earnest liberalism" that is "both preachy and slickly sentimental" (Nicholls 384). In maintaining the hope of overcoming alienation and finding an already existing community of like-minded individuals, American science fiction, especially in its Hollywood incarnation, differs strongly from both European science fiction and mainstream social realism, in which isolation and existential angst rule the day. Indeed, the movement from isolated individuality toward some form of social adjustment may well be the master plot of American science fiction.

What makes the friendship interesting in "Enemy Mine" is not that it follows this typical narrative pattern, however, but that the movement out of isolation is enabled by the mutual struggle of the two characters in adjusting to the ecology of the planet to which they have fallen. They need each other to survive. The environment proves the stronger enemy, the ultimate Other. The alienation they feel as a result of having evolved in different ecologies drives the alienation they feel from each other into insignificance. The weather is harsh. In the story, the sea near which the characters settle serves up regular tidal waves, and in the film, the atmosphere provides little protection from regular meteor showers, and the

native creatures appear as unintelligent lower forms of life with no com-
pulsions against eating anything in sight. The human and the Drac band
together in a primitive search for food and shelter. In the long winters,
hiding in a cobbled-together shelter from the threat of a cold and dangerous nature, the two intelligences gradually emerge from mutual aid into
trust and then friendship. Their alienation from nature drives them together. Davidge the narrator quotes Shizmaat on the topic: "Intelligent life
[makes] its stand against the universe" (107).

Through their combined ingenuity, close observation, and technical
understanding, the two intelligent beings solve the problem of survival
relatively easily, but their relationship goes further, ultimately reenacting
the defeat of nature by culture, for it is cultural exchange that provides the
means of solidifying and deepening the relationship between the two sur-
vivors. Here the theme of literacy enters. A book is the Drac's most prized
possession. It is a book of the oldest kind, a collection of sayings, the wisdom literature of a primarily oral culture just emerging into the literate phase
in the version of cultural history promulgated by literacy theorists like Ong
and McLuhan. The primary orality of the Dracs is demonstrated in the alien
protagonist's ability to recite his genealogy back to the origins of his race.
By learning to recite this genealogy under Jerry's careful instructions, Davidge
confirms his devotion to the Drac. This initiation into cultural practice pre-
pares the human being for the task he finally must accept, becoming surro-
gate parent to Jerry's offspring after the Drac dies during childbirth. Known
to the child by the honorific "Uncle," the protagonist takes on heroic pro-
portions by overcoming trials of race, place, and finally literacy. Before the
elder Drac dies, Jerry teaches Davidge to read Dracon and confers to the
keeping of his human friend the book of wisdom to be hung around the
neck, kept close to the heart, and used to ward off the curse of isolation.

We can interpret the story as an allegory for the emergence of the modern individual. His greatest physical and social accomplishments are represented in an adjustment to the condition of isolation in a threatening environment. His greatest comfort in the face of continuing alienation comes
from maintaining a virtual contact with what he most loves by way of literacy. In this allegory, literacy is not simply the ability to read and write
but the hard-won capacity to feel the weight of words in one's heart. The
written word becomes a portable means of access to cultural significance,
which somewhat ironically strengthens the individual as an isolate. Alienation becomes a matter of pride rather than a source of fear and loathing.
The difference one feels has to do with ethos, with the identification of
the individual with a cultural tradition, a past to be brought into the present
and preserved for the future.

Literacy, in McLuhan's provocative formulation—the isolated experience of being a committed writer or a dedicated reader—provides not just one impetus but the essential one in the evolution of individualism as we know it in modern times. In this sense, the alienated, individualistic, and often anarchic heroes that thrive in American science fiction may be read as images of the reader or as rhetorical appeals from the isolated writer to the isolated reader—one alien to another. The stereotype of the eccentric sci-fi fan, the dedicated reader viewed as antisocial nerd, very likely arises from the same cult of individualism. The alienation required by reading—the withdrawal from society made possible by silent reading—forms a structure of consciousness that welcomes thematic alienation in science fiction stories and supports the cultish iconoclasm of fandom. Or perhaps it is better to say that each of these phenomena supports the other. The discovery of links among individual fans and among fans and favorite authors, celebrated annually in hundreds of fan-sponsored conferences and websites, reenacts the discovery of common ground between alienated protagonists and sympathetic aliens in hundreds of narratives in the tradition, in both print and film.

Eventually among these celebrants of individuality and difference, forms of discipline develop. Ethical protocols emerge that taboo certain acts of self-serving and of group survival. In "Enemy Mine," the taboos run from the blind conformity of military society to the destructive self-centeredness of ecopolitical oppression.

At the beginning of the story, the human protagonist appears as a creature of the modern military. Propaganda has rendered him all but incapable of dealing with difference except in one way: kill or be killed. The individual is not an individual warrior but part of a killing machine, lacking flexibility and sensitivity to context, both social and natural. Friendship is interpreted narrowly, leaving only the possibility of loyalty to comrades, more oil for the successful war machine. Literacy serves only a narrow, instrumental function, providing training materials that work like computer programs for the human mind. In "Enemy Mine," the propaganda of Davidge's training sessions demonize the Dracs in the great tradition of military-inspired mass communication. Physical differences are emphasized—the scaliness, the smell of the enemy—and appropriately so, for in this discourse, human individuality is reduced to states of bodily presence. The body is the part of the individual required by the machine, so everything is directed toward its differentiation and protection.

In the broader perspective from which the story is told—that is, from the discourse of individualism as constructed in modern literacy—the sovereign person must learn to resist the kind of reduction the military imposes upon individuals and must learn that the body, while necessary for self-realization, is not sufficient. In the written version, the story suggests that once mobilized by war and propaganda, such beings cannot realize themselves except as a collective or nation-state endlessly opposed to a demonized enemy. Davidge cannot go home again once he has realized his own otherness. He is alienated by his former comrades as a "Dragger suck," the counterpart of the white American civil rights sympathizer in the 1960s, denounced by epithets like "nigger lover." And once returned to the Drac people, Jerry's progeny Zammis is hidden from his family and subjected to a battery of psychiatric tortures to rid him of his perverse sympathy for the human race. Ironies abound as Davidge travels as a private citizen to the planet Draco after a testy treaty has been negotiated between the humans and the Dracs, suffers through several episodes of racist abuse, proves himself to Jerry's father by reciting the genealogy, and with the old man's help, rescues Zammis and returns to the harsh environment of Fyrine IV to live with Jerry's descendants as a frontier settler. The original scene of his alienation becomes the place of salvation. The final realization is that the personal enemy of every individual is not otherness as embodied either in nature, harsh and demanding as it may be, nor in other living individuals, different as they may be. The enemy is rather the social collective that would reduce natural sociability to the mechanistic functions of war and conquest.

The film version develops a somewhat different set of values and taboos, which focus on the problem of exploitation. The Dracs appear as a model of natural sociability in the film, which nurtures a thematic seed from the short story—Jerry's insistence that Davidge lacks a centering identity because he cannot recite his own genealogy beyond two generations: "Davidge," he says, "how lost you must feel. You humans—how lost you must feel" (121). Of course, both beings are lost, but Jerry is lost only geographically while Davidge is lost geographically and spiritually. As he discovers new resources of selfhood in communion with his Dracon friends, he forms an ironic identification not only with these people, who are so remarkable for their spiritual depth, but also with the place against which he and his friend have tested and refined their mutual self-realizations. So in the story, it is no wonder that Davidge returns to the wilderness that he associates with his truest self, much in the manner that advocates of wilderness protection form an identification with the outdoors that expresses their discontent with urban, industrialized modern life. In the same movement we have seen in Janisse Ray's *Ecology of a Cracker Childhood*, Davidge undertakes a reinhabitation of the accursed place.

The film extends the critique of the harm that mechanistic oppression brings to individuals and communities by introducing a different enemy— pirates that come to unsettled worlds to mine the resources. Human beings who work their operations with Drac slaves, these people represent a perversion of individualism driven exclusively by the profit motive. Their alienation from others is complete and cynical; they bond together only for the sake of power and gain. In the film, Zammis is captured by such men and kept in captivity along with others of his race. The injured Davidge is rescued by his old squadron, several members of which join him as new comrades in his personal quest to rescue the young Drac. Now the title "Enemy Mine" takes on a new meaning as again the narrative elements of place and person run together. My enemy is an enemy mine, tearing ore from the planet and depriving slaves of personhood. The forces that plunder the planet are the same ones that exploit the people, or in Murray Bookchin's well-known formulation of "social ecology": "the very notion of the domination of nature by man stems from the very real domination of human by human" (1), which echoes the thoughts of the American Indian philosopher Vine Deloria Jr., whose works we considered in chapter 5.

The wilderness ethic, by which the "wholly other" of nature becomes a point of identification, the "holy other," the sacred wilderness for the individual estranged from the people and places of the so-called civilized world, is embodied in our short story as the hermit Davidge living out his days garbed in snake skin and feeding on smoked meat in the cave where he and Jerry awakened to the sacred communion of individuals. His only contact with intelligent life occurs in occasional meetings with Jerry's descendants, his carefully chosen and strictly limited community. By contrast, the film version ends with Davidge reciting Zammis's genealogy before the Dracon elders, bringing the young one back into his rightful social orbit and finding for himself a new tribal identification by which to resist the reduction of humanity to a social mechanism suited only for war and exploitation. His stand with nature is deeply connected with, and in some sense subordinate to, his devotion to the tribe.

What is most remarkable about "Enemy Mine" is that the narrative stem—one man's account of his transforming experience in the face of alienation from land and living being—can lead to the very different kinds of adjustment in the story and film versions. Both versions tend ironically to substantiate the right wing's complaint that environmentalists want us to return to living in caves, but of course the meaning of the cave is enriched and complicated. The film of "Enemy Mine" suggests that the hope of Western individualism lies in recovering the community of ancestors, connecting back with the world we have all but forgotten. The written version hints at the creation of a new way of life, starting over on new terms, recovering what is essential and discarding what is mean in life, like Thoreau reading the classics and making scientific observations as dual forms of meditation in his lakeside cabin built with his own hands.

Yet a crucial point remains. Both of these ways of hoping arise from the profoundly Western perspective of individualism, which begins with the ability to imagine oneself as isolated from the state, from the tribe, from nature, and even from one's former self, shedding the old skin, as Thoreau says, and feeling the world in new ways.

Reading and Writing Revisited: Literacy as a Humanizing Enterprise

With their racially sensitive approaches to literacy, the narratives of Douglass, Malcolm X, Gaines, and Longyear recall what the Brazilian activist and teacher Paulo Freire has called the "pedagogy of the oppressed." Freire accepts the premise that literacy advances the critical understanding of the individual and that individuation, while often leading to a sense of alienation and displacement, is crucial to leading a meaningful life in the modern world. Thus education becomes the foundation for raising the consciousness of classes of people kept in the dark by ignorance perpetuated in oppressive living and working conditions. Literacy becomes the first step in a program of liberation that helps people think about who they are in relation to others. In this sense, reading and writing give individuals the ability to step back and reflect on their lives. ·

Modern critical theorists, especially neo-Marxists and other socially oriented thinkers, have developed a powerful critique of the modern individual as a cog in the industrial machine. They argue that individualism is an illusion and that capitalist society depends upon people thinking they are free and individualistic when in fact they are driven by consumerism and other ideologies that benefit by their failure to form into collectives. Likewise, contemporary treatments of "identity politics" suggest that ethnic identity informs every aspect of life and that the so-called individual is merely an alienated and sad remnant of lost communities. According to this view, individualism and literacy are not neutral educational goals but are political tools of the establishment. If people learn to think according to the ideology of individualism and the educational program of the ruling classes, they learn to value the behavior of the other and to reject their own culture as inferior.[3]

The critique is strong enough to raise questions about making literacy and individualism the foundation of our communication model—rather than some other more communal model, perhaps a socialist model that discards individualism as a trick of bourgeois oppression. As a kind of compromise, I follow Paulo Freire in teaching reading and writing as social practice, but as an advocate of literate rhetoric, I must also insist that the work requires the figure of the silent reader and writer alone in his or her room putting pen to paper or hand to keyboard. Reflection on one's condition begins in this germinal state. Writers as different as Douglass, Malcolm X, Gaines, and Longyear appear to arrive at agreement on this point.

Modern rhetoric requires the image of this lonely and productive soul. The examples considered in this chapter fill out the image of this character, the singular literate seeking an audience within and beyond the local context of community, an atomistic individual looking to form strong molecular bonds.

9 ▸ Appeal Through Tropes

Trope is just another word for "figure of speech." Perhaps the most commonly recognized example in ordinary language is *metaphor*, a trope that identifies a person, thing, or concept with a logically dissimilar thing, as in "love is a rose."

I prefer the term *trope* to *figure of speech* because figures of speech are also figures of thought and figures of writing. *Trope* is more inclusive. In addition, I like that the Greek word *trope* literally means "turn," a definition picked up in our common expression "turn of phrase" and "turn of thought," not to mention "twist of plot."

The idea of *troping*, or turning a phrase, captures a truth about rhetorical appeals that we are liable to forget: They always involve swerves, indirections, substitutions, twists, and turns of meaning. Love is not a rose after all, so what do we gain rhetorically by identifying the one thing with the other? What's the appeal?

I have hinted along the way that appeals do more than please and plead. Tropes help us to classify and study other functions of appeals. They suggest how one position (author, audience, or value) can relate to another. An appeal may

- *identify* one position with another (metaphor)
- *associate* one position with another (metonymy)
- *represent* one position by another (synecdoche)
- *close the distance* between two positions and *increase the distance* of both from a third (irony).

This chapter, after briefly summarizing the treatment of tropes in the history of modern rhetoric, spends some time with each of these functions.[1] What we end up with is not only an expansion of the appeals theory and its analytical power but also a redefinition of the tropes as patterns of appealing. The chapter closes with a brief introduction to a critical method for analyzing tropes and determining not only what they reveal but also what they conceal.

Tropes in the History of Modern Rhetoric

In the European Renaissance of the sixteenth and seventeenth centuries, also known as the "early modern period," logicians and philosophers of science called rhetoric into question because of its tendency to pile up tropes, favoring eloquence over good sense. They mistrusted the twists and turns, the "excesses of rhetoric," and preferred a plainer, more direct style of communication. Building upon the ancient competition between rhetoric and philosophy and foreshadowing the way later scientists would dismiss the need for rhetoric, the Renaissance critics complained that the number of tropes identified by the old Greek and Roman masters had grown to a nearly uncountable number. How could all this technical fuss improve our understanding of language and the world?

Modern theorists of rhetoric responded by insisting that rhetorical language, including the use of tropes, is pervasive and unavoidable. All forms of knowledge and even conventional uses of language are built upon an original foundation of wordplay and figuration. As Friedrich Nietzsche provocatively puts it,

> What then is truth? A moveable host of metaphors, metonymies, and anthropomorphisms [personifications]: in short, a sum of human relations which have been poetically and rhetorically intensified, transferred, and embellished, and which, after long usage, seem to people fixed, canonical, and binding. (1174)

Along similar lines, in "Politics and the English Language," George Orwell reminds us that literal language consists of dead metaphors, and that clichés and slang are composed of metaphors in the process of dying. We tend to forget or ignore the metaphorical origins of common phrases like "feeling low" and slang terms like "getting high." A literalist approach to language might find it odd that "cool" and "hot" can mean the same thing in modern slang, but not a metaphorical approach. Metaphor is everywhere, and so is the kind of value-laden, emotional language usually associated with rhetoric, no matter how hard scientific and academic writers may try to avoid it. Richard Weaver thus insists that all language is "sermonic" and that rhetoric thus provides a necessary complement to science: "If science deals with the abstract and the universal, rhetoric is near the other end, dealing . . . with the particular and the concrete," the historical and emotional content of life (1353). Tropes tend to connect the abstract to the concrete—again, "love is a rose"—expressing the emotional quality of our relationship to the world.

A second response to the critique of rhetoric in modern philosophy and science has involved reducing the number of key tropes and revisiting their functions, considering tropes not merely as embellishments of language but as ways of thinking. Kenneth Burke follows the eighteenth-century scholar Giambattista Vico as one of the leaders in this movement. In a famous appendix to *A Grammar of Motives*, an essay entitled "Four Master Tropes," Burke connects four classical figures with four habits of mind or conceptual attitudes more easily recognized by modern readers: metaphor with *perspective*, metonymy with *reduction*, synecdoche with *representation*, and irony with *dialectic* (503). Other theorists have gone even farther in narrowing the field. The famous linguist and critical theorist Roman Jakobson focuses on two key tropes—metaphor and metonymy. And in *Metaphors We Live By*, the linguist George Lakoff and the philosopher Mark Johnson concentrate on the single trope of metaphor, which they consider to be a deep structure or foundational pattern of human cognition. Lakoff and Johnson are convinced that the brain itself functions metaphorically. And since human beings live by their wits, metaphor—by connecting abstractions and unfamiliar things to the root experience of the body—provides the underpinning for all thinking, planning, craft, and art. In this sense, we literally live by metaphors.

In the shadow of these powerful new approaches, the next four sections offer a slight reinterpretation of Burke's four master tropes that allows me to advance the theory of appeals. We begin with metaphor, which theorists like Lakoff and Johnson take as the root of all tropes.

Identification/Metaphor

Most people study metaphor first as a technique of poetry in high school. They learn to distinguish it from the technique of simile. According to this scheme, simile is a comparison that uses *like* or *as*—"My love *is like* a red, red rose," as the Scottish poet Robert Burns says—while metaphor is a comparison that omits *like* or *as:* "Love *is* a rose (but you'd better not pick it)," as the old country song says. A related term, *analogy*, is usually reserved for prose. We might say, for example, "Today let us compare the emotion of love to a rose, sometimes thorny but nevertheless beautiful and sensually pleasant."

This simple explanation of metaphor and its close relatives, while helpful in identifying the different figures of speech, doesn't take us very far. Instead of thinking of metaphor as a comparison that leaves something out, try thinking of it as an *identification*, a way of bringing together seemingly unlike things. In this sense, metaphor is a strong identification, while simile and analogy are more cautious attempts to link unlike things. In this way, we can see that metaphor is not merely one technique among many but is instead a crucial way of thinking, an attempt to bridge conceptual gaps, a mental activity at the very heart of rhetoric. Rhetoric itself, as Kenneth Burke suggests, is all about identification, finding common ground among persons, places, things, and ideas usually divided.

At the level of the word or phrase, then, metaphor offers clues to the rhetorical aim of whole discourses. Consider, for example, the metaphor in the opening line of "Ode to the West Wind" by the English poet Percy Bysshe Shelley: "O wild West Wind, thou breath of autumn's being" (l. 1). The line develops an identity between two things that everyday language tends to keep separate, in this case wind and breath. By bringing these things together, Shelley creates an important philosophical identity between human life and nature, one of the key themes of Romantic literature.

To grasp the full sense of his metaphor, think of it not as a comparison but as a ratio. Breath is to human (or animal) life as wind is to the season of autumn:

$$\frac{\text{Breath}}{\text{Human life}} = \frac{\text{Wind}}{\text{Autumn}}$$

The metaphor thus contains an appeal to the body that ultimately supports the key theme of the poem, a plea to think of human life as cyclical rather than linear. The poem closes with the line "If Winter comes, can Spring be far behind?" (l. 70). Like the wind, the spirit (a word whose Latin root means "breath" or "wind") returns to animate the earth again and again despite the passing of any particular year or human lifetime. The appeal to nature thus becomes a way of reconciling human beings to the passage of time.

Now recall the very first example in chapter 1, Wendell Berry's claim that "the disease of the modern character is specialization" (19). The claim involves a metaphor that, viewed as a ratio, would look like this:

$$\frac{\text{disease}}{\text{the body}} = \frac{\text{specialization}}{\text{character}}$$

Just as Shelley draws the reader closer to nature by identifying wind with breath, an essential need of the body, Berry makes specialization repellent by identifying it with disease, an uncomfortable and sometimes deadly bodily state. While Shelley's metaphor is positive and affirmative, Berry's is negative and divisive, but both involve compact appeals to the body.

According to Lakoff and Johnson, the cognitive power of metaphor—its significance not only as a trope but a way of thinking—has to do with the tendency of all metaphors to connect the world to the body, to relate unfamiliar things to the familiar experience of physical existence. This property is embedded not just in poetic language but in all speech and writing.

Our most common expressions perform the same function. When we say, "I'm feeling low today," we use a bodily metaphor to express a psychological state. As a ratio, it would look like this:

$$\frac{\text{low}}{\text{the body}} = \frac{\text{depressed}}{\text{the mind}}$$

"Depression" itself is merely a technical term for feeling low. When you are "low" or "down," your energy is lacking. You don't want to get out of bed ("get up"). You feel all your weight as the pull of gravity toward the earth. The ultimate "down" state is death. That kind of gravity leads to the grave (words which have the same etymological root, after all). No wonder then that when a patient is "really down," the psychologist worries about suicide. Also notice that, to take the full implication of the metaphor, there's no big division between mind and body but rather a continuity. When you're sick, you feel low; depression often has a physical root in illness, for example, some chemical shift in the brain. Metaphor tends to emphasize such continuities and deemphasize borderline distinctions.

Consider an example from Martin Luther King Jr.'s famous "Letter from Birmingham Jail":

> Actually, we who engage in nonviolent direct action are not the creators of tension. We merely bring to the surface the hidden tension that is already alive. We bring it out in the open where it can be seen and dealt with. Like a boil that can never be cured so long as it is covered up but must be opened with all its ugliness to the natural medicines of air and light, injustice must be exposed, with all the tension its exposure creates, to the light of human conscience and the air of national opinion, before it can be cured. (509)

Like many of the appeals to the body already studied, King's central metaphor of injustice as a boil that must be opened to be cured invokes the values of health, purity, freedom, and power—in this case, social health, purity of motive, freedom from oppression, and the power to heal. These values arise from the implied metaphorical identification of civil rights activists with doctors treating diseases of the body. Activists are not troublemakers but healers; they treat injustice the way a doctor would treat a painful boil, thus yielding this ratio:

$$\frac{\text{activists}}{\text{injustice}} = \frac{\text{doctors}}{\text{boils}}$$

The connection to the body is not always so direct. Sometimes we must find our way along several links in a metaphorical chain of implications. Such is the case with Orwell's appeal in "Politics and the English Language": "Our civilization is decadent and our language—so the argument runs—must inevitably share in the general collapse" (156). In Orwell's essay, the central metaphor is that bad language corrupts thinking in the same way that bad politics corrupts society. This ratio builds upon an implied metaphor that connects "decadent" thought and corrupt politics with the decay and ultimate collapse of the body—with death, that is. Roughly diagrammed the metaphorical complex looks like this:

$$\frac{\text{bad language}}{\text{weak thought}} = \frac{\text{corrupt politics}}{\text{decadent society}} = \frac{\text{decay}}{\text{dead (or dying) body}}$$

This kind of complex metaphorical development is precisely the sort of thing that leads Lakoff and Johnson to say that metaphor is foundational to human thought. Metaphors run throughout any discourse in a variety of directions, but they ultimately lead back to the body.

Along these lines we can also suggest that appeals to the body, built upon a network of metaphorical identifications, form the foundation for most of the other appeals:

- Appeals to time link metaphorically with the experience of the aging body.

- Appeals to place link with the spatial experience of the living body, including the perception of natural phenomena such as gravity, weather, topography, and the seasons. The body is the place of places, where the self resides.

- Appeals to gender link with the bodily experience of maleness or femaleness, including the awareness of bodily features and functions such as hormonal fluctuations as well as societal injunctions and limits on behavior.

- Appeals to race link with skin color and other physical signs of ethnic origin (eye and nose shape, body size, hair color, etc.).

Because of its power to invoke the aid of the body in understanding, metaphor deserves close attention in the crafting and analysis of rhetorical appeals.

Association/Metonymy

Because Lakoff and Johnson understand metaphor as the master trope, they treat metonymy and many other figures as subcategories of metaphor. Even scholars who want a stronger distinction among the figures admit that there is a lot of overlap and some confusion when people try to say whether something is a metaphor, a metonym, a synecdoche, or some other figure. Students often find the process maddening. There are good arguments on both sides for expanding or contracting the number of tropes.

Staying true to the ordinary-language approach, I would argue that it's not as important to get the technical name right as it is to discover how a trope functions within the context that it appears. My aim in expanding the number of tropes a little beyond metaphor is to give a sense of the variety of functions and kinds of appeals that tropes make possible at the level of word and phrase.

On the basis of the differing functions of metaphor and metonymy, the influential linguist and literary theorist Roman Jakobson has argued for keeping the two tropes separate and treating them as master tropes. In his studies of aphasia, in which people with brain damage lose different kinds of language functions, Jakobson notes two general classes of function loss: similarity disorders and contiguity disorders. People with similarity disorders have trouble seeing relationships among like things or concepts that most of us would recognize with little effort. People with contiguity disorders have trouble recognizing ordinary associations among related words or things, especially things close to each other or arranged in a sequence. On this basis, Jakobson argues that the functions of recognizing similarity and contiguity are fundamental to human thinking and that metaphor (the master trope of similarity) and metonymy (the master trope of contiguity) form the two poles of linguistic practice.

If metaphor works by identifying similar things, metonymy works by substituting a thing for a closely associated (contiguous) thing. For example, we refer to Queen Elizabeth II of England as "the crown," or the government of the United States as "Washington." The easiest (though not totally reliable) way to distinguish between metaphors and metonyms is to say that metaphors are about shared attributes between different things while metonyms are not. The breath and the wind in Shelley's metaphor are both composed of air, after all; health and moral character in Berry's metaphor are both conditions of the person. Everything in metaphor ultimately comes back to the body and suggests relationships that form into ratios. Metonyms usually do not work out as four-part ratios the way metaphors do, and they are about habitual associations rather than shared attributes or features. The crown has nothing to do with the Queen's body or her character. The shape and character of the American government has little to do with its location in Washington; it used to be in New York, after all, though we might argue that by moving the capitol southward, the founders of the nation were trying to give it a metaphorical significance, putting the capitol closer to the geographical center of the nation, making it the heart of the nation's body. Since we haven't moved the capitol westward as the nation expanded, however, such a metaphorical meaning is lost. (With a poet's sensibility to metaphoric value, Walt Whitman thought we should move the seat of government to Denver, but after the addition of Alaska and Hawaii, we might suggest Los Angeles.)

At the level of word and phrase we have already seen a few examples of metonymy at work. The Native American writer Linda Hogan, quoted in chapter 3, writes of "the language of this continent" (78), meaning the language of the people who live on this continent of North America. Thomas Paine, quoted in chapter 4, writes of "the times that try men's souls," when it is the conditions of war, not literally the times, that test people's souls. In Hogan's metonym, the place is substituted for the people, while in Paine's metonym, the times are substituted for the actions of the people. In one, we get an appeal to place; in the other, an appeal to time.

The entry on metonymy in the *Encyclopedia of Rhetoric and Composition* gives a good list of examples from news captions, popular songs, ads, and cartoons, showing how metonyms involve the substitution of one thing for another closely associated thing:

- In "Bernstein gives up baton," a symbol (baton) is substituted for the action symbolized (conducting an orchestra).

- In "Our face cream removes the years," a cause (passing time) is substituted for an effect (wrinkles).

- In "He took a swig of courage," an effect (courage) is substituted for a cause (whiskey).

- In "Bush bombs Iraq," a controller (Bush) is substituted for the controlled (U.S. Air Force).

- In "You're never alone with a poet in your pocket," a creator (poet) is substituted for a creation (book of poetry).

- In "The plane brought back ten body bags," a container (body bags) is substituted for the contained (dead soldiers).

- In "The hired gun confessed," an object used (gun) is substituted for the user (killer). (Davis, "Metonymy" 445)

The last examples show how, as Kenneth Burke suggests, metonymy can be reductive, functioning much as a stereotype does, reducing a whole person to an object. Similar examples from common language include the reference to business people as "suits" or women as "skirts," substituting the container for the contained and reducing individual people to stereotypic states of dress. The tendency of metonymy to objectify and depersonalize people can thus prove all too effective in negative appeals to gender and race.

Metonymy also often gives rise to the kinds of symbols, icons, and logos used as cultural indicators in everything from literature and psychology to advertising, sign-making, and brand names. Think of the giant plastic cows placed in the parking lots of steak houses, the icon of a knife and fork used to indicate restaurants on interstate highway signs, the logo of a dinosaur to stand for a museum of natural history. In religion, the cross, an element from the story of Jesus, becomes a symbol for Christianity. In world politics, a flag symbolizes a nation.

In the novel *Moby-Dick*, a great white whale stands for a whole complex of meanings and states of being. The narrator Ishmael sees the whale as a pure state of nature, ultimately inscrutable to human understanding. But Captain Ahab associates the whale with all his troubles in life, which began, as he sees it, when a white whale bit off his leg. If he destroys the whale, he reasons, he destroys his own failure. Some would say that the whale is a metaphor for his trouble, but that's not quite right. Notice how the whale shares no real attributes with Ahab's failure, but is rather associated with the failure by a series of events. Psychologists often deal with this kind of obsessive focus on something associated with a mental state. A patient may develop an irrational repulsion to some food that was served on the night his parents announced their divorce, for example.

The symbolic use of metonymy suggests its cognitive dimension, its important place in human thinking as well as in rhetoric. One more conceptual association is worth mentioning in the study of rhetoric: the appeal to authority. We might say, "I believe in the Bible," or "I believe in the Koran," for example. We don't literally believe in the books as material objects but in the messages they carry. We substitute the container for the contained and often treat the container as a holy thing. Some people refuse to allow the Bible to be placed on the ground; some wash their hands before opening the Koran.

Young students often treat published authors with the same authority, as if publication and placement in the library (contiguity with the temple of learning, in a manner of speaking) were an indicator of truth and value. And even experienced authors will refer to predecessors with a kind of reverence. Remember how in chapter 2 we saw Robert Putnam hold up Tocqueville as an established authority in the history of democracy? The mere mention of Aristotle in many rhetorical circles suggests authority and credibility—an association with a long and venerable tradition. In other circles, you can gain adherents to your cause by invoking science. Nine out of ten doctors, an ad might say, prefer our product. The modern scholar, says Nietzsche, "builds his hut right next to the tower of science so that he will be able to work on it and to find shelter for himself beneath those bulwarks" (1177).

So it is with all citation of authorities. We seek protection from personal attack by metonymically allowing authoritative voices to substitute for our own.

Representation/Synecdoche

Synecdoche also involves acts of substitution and closely resembles metonymy. Some would say it is a subspecies of metonymy, but I think it is useful to maintain a slight distinction in function.

The best way to distinguish between metonymy and synecdoche is to say that metonyms involve relationships with things external to, or not a necessary component of, the main subject. (The crown is external to the queen; Washington is not a necessary component of the U.S. government.) By contrast, synecdoche involves using some internal part or necessary component to stand for the subject. If I say, "My heart is not in my writing today," I mean my whole self. By using "heart" to stand for the whole self, however, I focus attention on emotions.

One of my all-time favorite synecdoches in poetry shows how the trope functions. In the poem "I Heard a Fly Buzz When I Died," Emily Dickinson imagines a persona on her deathbed, looking around the room and seeing in her dying moment a fly buzzing at the window pane. Just before she sees this odd symbol of stirring life (a metonym), she looks up and sees her family and friends crying over her in the traditional nineteenth-century death watch. She says, "The Eyes around—had wrung them dry" (223). She means that the people have wept till they can weep no more; they've wrung themselves dry. By referring to people as "eyes," using a part to stand for the whole, she focuses on the part of the body that we look into to determine how others feel. The poet's wordplay hints at the old saying that the eyes are the windows of the soul. The family and friends look into the eyes of the dying one to see if she still has life in her while she watches them watching her to understand her own state. The synecdoche draws our attention to the act of watching and the means of watching—the eyes.

Though ancient theorists of rhetoric considered a wide range of relationships under the heading of synecdoche, I want to focus on only one: the relationship of the part to the whole. I am using a synecdoche when I tell my neighbors that I will "lend a hand" in helping with their garden. Of course I will use my whole body, not just my hand, but I focus on the most active part. When the person on the shore says, "There are ten sails coming this way," there are really ten complete boats, but the trope focuses on the visible part of the boats.

Other good examples appear in the entry on synecdoche in the *Encyclopedia of Rhetoric and Composition:*

- We don't have wheels (a car).
- New blood (bodies) in Congress inspires hope.
- This is where the rubber (tires) meet the road.
- There's a compound fracture in the emergency room and a heart attack in Room 4 (patients with these maladies). (Davis, "Synecdoche" 712)

The main function of synecdoche in these and all other cases is to simplify and focus the attention. It is a device of emphasis.

To go beyond the level of word and phrase, we might suggest that whenever we pick out some element of a set to stand for the whole, we have acted synecdochally. The rhetorical use of examples—or what Kenneth Burke called "representative anecdotes"—are synecdoches that work at the conceptual level. Say you are writing a paper on problems in education and, for an example, you choose a story about a bad teacher you had in high school. Your example serves a representative function; your hope is that your readers will have had similar experiences that, taken together with yours, form something like a data set. Your story is a representative part of the whole set. If you are working from an actual data set rather than this kind of hopeful one, you try to choose the best data point as an example to appeal to the values you want to reinforce without alienating your intended audience. From many stories about citizens' declining participation in public life, for instance, Robert Putnam (discussed in chapter 2) chooses the bowling story as a point of emphasis in his essay because it allows him to create a relatively nonthreatening, "whimsical" example of participation in public life. He makes his point by giving us a strong visual image of community life that is not only morally commendable but also memorable.

Distance/Irony

The most complex and difficult of the four master tropes is irony. Novices to rhetorical analysis and literary criticism generally find it to be one of the hardest concepts to comprehend and put to use. But the practice of irony is so common and so crucial in much of modern rhetoric that it should not be neglected.

Irony is a trope that involves inversions and reversals. It turns standard meanings and expectations upside down. It often involves saying one thing and meaning another. In the infamous essay "A Modest Proposal," for example, the eighteenth-century satirist Jonathan Swift says that the rich people of England should eat the poor children of Ireland. What he really means is that the rich should care for the poor instead of figuratively "devouring" them with their policies of neglect and exploitation.

Like the other tropes, irony works at the level of individual phrases and at the larger level of whole discourses. Unlike the other tropes, it depends almost completely on contextual cues. When a teacher says to a class, for example, "You've studied so hard!" the teacher can mean something positive or something very critical. If said while the teacher is turning back a set of very bad papers, the tone of the remark will appear ironic, even sarcastic.

At the level of the phrase, irony often appears as sarcasm. But in context, irony always has a moral force. By saying "You've studied so hard," the teacher is not merely complaining that the students did poorly on the papers but also pointing the way to what they should have done (study harder).

More important than acknowledging the moral force in understanding irony, however, is the need to realize its dependence on context. A transcript of the teacher's statement to the students would not reveal the irony. Someone trying to figure it out would need a tape to hear the tone of voice, or insider knowledge of the grade book to know what was really intended.

Tone and insider perspective—these are the crucial elements of irony. Tone is usually defined as an author's attitude toward subject matter (the failed tests) and audience (the students). Ironic tone is conveyed by setting up a condition of unequal knowledge. Before they look at their papers, the students may think the remark is complimentary, but after they peek at their grades, they realize the irony. The "before" condition stands in contrast to the "after" condition because in the process they have gained new knowledge that allows them to realize the irony. Irony generally contrasts a naive position with a position of greater wisdom. In this case, the rapid shift from "before" to "after" does not allow the students to adjust to the new state of knowledge and thus will likely offend them. That's the way sarcasm usually works (and that's why using it too often is a notorious avenue to bad evaluations from angry students).

One way to get a handle on the rhetoric of irony is to use the approach of the triple persona, developed earlier in the discussion of gender in chapter 7. The approach is based on our ordinary understanding of pronoun grammar. Rhetorical irony involves creating an inner circle of a first and second persona—"I" and "you." The idea is to bring "I" and "you" into alignment under the banner of shared values—or in the case of the appeal to gender, a shared situation of struggle or oppression—to create a plural first persona, a "we"—and then to designate a third persona, "them." "We" stand against "them," the oppressors or their accomplices.

The example of the episode with the student papers turns out to be a weak one in this sense, but it still works. The "I" (teacher) and "you" (students) become a "we" position occupied by the teacher and the students in their knowledgeable ("after") state. The "they" position is occupied by the students in their naive ("before") state. This kind of irony is sometimes called "dramatic irony" because it emerges in the unfolding of dramatic events. A change must occur before the irony can be revealed. In this case, the change probably doesn't occur, and the students reject the "we" position.

Swift's "A Modest Proposal" offers a better example. As we begin to read, the "I" of the discourse appears to us as a social reformer. We may take the "you" position as the addressee for a while, but as the proposal becomes more and more preposterous, we begin to pull away, and as we do, we perceive that the author is winking at us. The first persona "I" of the essay is not the author at all but an invention of the author, an absurd mask. Likewise the "you" is not the intended audience (the reader) but the very people whose values the author is attacking, the neglectful and exploitive rich. As we pull away, we join the author in an inner circle of knowledge, a "we." The "I" of the proposer and the "you" that stands for the oppressors become together the "they" against which we take our stand with the author.

How do we know the author is winking when we can't see him? This question haunts students of irony and has prompted at least one book-length answer (Wayne Booth's *A Rhetoric of Irony*). The short answer is we grasp irony by insights into context and tone. If we know something about Jonathan Swift's political leanings, we can quickly grasp his intent. Even if we don't, however, we can pick up his tone by the way he manipulates the positions of value. When the "I" of the essay suggests cannibalism as a solution to the problem of hunger and poverty, he violates not only the rules of logic but also the root values of human life even as he promotes the entrepreneurial spirit and the values of hard work and ingenuity. Some values always take priority over others. Swift's irony allows the undeniable value of every human life to take priority over the lesser values promoted by his persona the proposer. The audience is left to reflect on the way that the values of hard work and productivity often mask exploitive attitudes even when they are not taken to the extremes of "A Modest Proposal." The hope is that the "we" of the essay endures as a political "we" in public life.

The ironic appeal, involving as it does the development and maintenance of emerging communal relationships, proves extremely important in the destabilized, ever-shifting social relations of modern times. In allowing the audience to "see through" the mask of the persona, Swift teaches the audience to adopt a critical attitude, to pull away from the complacency and ignorance that accepts all proposals at "face value." What are the hidden values, the hidden agendas driving the argument?

In the chapter on gender, we saw the same process at work as writers like Friedan and Hochschild urge us to unmask the advertised images that seem to speak for women's desires—the ultrafeminine figures of passivity that promise women happiness and contentment, and later the supermoms that promise power and freedom. By showing these images to be puppets of the advertisers, the feminist critics reveal the real purpose of the ads: to stabilize markets by invoking fantasies and glossing over the hard questions raised by the division of home and workplace and the strain that advancing education and modern economic forces place upon the institutions of marriage and the family. If we choose to accept the unmasking of the images, we move to a new position of understanding. We join a community of understanding and feel distanced from our old naiveté.

Wit and Judgment: Cultivating Critical Distance

The skeptical attitude suggested in the practice of irony hints toward a critical method that goes back to Plato and that took on new force in the early modern treatment of *wit* and *judgment*. In the tradition of the English philosopher John Locke, *wit* involves the recognition of similarities, sometimes surprising similarities; *judgment* involves the recognition of difference. Metaphor, metonymy, and synecdoche tend to be tropes of wit; irony involves both wit and judgment—the closing of distance within the "we" group (similarity) and the increasing of distance (difference) between "we" and "they."

When the women in Hochschild's study look at the advertised images of supermom and say, "That's not me," they reject the identity (metaphor) offered to them by the advertisers. They refuse to accept her even as a representative woman (synecdoche) when they say, "That's not like anyone I know." The women are exercising their judgment in rejecting the wit of the advertisers, their suggestion of a similarity.

We can expand this skeptical practice into a simple critical method for testing the robustness of tropes. Apply this general rule: *If someone says that two things are similar to one another, try thinking of their differences. If someone says that two things are different, try thinking of them as similar.*

Compare two examples we've seen of tropes of wit, both involving appeals to health: Wendell Berry's claim that the specialization of modern life is a disease, and Martin Luther King's claim that racial injustice is a boil that needs to be lanced. If we look for the healthy qualities of professional specialization, we might eventually come to say that the case is not quite so clear-cut as Berry's metaphor suggests; we might even reject the trope as an overstatement. We can die from bad health, after all, but probably not from specialization. But King's metaphor stands up better to our scrutiny. It's hard to find anything healthy about racial injustice. Like bad health, it can kill.

We can work the same way with judgments. When we hear the old interview in which the Vietnam-era general said that Asian people are not like westerners because they don't have the same regard for human life, we can object that they are like us because they do. The makers of the film *Hearts and Minds* take exactly this approach when they juxtapose the clip of the general's remark with a clip of Vietnamese villagers weeping over their dead. They create an ironic reversal, allowing us to see how wrong the general actually is. Likewise, the whole of Ernest Gaines's novel *A Lesson Before Dying* is devoted to showing that, contrary to what the lawyer says in the trial of the young black man, an illiterate person is not a hog but a human being like the rest of us.

The contrariness of this kind of skeptical analysis can make you into a pretty cynical person if you practice it continually and never retrace your steps. That's not my goal. I like to think that, by putting ideas to the test this way, we can get a little distance that might help us understand both sides of an issue (or see many sides that we might have neglected by reducing everything to two sides, as in a war). You can always go back to your original position, but that little exercise in distance might ultimately be the key to communication with people who differ from you. It might also be the first step in intellectual growth.

10 ▸ The Appeal of Narrative

Take another look at a sentence from chapter 2: "Depending on the audience, the fact that the number of alcohol-related deaths on county roads rose from twenty-two to thirty-three last year might have less impact than the story of a high-school couple killed on the way to the senior prom by a drunk driver." In that chapter, we noted that classical rhetoric associated the use of data in arguments with expert discourses in philosophy or science designed for an insider audience. The same tradition suggests that for a general audience in the public forum, data might not be as effective as short illustrations or examples.

Illustrations, examples, and anecdotes take a narrative form, linking together actors and scenes in a chronological sequence of events. They tell a story. People tend to think of experience itself as having a narrative form—they say, for example, that they live out their "life stories," and they speak of events as "episodes" in life—so that all appeals to personal experience or to the observed experiences of others rely on narrative, on storytelling.

As chapter 2 suggests, we can think of data as severely compressed examples, stories reduced to attributes of similarity and placed in relation to other stories. I can tell the story of going to vote yesterday—how I lost my car keys but still walked to the polls in the rain because I was determined to vote against the incumbent mayor of my town whose policies I disagree with. Or my story can be reduced to a data point, in which case I become one of the 2,341 votes registered for the challenger against the incumbent.

Following the classical tradition, scholars in modern rhetoric and discourse theory have made much of the difference between telling a story and making an argument with data and other rational forms.[1] Walter Fisher goes so far as to argue that people who prefer arguments from data operate under a different worldview or "paradigm" from people who prefer narrative-centered discourses. What Fisher calls the "rational world paradigm" thus competes with the "narrative paradigm." Jean-François Lyotard takes a similar position. Science (by which he seems to mean all specialized academic or expert studies in modern times) tends to use "denotative" discourse that builds arguments with theory and data instead of narratives. Even so, says Lyotard, the scientific disciplines must use narratives to communicate with outsiders because denotative argument is too hard (or too boring) for the nonexpert to follow.

The development of science as an authoritative discourse in modern times therefore favors data-driven arguments over the telling of stories. But narrative remains a considerable force, a dominant form in news reporting as well as entertainment—magazine stories, novels, movies, and television programs, for example. Narratively structured examples retain a prominent place in such staples of rhetorical practice as political speeches, sermons, and teaching. Testimonial stories play an important role in advertising, religious inspirational literature, self-help books, and courts of law. The emergence of democratic attitudes in societies with near-universal access to education also supports storytelling on a wide scale. If everyone's experience is potentially as valuable as everyone else's, then everyone has a story to tell.

Examples and illustrations are short enough to function more or less as slightly expanded data points, but what happens when narrative becomes the primary structuring device in the whole essay, speech, film, or book? This chapter considers the appeal of these longer narratives and their rhetorical functions. It begins with questions about the motives of storytelling—above all, why do we tell stories?—then proceeds to discuss the community-building and audience-empowering functions of narrative.

Rhetorical Motives in Storytelling: The Situation

I have defined rhetoric (in the preface) as *a concern for audience manifested in the situation and form of a communication*. Traditional theorists divide rhetoric from poetics by suggesting that rhetoric aims to move people to some kind of action or at least to inspire a change of mind or attitude toward a subject, while poetics deals with literature and other creative arts that aim mainly to entertain and even divert us from the serious business of life. Storytelling tends to get placed under the heading of poetics in classical studies. Aristotle, for example, has much more to say about narrative in his influential book on poetics than in his equally famous treatise on rhetoric.

But scholars in modern rhetoric, such as Wayne Booth, have shown that even entertainment involves some degree of rhetorical concern—a pitch to a certain segment of the audience, for example, as when a TV network chooses programs to attract women during the day, men on Saturday afternoons, and families during evening prime time, or another network directs its entire programming schedule to women (the Lifetime channel) or to children (Nickelodeon) or to men (Spike TV). So in taking on the question of rhetorical motives in storytelling, we want to know what there is in the *situation and form* of a narrative that shows the concern for audience.

Let's start with the situation. Let's indulge, for a moment, in a little fantasy, a kind of primal narrative scene. Imagine that you're a boy or girl sitting around a village or tribal camp one evening when the adults return from a hunting trip, bringing in the carcass of a huge bear. The hunters are all muddy and smeared with blood and are shaking their spears and arrows, whooping in celebration of their success. You join in as the dead beast is skinned, butchered, cooked, and eaten.

After the great feast, you're all sitting around the campfire with full bellies. Now you get to hear the story of the hunt. Perhaps all the hunters share parts of the tale. Maybe they act it out, with one wearing the skin of the dead bear. Maybe the one who delivered the killing blow has the honor of telling the tale, or maybe the oldest and wisest of the hunters gets the nod.

The main point is, the story must be told. Why? In his *Poetics*, Aristotle suggests that human beings are imitative animals—we love mimicry—so we take delight in imitating nature, recreating events in stories, literature, drama, painting, and the other arts. In a similar vein, Freud suggests that we repeat, sometimes compulsively—in our conversations, dreams, and art— not only pleasurable events or themes, but even traumatic ones. We entertain ourselves with stories, then, because it is our nature to do so. Stories appeal to us.

One of the conclusions that the study of appeals leads toward, however, is that if something appeals in the sense of giving pleasure, it is likely involved in an appeal that someone—an author, or in this case, a storyteller—is making in another sense, in the sense traditionally associated with rhetorical appeals, a pleading, an appeal to an audience on the basis of shared values.

What, then, are the rhetorical motives for storytelling? What's the appeal? We might suggest three possible overlapping motives:

- The storytelling builds community. Those who participated in the hunt or witnessed it report to those who did not, allowing them to join in the event vicariously and thus feel included. In everyday life, this kind of story gets told hundreds of times daily when a family member comes home and somebody asks, "How was your day?"

- The storytelling reinforces values. The storyteller may emphasize the bravery and skill of the hunters; or if the teller is a shaman, he or she might attribute the success of the hunt to the good prayers and reverence of the hunters as they entered the woods. The listeners may be reminded of other hunts or of legendary hunters who embodied the community's most cherished values.

- The storytelling performs a training function. Young listeners learn not only about values but also about practical skills and behaviors. The teller might caution against approaching the bear in the way one hunter did, who was mauled before the others could subdue the animal. Again, this kind of story-teaching takes place every day in hundreds of households. A parent says to a child, "Let me tell you what could happen if you play with fire."

Of the examples we have seen in previous chapters, the narrative of ex-slave Frederick Douglass best illustrates these motives. Douglass attempts to build community with his predominantly white Christian audience by revealing the contradictions between Biblical injunctions and the practice of slavery and by arguing that the institution of slavery corrupts the white slaveholder as much as the black slave. He reinforces the values of hard work, determination, and education. And he uses his narrative to teach the audience about the horrors of slavery about which they may have little knowledge—the near starvation of some slaves, the indiscriminate separation of families, the practice of keeping slaves purposely ignorant, to name a few.

Another good example comes from the theoretical literature on the insider and outsider discourses of science. In discussing how modern science favors "denotative" or data-driven arguments as an insider discourse, Lyotard mentions that science turns to narrative as a recruiting and teaching discourse. The technical literature of science requires an expert audience to receive the information of expert authors. But a person is not born an expert; some bridging communication is needed. So like the hunter, the scientist (or the scientist's representative, the science writer) returns to the public forum (village) to tell the story of great deeds in the laboratory and field. Think of all the science-is-fun programs on television, full of amazing tales about heroic discoveries and strange creatures and natural occurrences. Science textbooks mix in history and flashy images as well. I remember reading an odd story in a physics book once, in which the great Italian scientist Volta was said to have placed an electrode in each of his ears. He reported hearing a sound like that of boiling soup. The story appealed to my taste for eccentricity and kept my wandering attention intact for a few more pages. It definitely stuck in my memory more effectively than the rest of the chapter on electrical current. Some magazine editors have suggested that the heroic narratives of science fiction also perform a recruiting function. As evidence that it sometimes works, I knew a student who said she took on a double major in bioengineering and psychology to become the world's first "robopsychologist," an idea she got from reading about the character Susan Calvin in Isaac Asimov's robot stories. I was myself enticed into a chemistry major by reading biographies of people like Alexander Fleming and Marie Curie. Once I grasped the reality of laboratory work in college, however—the tedium of watching endlessly dripping titrations—I realized that it was the stories and not the science that I was most interested in. The hope is that the few who can endure the demands of the laboratory and the conceptual demands will become the scientists of the future. The motive of television, science fiction, and textbook narratives is simply to get potential recruits to take that first step into the laboratory.

Author Position 1: Bearing Witness (Metonymy/Association)

"I am the man, I suffer'd, I was there," says Walt Whitman in "Song of Myself" (*Leaves of Grass* 59). Embodying the values of "bearing witness," a concept he learned from his Quaker upbringing, Whitman claims a position of privilege as an author. And yet he also insists that in a democratic society, potentially everyone has the same privilege (and duty) to speak out, to tell his or her personal story. "I speak the pass-word primeval, I give the sign of democracy," he writes, "By God! I will accept nothing which all cannot have their counterpart of on the same terms" (48).

Along the same lines, Lyotard suggests that unlike scientific discourse, anyone can participate in community narratives; everyone is a potential storyteller. But we need to add that certain storytellers have more power to appeal—those with special experiences that set them apart and those who have witnessed important events. The author position in a narrative appeal, we might say, is enhanced by a direct association—a metonymic connection—with the actions narrated.

As a victim of and witness to slavery, Frederick Douglass claims a special hold on the audience's attention. A storyteller with firsthand experience of slavery, he made a strong appeal to potential recruits for the abolitionist movement in the North. All people with avenues to special experiences beyond the normal cycle of everyday life—victims of crimes, eye witnesses, news reporters, travel writers, celebrities, public leaders—attract readers and listeners who long to be a part of a wider community, who seek new insights into life, who wonder about their relationship to the rest of the world.

In this light, it is easy to see why the most appealing stories mix the exotic with the familiar or make the familiar seem somehow new. They bring *information*, which the anthropologist Gregory Bateson defines as *a difference that makes a difference.*

Consider, for example, the author position in some of the narratives we have studied in previous chapters:

- The social critic Wendell Berry uses his perspective as the owner of a small family farm to criticize the condition of people in the specialized professions of the modern world. His audience is presumably composed primarily of the kind of people whose condition he laments, people who know little or nothing of farm life (chapter 1).

- Memoirist Richard Rodriguez tells his story as a Mexican American who emerges from a traditional family into the literate culture of the modern writer. He brings a new cultural perspective to readers with whom he hopes to form a new community (chapter 3).

- Essayist Leslie Marmon Silko, writing for a predominantly Anglo-American, educated, and thoroughly modern audience, tells how her own more traditional Laguna people maintain a close connection to the land by telling mythic tales connected to real places (chapter 5).

- Journalist Jonathan Kozol tells of his visits with children of the inner-city poor, whose living conditions contrast strongly with most of the people who read his articles and books (chapter 6).

- Sociologist Arlie Russell Hochschild tells of her own experience as a working mother who brings her child to her university job as a way of establishing common ground with the working mothers she studies in *The Second Shift* (chapter 7).

- Malcolm X recounts his life of hustling and crime, his prison time, his conversion to Islam, and his subsequent discovery of self-respect and a proud racial identity as a way of holding out hope for his own people and challenging the white world to recognize the abilities and promise of African Americans and other oppressed people (chapter 8).

All of these witnesses attempt to change the perspective of the audience by telling stories that readers are supposed to receive as vicarious experiences. The readers have not had the opportunity to live on a farm, grow up Mexican American, hear stories from the elders of Laguna Pueblo, visit the inner-city poor, carry their babies to work, or become a powerful figure in religion and politics. But they can "try on" the experience imaginatively. The authors use this reader curiosity to question the boundaries of community and bring new understanding of outsiders. It is a very old and very valuable rhetorical practice.

Author Position 2: Making Ironic and Mythic Connections (Metaphor/Identity)

In the same way that authors of journalism, personal essays, and other nonfiction narratives bear witness to events that make the exotic world more familiar or the familiar world seem strange, authors of novels, plays, ballads, and other creative narratives invent narrators or tell of characters whose experiences *defamiliarize* the worlds in which their audiences usually dwell. Instead of bearing witness to the actual events, these imaginative narratives create a parallel reality. Instead of association (metonymy), the rhetorical appeal of such narratives works metaphorically. If the narrative succeeds, the audience forms an identification with either the characters or the author.

A good example is Jonathan Swift's "A Modest Proposal." Swift was an official of the Church of England in Ireland and was horrified by the conditions of the poor there. He might have written journalism like that which Jonathan Kozol wrote over two hundred years later, but Swift chose a different approach. He created a persona, a narrator who puts forth a preposterous proposal that he seems to feel his audience will accept with no questions asked. He proposes to raise the Irish children for meat, which their parents can sell to the rich as a delicacy and thereby improve their condition. In the parallel universe of the proposer and his ideal audience, cannibalism is not taboo, at least not among the lower classes, who are little better than animals anyway. Swift appeals to the audience first to see the proposal as part of an absurd story that can't really take place, and second to *see through* the story that the reality of English-Irish class relations is not so different. The parallel world is all too close to the real world. The first movement is to judge and separate. The second movement is to identity the two worlds. In one, landlords metaphorically "devour" their tenants. In the other, the landlords literally devour their tenents.

By allowing the audience to do some of the interpretive work, Swift appeals not only to their sense of morality but also to their intelligence. Smart people like us, he seems to say to the audience, can see through this sham. Thus he creates an inner circle that includes himself and his audience, a circle separated from the abusers of the poor by morality and good sense. Swift and his readers look with withering irony upon the way the privileged treat the poor.

We have also seen how authors will use first-person ("I") narrators who tell their story from the perspective of older, wiser people looking back on an experience in which they underwent an important change. Such is the case with both Willis Davidge in Barry Longyear's story "Enemy Mine" and Grant Wiggins in Ernest Gaines's novel *A Lesson Before Dying* (both discussed in Chapter 8). It is not by accident that both narratives involve the narrators' adjustment to a new community whose old boundaries, particularly the divisions of race and education, have been redefined. The literate situation of isolation in the act of reading forms a parallel to the isolation of Davidge on the desolate planet ("Enemy Mine") and the educated Wiggins in his community of undereducated and underprivileged rural African Americans *(A Lesson Before Dying)*. Through these narrators, the authors appeal to readers to open their minds and expand their own communities to develop new identifications and perhaps new identities.

One other form of identification needs mentioning. Identification some-times occurs not only at the narrator-character and author-audience lev-els but also at the level of the whole narration. The scenes, characters, ac-tions, and thematic patterns of one story may recall the elements of a well-known story. In Frederick Douglass's day, biblical stories of the cap-tivity, exile, and exodus of the Jews had a mighty appeal to the newly Christianized slaves, producing some classic works of African American music, poetry, and literary art on the theme of "Let My People Go." From the earliest field chants and spiritual songs to high modern musical, liter-ary, and rhetorical performances such as James Weldon Johnson's *God's Trombones*, James Baldwin's *Go Tell It on the Mountain*, Martin Luther King's "I Have a Dream" speech, and the recent references to the Babylonian cap-tivity in reggae music, the theme of lost freedom resonates. The story of how the Jews were enslaved and then freed by their inspired leaders forms a parallel first with the striving of slaves toward freedom and later with the striving of the displaced people toward full membership in their com-munities and self-realization as individuals.

Narratives that form mythic links in this way allow authors to appeal by suggesting links with historical and spiritual depth. A few examples we have seen so far include the following:

- Linda Hogan's appeal to European Americans to connect the sto-ries of Greek mythology to those of the old Native American sto-ries portraying the earth as a living being (chapter 3).

- Abraham Lincoln's allusion to the American Revolution in his me-morial to the Civil War dead in his "Gettysburg Address" (chapter 4).

- Aldo Leopold's use of the myth of Odysseus in his introduction to "The Land Ethic" (chapter 4).

- Leslie Marmon Silko's use of ancient Pueblo and Navajo stories as a parallel to her character Tayo's experience in surviving World War II (a narrative that may have been based on stories she heard from her father, who served in the Philippines) (chapter 5).

The Audience Position: Participation and Empowerment

Swift's appeal to an intelligent audience capable of picking up his irony involves a great deal of faith in the reader. The risk is that if you leave too much to the audience, if you don't explain the mythic connection or the main point of your implied argument, you may end up telling a good story but failing to get the point across. Most literary artists have no problem taking the risk. Even if the audience fails to pick up the themes, the story may accomplish its goal of entertaining. The Roman poet Horace said that art should be both sweet and useful—it should please and plead, in other words—but modern creative writers would rather err on the side of sweetness at the cost of utility just as modern technical writers would rather err on the side of utility. Rhetorical narratives tend to take the middle ground. The hope is that, if they fail to teach a precise lesson, perhaps they will build a communal relationship with the audience that may establish a foundation for further communication.

As an illustration, consider one of my own efforts at storytelling. I'm occasionally invited to speak to groups of teenagers, and I've found that I have better luck holding their attention if I tell a story than if I try to lecture or sermonize. On several occasions I've tried to discuss a phenomenon that's undoubtedly well documented in the literature on adolescent psychology and sociology—violence among adolescent males. I could cite statistics on increased fighting at school or surveys of psychologists who remark on the tendency of boys to pull away from the family at puberty, to question the authority of parents. The road to personal independence, I could show with the help of this information, often leads boys to violence.

Instead, I tell them a story. I take an indirect approach and tell them I want to show them a sample of personal writing that I hope will encourage them to take up writing projects of their own. Even if they never finish them—the story comes from a manuscript of mine that I work on endlessly—they might learn something about themselves by treating themselves as characters in a narrative. This is how the story goes:

> I remember the day when the consequences of fighting became a reality for me. A boy older than me, but much smaller, decided I was easy prey. Maybe I carried too many books or talked too glibly, or maybe he decided I was just a nice big target for him to show others how tough he was. And he was tough, no doubt, an experienced and capable fighter. He probably learned how to defend himself at home.
>
> His name was Jaime, pronounced in the Spanish way as "Hi-me." His real name was James Hedges, but everybody called him Jaime for some reason. It pissed him off, of course, as everything seemed to. To this day, I can't remember what I said to him on the bus as I tried to get him to leave me alone. I only remember him saying, "Did you call me a son of a bitch? When we get to your stop, I'm going to kick your ass."
>
> He followed me off the bus and challenged me at the street corner, his hands up in the guard of an experienced boxer. I handed my books to my friend and turned to face him, again feeling that focus

I'd felt before. But this one was too fast. Before I could even raise my hands, he had delivered six or seven well-aimed punches to my face and head.

I remember bowing, as if in prayer, my vision blurred with tears and blood. I heard him say something really sharp and loud and felt the crowd diminish around me, my friend handing me my books and walking away.

I stumbled home, entered through the garage door, and went up the short flight of stairs to the kitchen. My little sister was already there, having an after-school snack at the table. Her face registered the shocking condition of my own face. She sat there staring as I tried to wash the hurt and embarrassment away in the kitchen sink, and then she said, "What happened?"

"Just shut up!" I yelled and ran to the bathroom I shared with my brother and locked the door and cried and washed some more.

Within minutes, Mother was at the door, demanding to be let in. I opened the door to her stunned expression. She insisted on knowing everything, and as soon as she learned the name of the boy involved, she hurried me into the car and headed toward his house. The tears—now driven from my eyes by the humiliation of having my mother confront my enemy—would not stop. I would not leave the car when we arrived, so she went to door of the Hedges house by herself. I saw Jaime appear. He seemed so small in the face of Mother's anger. His mother was not home, he said; she was at work. Mother told him to call her and have her come to our house immediately unless she wanted some real trouble.

The next hour was a blur to me. I had a bad headache and a troubled mind. Mother's protective care had pulled me so close to her that I lost all perspective on what was happening.

When Mrs. Hedges and Jaime were finally admitted to the den and the four of us sat in a small circle of extreme discomfort, I did not raise my eyes from the floor until Mother put a question to me: "Is that true, son?" Mrs. Hedges, a tough woman at least ten years older than Mother with a face like a hatchet, had said, "He called my boy a son of a bitch, and we don't stand for that kind of talk."

I did not hesitate to look Mother in the eye and say "No!" even if it was a lie. At that moment I hated everybody in the room. I hated this terrible woman and her rough son for intruding in my life, and I hated Mother too. She had drawn me so close I was humiliated, then seemed just as suddenly to doubt me and my victimized state, as if any words I said might have justified the beating this foul-mouthed boy had given me. And of course, I hated myself for failing both as a fighter and a son.

When the Hedges left in a huff, nothing decided because no one believed anyone else, Mother continued to vacillate between the roles of protector and inquisitor. The tears kept coming and my head pounded. I could see the sympathy in her eyes, but I could also see the warring systems of values. One said that nothing excuses violence on this order. The other said honor must be protected, even with violence. I probed my memory for what I had said, and I revised my lie. "Honestly I can't remember what I said," I told her in frustration.

"Well, it matters," she said. "You can't just say anything you want to anybody, and you certainly can't go around insulting people's mothers"—but then she added, with a mouth full of spite, "even if they deserve it."

I lay on the sofa in the den and drifted toward a disturbed sleep. I awoke when I heard Dad clearing his throat as he walked up to me, his doctor's bag in his hand. As he looked into my eyes and ears with his little lighted instruments and put the old stethoscope to my chest, he asked me to tell him what had happened as simply as I could. I did my best. I was tired of telling the story. He gave me some aspirin to take and told me just to relax. Then he went upstairs.

He came back in a few minutes with a cold drink for me. "You might have had a little concussion," he said. "He must have hit you pretty hard." I nodded. I needed his sympathy as much as I needed air to breathe.

He gave it freely, but like Mom, he seemed to be in conflict, too. I read him as closely as I could with the limited understanding of a thirteen-year-old boy in a man's body.

"I talked to Mr. Wright," he said, meaning his lawyer. "He says that no matter what words were passed, the boy had no right to hit you and could go to jail if we pressed charges." I started to cry again.

"Now hang on, Jim," he said. "I know you don't want to do that, and neither do I. We want to put this thing behind us." He paused till I got control again. "What I'm telling you is that you don't have to fight with your fists. There are other ways to protect yourself. Now if you think that you have to fight, then let's you and me get some gloves and start practicing. But I don't think that's the way to go. That's not the way we raised you. We want to live another way. Do you understand?"

"Yessir," I said. He nodded, and that was the end of the talk.

But, of course, I didn't understand. Mother and Dad's ways of thinking seemed so abstract, so careful of consequences, and what I understood least of all, so conflicted. They seemed nearly as confused as I was. Now I know, of course, that they were so shocked out of their usual routine by having their son come home with his face beaten bloody that their world, like mine, was deeply threatened.

I also know that, for Mother at least, two worlds had collided: the life that she had lived with her own father, the tough little fighting man—a life built on concepts like duty and honor and the violence that upholds duty and honor—and the life that she was living with Dad, a life guided closely by modern ethical codes and professional behavior, and protected by a tight family circle within the concentric circles of church, school, and law. In the end, she turned everything over to Dad.

Neither one of them would ever know how strange the whole thing was for me, how the day after the fight, both eyes blackened, lips swollen and crusted with the new cuts, knots raised on my forehead where Hedges had struck me with the big rings he wore on his fingers, I went to school to be greeted by a tearful girlfriend who heard rumors that I had been hospitalized with a concussion, by awestruck friends and even teachers who seemed to admire me for standing up to Hedges even though I had been shamed, and strangest of all: one of Hedges's own companions came up to me as I stood in my position as a hall monitor and told me to let him help me if Hedges ever bothered me again. I had no idea what to make of that.

With Hedges himself, I avoided him and waited. A year later, a chance for revenge presented itself, and I took it.

We both went out for the junior varsity football team. In a scrimmage game, he was on the opposing team, playing defensive back, as I lined up at right offensive tackle, a position which I had held the year before and at which I had gained a good level of skill. On a running play to the left side, my assignment was to go downfield and block the defensive back, and as I broke through the line, I saw Hedges watching the action come toward him without any view of my approach. There was my chance. I came in at full speed and leveled him with a cross body block right in front of the coach. As I was walking back to the huddle, I heard the coach yelling at Hedges as he lay stunned on the ground.

Two weeks later, he was cut from the team, and I was the starting right tackle. I don't remember ever seeing his ugly face from that time on. He disappeared from my life.

While it's surely no literary masterpiece, the story has never failed to rivet the attention of my young audiences. What's the appeal? The boys tell me it speaks to their experience (engaging the metaphoric/identifying functions of narrative); the girls say it gives them insight into what it's like to be a boy (bearing witness and thus engaging the metonymic/associative functions).

Look at it as a story about storytelling (a good approach to the analysis of narrative: begin with a story about storytelling). Here's a man in late middle age reading to a group of high-school students. He's not lecturing—reducing lives like their own to a series of numbers that he can compare and contrast. He's not preaching, connecting a Bible story with a little story from modern life to urge them toward moral behavior. He's not judging, lording over the story of adolescent misbehavior, waiting impatiently to arrive at a sentence for the crime. On the contrary, he's offering a confession and inviting the audience to judge him.

An interesting result of this storytelling is that the young people do not judge the persona of the story very harshly. They see him caught up in the kinds of struggles they face every day. They nearly always see how loneliness and violence go hand in hand and that some kids do better at street fighting, while others—the successful hall monitors and football players—work the system to satisfy their competitive and often vengeful desires.

If you try to make such points explicitly, you might not have the same success. Mentioning the abstract term "violence," for example, will likely generate all kinds of preconceived notions or prepackaged lessons. If you criticize organized sports and "healthy competition" as every bit as violent as brawling in the street (though perhaps not as threatening to human life), you're pushing against an entire institutionalized system of morality and fair play. The story lets the audience make the connections and form the judgments. It strongly implies the judgment about systemized violence, but it doesn't push it too hard.

A truism among creative writer teachers (and a point that gets a great deal of attention from Wayne Booth in his *Rhetoric of Fiction*) is that *a good story doesn't tell, it shows*. It doesn't say that a certain character is devious and manipulative. It shows him in acts of trickery and deceit. It shows him telling one friend one thing and a second friend something entirely different. This kind of story increases audience participation. The audience is permitted not only to identify with one character or another, but also to apply previous experiences of characters like the ones in the story in forming judgments and generalizations.

The dictum to show rather than tell is a standard of storytelling particularly associated with modern literary narratives. In ancient and medieval times, it was common to attach a chapter or moral that explains the story to the audience (remember Aesop's *Fables?*). In Victorian novels, the narrator often addresses the audience directly ("Dear reader") to advocate a certain view of a situation or character—a technique revived among writers classified as "postmodern" (such as Vladimir Nabokov).

The preference for dramatizing rather than preaching a point reached a zenith in the high modernism of the early twentieth century, under the influence of literary realists like Ernest Hemingway. Interestingly, the people of this era cherished the ideals of democracy and freedom, ideals embattled on many fronts. To my mind, it makes perfect sense that democratic ideals and a rhetoric that lets audiences make up their own minds go hand in hand.

Compensation in Narrative and the Horizon of Success in Rhetoric

We have barely scratched the surface of narrative rhetoric and have already exposed numerous possibilities. Perhaps the main point to remember is that narrative offers a powerful approach to community building through its metonymic (associative) and metaphoric (identification) functions.

Like all rhetorical techniques, however, narrative has its limits. It is clear enough that, from the perspective of a nonexpert audience, scientific writing and other "academic" discourses built on data and theory tend to be abstract, reductive, dry, and rational, while narrative is rich, easy-to-follow, and full of possibilities for association and identification. But we should not forget the advantages of data-driven arguments. Above all, they get to the point faster, while narrative tends to wander here and there and proceed at a leisurely pace. Narrative makes a strong appeal to time—in many ways it is a trope of time, an artistic re-creation of events structured chronologically—but data can save time by making the point faster or clearer. Moreover, narrative risks swamping the point in marginally relevant detail—the color of a character's eyes, the weather on the day of the event recounted—stuff that might delight but also distract the reader and make the main argument unclear.

What emerges here is a point worthy of a conclusion: what Emerson called the law of compensation. Every gain in life involves a compensatory loss; with every loss, something is gained. Try as we might, there are no easy and failsafe methods in rhetoric. Rhetorical success is a receding horizon.

That's why rhetorical criticism must always be the counterpart of rhetorical practice. What worked last time may not work this time. We take a risk and then apply the analysis of self-criticism. The goal is not to reach the horizon but to realize the human possibility along the way.

Notes

Works Cited

Index

Notes

1. A General Introduction to Rhetorical Appeals

1. For more on this point, see chapter 3. I'm not sure exactly how ethos, pathos, and logos came to be called "appeals." While Aristotle talks at some length about each of the terms, he seems to say very little about the general category to which they belong. In the *Rhetoric* (book 1, chapter 2, paragraph 2), he defines what we have come to call appeals *(pisteis)* by dividing them into two categories: one called "entechnic," "artistic," or "intrinsic," the other called "atechnic," "inartistic," or "extrinsic" (*On Rhetoric* 37, 37n). The atechnic category includes accounts from witnesses and "testimony of slaves taken under torture" (37). The artistic category, the proper concern of rhetoric according to Aristotle, includes ethos, pathos, and logos. They are "artistic" in the sense that, while rhetors "use" the inartistic *pisteis,* they "invent" or "discover" or "provide" *(heurein)* the artistic (37, 37n). As I've suggested here, no widely accepted translation of Aristotle's text uses the term *appeal* to name either the artistic or inartistic categories. In the still much-used translation of W. Rhys Roberts, ethos, pathos, and logos are called "modes of persuasion"—a technically accurate but not particularly memorable rendering, though one still preferred by some scholars with a strong sense of faithfulness to the original (see, for example, Johnson 243; and Swearingen 124). The entry on "Aristotle's Rhetoric" in the *Stanford Encyclopedia of Philosophy* (section 5) uses the phrase "means of persuasion," which places ethos, pathos, and logos at the center of the treatise since Aristotle defines rhetoric itself as the process of finding the available means of persuasion. But again, this usage has not found its way into the ordinary usage of the scholarly community. Ethos, pathos, and logos are sometimes called artistic "proofs" (see, for example, Kennedy's translation 82). But to use the term "proof" runs counter to modern usage—writers or speakers aren't supposed to "invent" proof in an argument—a difference that probably accounts for the tendency in modern rhetoric and composition to substitute the term *appeal* not only in textbooks, where the term prevails above all others, but in many scholarly sources (see, for example, Yoos 410; Colavito 494; and Kinneavy, *"Pistis,"* as well as Kinneavy's influential *A Theory of Discourse*). Yet the weight of scholarly opinion suggests that "appeal" may not be a good translation for Aristotle's *pistis.* In the notes to his authoritative translation, Kennedy sticks with the term "proof," but in the main text, he declines to translate the Greek term at all and simply refers to atechnic and entechnic pisteis (Aristotle, *On Rhetoric* 37, 37n). On the basis of these sources, I would contend that contemporary usage

of the term *appeal* in rhetorical analysis tends to depart from Aristotle except when we confine ourselves to doing neo-Aristotelian analysis of ethos, pathos, and logos, and even then, we may be adding new layers of significance to the terms and ignoring old meanings by referring to these "modes" or "means" of persuasion as "appeals." Yet the very drift toward a preference for the term suggests its resonance for contemporary rhetoricians and the need for a revised model, such as this book offers, that accounts for the meaning and overtones of the word, in a way that the recourse to the Aristotelian terms does not.

2. My main source in discussions of word origins is Douglas Harper's *Online Etymology Dictionary* (from which I quote) with occasional reference to the *Oxford English Dictionary.* I got early help in developing the etymologies from my esteemed student Georgina Kennedy and my friend and colleague Chris Holcomb.

3. A particularly influential and rhetorically sophisticated example is William Gibson's novel *Neuromancer.*

2. Appeals to Authority and Evidence

1. To name only three of many excellent examples, see Alan Gross, *The Rhetoric of Science;* Dierdre McCloskey, *The Rhetoric of Economics;* and Jeanne Fahnestock, *Rhetorical Figures in Science.*

2. This is the famous position of the philosopher of science Karl Popper. See *The Open Society and Its Enemies.* Another now classic work in this field, Thomas Kuhn's *The Structure of Scientific Revolutions,* offers the best discussion of how the authority of scientific theories or "paradigms" undergo continuous scrutiny and often get overturned.

3. See Kennedy's discussion of Augustine in *Classical Rhetoric and Its Christian and Secular Tradition from Ancient to Modern Times.*

3. Rhetorical Situations

1. My reading and discussion of Aristotle are influenced strongly by the work of George Kennedy, both his translation of the original and his *Classical Rhetoric and Its Christian and Secular Tradition from Ancient to Modern Times.* Renato Barilli's *Rhetoric* has also proved invaluable.

2. See Booth, *The Rhetoric of Fiction;* Ong, "The Writer's Audience Is Always a Fiction"; Black, "The Second Persona"; and Jane Tompkins, ed., *Reader-Response Criticism.*

4. Appeals to Time

1. For a brief account of the interesting coincidence of Aristotle's treatment of time and genre and that of modern technical writing, see Killingsworth and Gilbertson, "Rhetoric and Relevance in Technical Writing."

2. For a provocative and engaging, if somewhat oversimplified, account of these times, see I. F. Stone's *The Trial of Socrates*. Also see Kenneth Burke's treatment of politically charged language and sustained appeal of a text over time in *Counter-statement*.

3. For an outstanding study of rhetoric in historical context, see Garry Wills's *Lincoln at Gettysburg*.

5. Appeals to Place

1. Burke has inspired many explications for readers who need some help with his challenging writings. The ones I've found most helpful may be found in Richard M. Coe, *Form and Substance: An Advanced Rhetoric;* Timothy W. Crusius, *Kenneth Burke and the Conversation after Philosophy;* and, on dramatism in particular, David Blakesley, *The Elements of Dramatism*. I especially recommend Coe and Blakesley for students new to the study of Burke.

2. Recent scholarship in rhetoric and literary criticism calls for a reevaluation of how place functions in discourse. Place occupies various analytical positions in these studies. It can take the position of a theme or topic, as in the focus of environmental rhetoric and ecocriticism on political ecology with its concern over the preservation of specific places (Killingsworth and Palmer; Glotfelty and Fromm). It can also take the position of the setting or context of any discourse, as in ecocomposition, in which place becomes one element among many in an "ecology of writing" (Cooper; Dobrin and Weisser). But neither the thematic nor the contextual view fully accounts for the way that place functions as a source of identity and inspiration in rhetorical appeals, when authors identity their own perspective with a particular region or locale or when they offer scenic images (appealing places) and invite identification from the audience.

3. Lest we too quickly dismiss hooks's observations as a phony idealization of country life, we should also consider the similarity of her remarks to those of the journalist and social critic Jonathan Kozol, who has studied the plight of poor children both in the rural south and the inner-city north. The houses he visited in New York City, he says, "are often as squalid as the houses of the poorest children I have visited in rural Mississippi, but there is none of the greenness and the healing sweetness of the Mississippi countryside outside their windows, which are often barred and bolted as protection against thieves" (4–5). See the discussion of Kozol's own appeals in chapter 6. See also the tonal differences between the urban intensity of Malcolm X's rhetoric in contrast to the rural narrative of Ernest Gaines in the discussion of appeals to race in chapter 8.

6. Appeals to the Body

1. In addition to many articles and chapters in the fields of environmental rhetoric and ecocriticism (see note 2 for chapter 5), an entire book has

been devoted to the study of Carson's rhetoric: Craig Waddell's collection *"And No Birds Sing."*

2. The representation of the body in discourse has attracted a good deal of scholarly attention lately. "Body criticism" in literary studies emerges into the study of rhetoric in Jack Selzer and Sharon Crowley's collection of essays *Rhetorical Bodies.* Selzer's introduction is particularly useful. Studies in women's rhetoric have taken a particular interest in appeals to the body. See, for example, the comments on "physicality" and "writing the body" in Joy Ritchie and Kate Ronald's introduction to *Available Means: An Anthology of Women's Rhetoric(s)* (xxvi). For more on appeals to the body in the rhetoric of gender, see chapter 7. The body also figures importantly in the treatment of race in chapter 8 and tropes in chapter 9. Chapter 9 argues that, in modern rhetoric at least, appeals to the body through metaphor are foundational to all other appeals.

3. I develop these themes further in *Whitman's Poetry of the Body: Sexuality, Politics, and the Text.* My latest book, *Walt Whitman and the Earth,* considers appeals to the body in relation to appeals to place and discusses the further relation of environmental rhetoric to "ecopoetics."

4. My discussion of the restrained style of social realism is influenced by a provocative analysis of Hemingway's style in the fine old textbook by Charles Kay Smith, *Styles and Structures: Alternative Approaches to College Writing.*

5. The concept of "subvocalization," well known to linguists, suggests that reading is never altogether silent despite our efforts to make it so in elementary school. The vocal chords continue to move and flex, producing an inner "voice" that we feel in our bodies as well as hear in our minds. For an even bolder version of the kind of appeal that Mairs's work embodies, see Nomy Lamm's writings on fatness. "Sometimes I feel my whole identity is wrapped up in my fat," she writes (460). I am indebted to my former student, Professor Amy Childers, for many stimulating conversations on the question of "voice" in writing, a topic on which she wrote a fine dissertation. I'm sorry we never got around to discussing Nancy Mairs and Nomy Lamm. I am indebted to another excellent student, Courtney Beggs, for calling my attention to Lamm and "fat studies" in general.

7. Appeals to Gender

1. Recent years have seen an outpouring of excellent studies in women's rhetoric. From early writings on women's right to speak in public forums (ranging from church to political assemblies) to recent studies of women's claim on special insights and forms of discourse, the field of study is wide open to new possibilities. A good place for novices to begin is the survey in Joy Ritchie and Kate Ronald's collection *Available Means: An Anthology of Women's Rhetoric(s).* The best scholarly work includes the collection of studies edited by Andrea Lunsford, *Reclaiming Rhetorica,* and the mono-

graphs *Man Cannot Speak for Her* by Karlyn Kohrs Campbell and *Rhetoric Retold* by Cheryl Glenn. As with the "masculine" tradition, much work remains to be done in modern women's rhetoric.

2. The rhetoric of the image has received increasing attention since the advent of photography, motion pictures, and television. As Kevin DeLuca argues, "Although rhetorical theorists from Aristotle through Bacon to Perelman have recognized the importance and power of 'bringing-before-the-eyes,' 'making pictures,' and 'creating presence,' today 'in the age of television, dramatic, digestive, visual moments are replacing memorable words'" (17). In this study of the use of images in environmental activism, DeLuca is quoting another key authority on political imagery, Kathleen Hall Jamieson. See especially her book *Eloquence in the Electronic Age;* also Medhurst and Benson's *Rhetorical Dimensions in Media.* One development that often goes unnoticed in media studies such as these is that, far from a simple replacement of written language as the favored mode of delivering political messages—the old cliché that a picture is worth a thousand words—the intensification of *visual imagery* in modern and postmodern culture is accompanied by a new emphasis on and refinement of *verbal imagery* in such writings as those I use for examples in this chapter. See also chapter 6, especially the section on "The Body Embattled."

3. The best introduction to French feminism for students of language and literature remains Toril Moi's *Sexual/Textual Politics.* On the question of hysteria, see Monique David-Ménard, *Hysteria from Freud to Lacan: Body and Language in Psychoanalysis;* and Martha Noel Evans, *Fits and Starts: A Genealogy of Hysteria in Modern France.*

8. Appeals to Race

1. Those wishing to pursue work in African American rhetoric will find an excellent starting place in *Understanding African American Rhetoric: Classical Origins to Contemporary Innovations,* edited by Ronald L. Jackson, Elaine B. Richardson, and Orlando L. Taylor. I have also found the work of Bradford T. Stull very insightful, both his chapter on race in *The Elements of Figurative Language* and his monograph *Amid the Fall, Dreaming of Eden: Du Bois, King, Malcolm X, and Emancipatory Composition.*

2. It is unclear to me whether Malcolm considered his book finished at the time of his death. What is clear is that Haley's epilogue turns attention back to the problems that Malcolm had with his former associates in Elijah Muhammad's organization. It makes a good story, one that we all want to hear, no doubt, but I think it unfortunately clouds the religious and political appeal that Malcolm makes at the end of the main narrative. Haley should always be remembered and appreciated as the author who made this book possible, but his journalistic instinct for a good story, while it surely helped make the beginning of the narrative one of the most read-

able and attractive treatments of Black Nationalism, may have blunted the final appeal of Malcolm's far-reaching spiritual vision and racial insights.

3. For a good introductory investigation into the rhetorical implications of Marxism, see James Arnt Aune, *Rhetoric and Marxism*.

9. Appeal Through Tropes

1. Besides the scholarship I mention directly in the text of this chapter, Bradford T. Stull's useful introduction *The Elements of Figurative Language* has influenced my understanding of tropes. Over the years, I have also drawn often upon Richard Lanham's *A Handlist of Rhetorical Terms*. I recommend both texts to the novice student of tropes. For a subtle use of classical tropology applied to modern texts, see Jeanne Fahnestock's *Rhetorical Figures in Science*.

10. The Appeal of Narrative

1. For an outstanding summary of general trends in scholarship, see the entry on "Narrative Theory" by Elizabeth Patnoe and James Phelan in the *Encyclopedia of Rhetoric and Composition* (Enos). The second edition of Gerard A. Hauser's *Introduction to Rhetorical Theory* includes a good chapter on narrative that builds upon the work of Walter Fisher.

Works Cited

Aristotle. *On Rhetoric: A Theory of Civil Discourse*. Trans. and ed. George A. Kennedy. New York: Oxford UP, 1991.

———. *Rhetoric*. Trans. W. Rhys Roberts. Available online at <http://classics.mit.edu/Aristotle/rhetoric.html>.

———. *The Rhetoric and Poetics of Aristotle*. Intro. Edward P. J. Corbett. New York: Modern Library, 1984.

"Aristotle's Rhetoric." *Stanford Encyclopedia of Philosophy*. Available online at <http://plato.stanford.edu/entries/aristotle-rhetoric/>.

Aune, James Arnt. *Rhetoric and Marxism*. Boulder: Westview, 1994.

Barilli, Renato. *Rhetoric*. Trans. Giuliana Menozzi. Minneapolis: U of Minnesota P, 1989.

Barnhill, David Landis, ed. *At Home on the Earth: Becoming Native to Our Place: A Multicultural Anthology*. Berkeley: U of California P, 1999.

Barton, David. *Literacy: An Introduction to the Ecology of Written Language*. Oxford: Blackwell, 1994.

Bateson, Gregory. *Steps to an Ecology of Mind*. New York: Ballantine, 1972.

Bergland, Renée L. *The National Uncanny: Indian Ghosts and American Subjects*. Hanover: UP of New England, 2000.

Berry, Wendell. *The Unsettling of America: Culture and Agriculture*. San Francisco: Sierra Club, 1977.

Bitzer, Lloyd F. "The Rhetorical Situation." *Philosophy and Rhetoric* 1 (1968): 1–14.

Bizzell, Patricia, and Bruce Herzberg, eds. *The Rhetorical Tradition: Readings from Classical Times to the Present*. 2nd ed. New York: St. Martin's, 2001.

Black, Edwin. "The Second Persona." *Quarterly Journal of Speech* 56 (1970): 113–19.

Blakesley, David. *The Elements of Dramatism*. New York: Longman, 2002.

Bookchin, Murray. *The Ecology of Freedom*. Palo Alto: Cheshire, 1982.

Boorstin, Daniel J. "The Rhetoric of Democracy." *Hidden History: Exploring Our Secret Past*. New York: Vintage, 1989. 127–37.

Booth, Wayne C. *The Rhetoric of Fiction*. 2nd ed. Chicago: U of Chicago P, 1983.

———. *A Rhetoric of Irony*. Chicago: U of Chicago P, 1974.

Buell, Lawrence. *The Environmental Imagination: Thoreau, Nature Writing, and the Formation of American Culture*. Cambridge: Harvard UP, 1995.

Burke, Kenneth. *Counter-statement*. Berkeley: U of California P, 1968.

———. *A Grammar of Motives*. Berkeley: U of California P, 1969.

———. *A Rhetoric of Motives*. Berkeley: U of California P, 1969.

Campbell, Karlyn Kohrs. *Man Cannot Speak for Her.* New York: Greenwood, 1989.

Carson, Rachel. *Silent Spring.* New York: Fawcett, 1962.

Cicero. *De Oratore.* Trans. E. W. Sutton and H. Rackam. Loeb Classical Library 349. Cambridge: Harvard UP, 1977.

Coe, Richard M. *Form and Substance: An Advanced Rhetoric.* New York: Wiley, 1981.

———. "Metaphor." Enos 438–44.

Colavito, Joseph. "Pathos." Enos 492–94.

Cooper, Marilyn. "An Ecology of Writing." *College English* 48 (1986): 364–75.

Corbett, Edward P. J. *Classical Rhetoric for the Modern Student.* 2nd ed. New York: Oxford UP, 1971.

Crusius, Timothy W. *Kenneth Burke and the Conversation after Philosophy.* Carbondale: Southern Illinois UP, 1999.

David-Ménard, Monique. *Hysteria from Freud to Lacan: Body and Language in Psychoanalysis.* Trans. Catherine Porter. Ithaca: Cornell UP, 1989.

Davis, Sheila. "Metonymy." Enos 444–46.

———. "Synecdoche." Enos 712–13.

Deloria, Vine, Jr. *God Is Red: A Native View of Religion.* 2nd ed. Golden: Fulcrum, 1992.

DeLuca, Kevin Michael. *Image Politics: The New Rhetoric of Environmental Activism.* New York: Guilford, 1999.

Dobrin, Sidney I., and Christian R. Weisser. *Natural Discourse: Toward Ecocomposition.* Albany: State U of New York P, 2002.

Dickinson, Emily. *The Complete Poems of Emily Dickinson.* Ed. Thomas H. Johnson. Boston: Little, 1960.

Donne, John. "No Man Is an Island." Peterson et al. 315–16.

Douglass, Frederick. *Narrative of the Life of Frederick Douglass: An American Slave.* New Haven: Yale UP, 2001.

Emerson, Ralph Waldo. "Compensation." *Essays and Lectures.* Ed. Joel Porte. Washington, DC: Library of America, 1983. 283–302.

Enemy Mine. Dir. Wolfgang Peterson. Twentieth Century Fox, 1985.

Enos, Theresa, ed. *Encyclopedia of Rhetoric and Composition: Communication from Ancient Times to the Information Age.* New York: Garland, 1996.

Evans, Martha Noel. *Fits and Starts: A Genealogy of Hysteria in Modern France.* Ithaca: Cornell UP, 1991.

Fahnestock, Jeanne. *Rhetorical Figures in Science.* New York: Oxford UP, 1999.

Faulkner, William. Nobel Prize Award Speech. Peterson et al. 319–20.

Fisher, Walter R. *Human Communication as Narration: Toward a Philosophy of Reason, Value, and Action.* Columbia: U of South Carolina P, 1987.

Freire, Paulo. *Pedagogy of the Oppressed.* Trans. Myra Bergman Ramos. New York: Continuum, 1990.

Freud, Sigmund. *Civilization and Its Discontents.* Trans. James Strachey. New York: Norton, 1989.

Friedan, Betty. *The Feminine Mystique.* New York: Norton, 1963.

Frost, Robert. "The Road Not Taken." Available online at <http://www.poets.org/poems/poems.cfm?prmID=1645>.

Gaines, Ernest J. *A Lesson Before Dying.* New York: Knopf, 1993.

Gibson, William. *Neuromancer.* New York: Ace, 1984.

Glenn, Cheryl. *Rhetoric Retold: Regendering the Tradition from Antiquity Through the Renaissance.* Carbondale: Southern Illinois UP, 1997.

Glotfelty, Cheryll, and Harold Fromm, eds. *The Ecocriticism Reader: Landmarks in Literary Ecology.* Athens: U of Georgia P, 1996.

Greer, Germaine. *The Female Eunuch.* New York: McGraw, 1971.

Gross, Alan G. *The Rhetoric of Science.* Cambridge: Harvard UP, 1990.

Harper, Douglas, ed. *Online Etymology Dictionary.* Available at <http://www.etymonline.com/index.html>.

Hauser, Gerard A. *Introduction to Rhetorical Theory.* 2nd ed. Prospect Heights: Waveland, 2002.

Hemingway, Ernest. "From *A Farewell to Arms.*" Peterson et al. 317.

Hirschman, Albert O. *The Rhetoric of Reaction: Perversity, Futility, Jeopardy.* Cambridge: Harvard UP, 1991.

Hochschild, Arlie Russell, with Anne Machung. *The Second Shift.* 2nd ed. New York: Avon, 1997.

Hogan, Linda. "Hearing Voices." Hunt 77–82.

hooks, bell. "Homeplace (A Site of Resistance)." Ritchie and Ronald 383–90.

———. "Touching the Earth." Barnhill 51–56.

Hunt, Douglas, ed. *The Dolphin Reader.* 6th ed. Boston: Houghton, 2003.

Jackson, Ronald L., II, and Elaine B. Richardson, eds. *Understanding African American Rhetoric: Classical Origins to Contemporary Innovations.* London: Routledge, 2003.

Jakobson, Roman. "The Metaphoric and Metonymic Poles." *Fundamentals of Language.* Ed. Roman Jakobson and Morris Halle. Hague: Mouton, 1956. 54–82.

———. "Two Aspects of Language and Two Types of Aphasic Disturbances." *Language in Literature.* Ed. Krystyna Pomorska and Stephen Rudy. Cambridge: Harvard UP, 1987. 95–114.

Jamieson, Kathleen Hall. *Eloquence in an Electronic Age.* New York: Oxford UP, 1988.

Johnson, Nan. "Ethos." Enos 243–45.

Kennedy, George A. *Classical Rhetoric and Its Christian and Secular Tradition from Ancient to Modern Times.* 2nd ed. Chapel Hill: U of North Carolina P, 1980.

Kerouac, Jack. *The Dharma Bums.* New York: Viking, 1958.

Killingsworth, M. Jimmie. *Walt Whitman and the Earth: A Study in Ecopoetics.* Iowa City: U of Iowa P, 2005.

———. *Whitman's Poetry of the Body: Sexuality, Politics, and the Text.* Chapel Hill: U of North Carolina P, 1989.

Killingsworth, M. Jimmie, and Michael Gilbertson. "Rhetoric and Relevance in Technical Writing." *Journal of Technical Writing and Communication* 16 (1986): 287–97.

Killingsworth, M. Jimmie, and Jacqueline S. Palmer. *Ecospeak: Rhetoric and Environmental Politics in America.* Carbondale: Southern Illinois UP, 1992.

King, Martin Luther, Jr. "I Have a Dream." Available online at <http://www.americanrhetoric.com/speeches/Ihaveadream.htm>.

———. "Letter from Birmingham Jail." Peterson et al. 503–15.

Kinneavy, James L. "Kairos: A Neglected Concept in Classical Rhetoric." *Rhetoric and Praxis.* Ed. Jean Dietz Moss. Washington, DC: Catholic U of America P, 1986. 79–105.

———. "*Pistis.*" Enos 521–22.

———. *A Theory of Discourse: The Aims of Discourse.* Englewood Cliffs: Prentice, 1971.

Kozol, Jonathan. *Amazing Grace: The Lives of Children and the Conscience of a Nation.* New York: Crown, 1995.

Kuhn, Thomas. *The Structure of Scientific Revolutions.* 2nd ed. Chicago: U of Chicago P, 1970.

Lakoff, George, and Mark Johnson. *Metaphors We Live By.* Chicago: U of Chicago P, 1980.

Lamm, Nomy. "It's a Big Fat Revolution." Ritchie and Ronald 454–61.

Lanham, Richard A. *A Handlist of Rhetorical Terms.* 2nd ed. Berkeley: U of California P, 1991.

Le Guin, Ursula K. *The Left Hand of Darkness.* New York: Berkley, 1976.

Leopold, Aldo. *A Sand County Almanac and Sketches Here and There.* Spec. commem. ed. Illus. Charles W. Schwartz. Into. Robert Finch. New York: Oxford UP, 1989.

Lincoln, Abraham. Gettysburg Address. Peterson et al. 317.

Longyear, Barry. "Enemy Mine." *Super Hugos Presented by Isaac Asimov.* Riverdale: Baen, 1992. 101–70.

Loving, Jerome. *Walt Whitman: The Song of Himself.* Berkeley: U of California P, 1999.

Lunsford, Andrea, ed. *Reclaiming Rhetorica.* Pittsburgh: U of Pittsburgh P, 1995.

Lyotard, Jean-François. *The Postmodern Condition: A Report on Knowledge.* Trans. Geoff Bennington and Brian Massumi. Minneapolis: U of Minnesota P, 1984.

Malcolm X and Alex Haley. *The Autobiography of Malcolm X.* Fwd. Attallah Shabazz. New York: Ballantine, 1999.

Mairs, Nancy. "Carnal Acts." Ritchie and Ronald 391–400.

McCloskey, Dierdre N. *The Rhetoric of Economics.* 2nd ed. Madison: U of Wisconsin P, 1998.

McLuhan, Marshall. *Understanding Media: The Extensions of Man.* New York: McGraw, 1964.

Medhurst, Martin J., and Thomas Benson, eds. *Rhetorical Dimensions in Media: A Critical Casebook.* 2nd ed. Dubuque: Kendall, 1991.

Moi, Toril. *Sexual/Textual Politics: Feminist Literary Theory.* London: Methuen, 1985.

N[icholls], P[eter]. "Enemy Mine." *The Encyclopedia of Science Fiction*. Ed. John Clute and Peter Nicholls. New York: St. Martin's, 1995. 384.

Nietzsche, Friedrich. "On Truth and Lies in the Nonmoral Sense." Bizzell and Herzberg 1171–79.

Ong, Walter J. *Orality and Literacy: The Technologizing of the Word*. London: Methuen, 1982.

———. "The Writer's Audience Is Always a Fiction." *PMLA* 90 (1975): 9–21.

Orwell, George. "Politics and the English Language." Hunt 156–69.

Paine, Thomas. *The American Crisis No. I* (1776–1883). The Secular Web Library. Available online at <http://libertyonline.hypermall.com/Paine/Crisis/Crisis-TOC.html>.

Patnoe, Elizabeth, and James Phelan. "Narrative Theory." Enos 454–57.

Peterson, Linda H., John C. Brereton, and Joan E. Hartman, eds. *The Norton Reader: An Anthology of Nonfiction Prose*. Shorter 10th ed. New York: Norton, 2000.

Plato. *The Collected Dialogues*. Ed. Edith Hamilton and Huntington Cairns. Princeton: Princeton UP, 1961.

Pollitt, Katha. "For Whom the Ball Rolls." Hunt 214–16.

Popper, Karl R. *The Open Society and Its Enemies*. 2 vols. Princeton: Princeton UP, 1966.

Putnam, Robert D. "Bowling Alone: America's Declining Social Capital." Hunt 197–214.

Ray, Janisse. *Ecology of a Cracker Childhood*. Minneapolis: Milkweed, 1999.

Rich, Adrienne. "Claiming an Education." Hunt 27–31.

Richards, I. A. *The Philosophy of Rhetoric*. New York: Oxford UP, 1936.

Ritchie, Joy, and Kate Ronald. *Available Means: An Anthology of Women's Rhetoric(s)*. Pittsburgh: U of Pittsburgh P, 2001.

Rodriguez, Richard. "Mr. Secrets." Hunt 124–40.

Schneider, Stephen. *Global Warming: Are We Entering the Greenhouse Century?* San Francisco: Sierra Club, 1989.

Selzer, Jack, and Sharon Crowley, eds. *Rhetorical Bodies*. Madison: U of Wisconsin P, 1999.

Shelley, Percy Bysshe. "Ode to the West Wind." Available online at <http://www.bartleby.com/101/610.html>.

Silko, Leslie Marmon. *Ceremony*. New York: Viking, 1977.

———. "Landscape, History, and the Pueblo Imagination." Barnhill 30–50.

Skocpol, Theda. "Unsolved Mysteries: The Tocqueville Files." *American Prospect*. 7.25 (Mar. 1–Apr. 1, 1996): 1–9. Available online at <http://www.prospect.org/print/V7/25/25-cnt2.html>.

Smith, Charles Kay. *Styles and Structures: Alternative Approaches to College Writing*. New York: Norton, 1974.

Snyder, Gary. *A Place in Space: Ethics, Aesthetics, and Watersheds*. Washington, DC: Counterpoint, 1995.

———. *Turtle Island*. New York: New Directions, 1974.

Stone, I. F. *The Trial of Socrates*. Boston: Little, 1988.

Stull, Bradford T. *Amid the Fall, Dreaming of Eden: Du Bois, King, Malcolm X, and Emancipatory Composition.* Carbondale: Southern Illinois UP, 1999.

——. *Elements of Figurative Language.* New York: Longman, 2001.

Swearingen, Jan. *Rhetoric and Irony: Western Literacy and Western Lies.* New York: Oxford UP, 1991.

Tompkins, Jane P., ed. *Reader-Response Criticism: From Formalism to Post-Structuralism.* Baltimore: Johns Hopkins UP, 1980.

Waddell, Craig, ed. *"And No Birds Sing": The Rhetoric of Rachel Carson.* Carbondale: Southern Illinois UP, 2000.

Weaver, Richard. "Language Is Sermonic." Bizzell and Herzberg 1351–60.

Whitman, Walt. *Leaves of Grass.* 1891–92. Deathbed Ed. *The Walt Whitman Archive.* Ed. Kenneth M. Price and Ed Folsom. Available online at <http://jefferson.village.Virginia.EDU/whitman/>.

——. *Specimen Days. Complete Poetry and Collected Prose.* Washington, DC: Library of America, 1982: 689–926.

Wills, Garry. *Lincoln at Gettysburg: The Words that Remade America.* New York: Simon, 1992.

Yoos, George E. "Logos." Enos 410–14.

Index

absurd, sense of, 110

action, 83

action, symbolic, 52

advertising: appeals to body and, 69–70, 82–83; newness and, 39–40; rhetorical risk and, 8–10; women's movement and, 87–88

African Americans, 65–66, 101, 143. *See also* "I Have a Dream" speech; King, Martin Luther, Jr.

agent, 52, 54

air-tight cases, 14, 15

alienation, 41, 115–16; from body, 78–79

almanac genre, 46

Amazing Grace: The Lives of Children and the Conscience of the Nation (Kozol), 74

American Civil War, 43, 76–77

American Crisis, The (Paine), 42, 43

American Revolution, 42

analogy, 123

anaphora, 45–46, 64, 95

angle, 10

aphasia, 127

appeals: definitions, vii–viii, 2–3, 153–54n1; model of, 1–5, 26–28. *See also individual types of appeal*

Aristotle, 1–2, 14–15, 24–25, 129, 137, 153n1

artistic proofs, 25, 153n1

association, 121, 126–30, 140–41. *See also* metonymy

attention, 36

attitudes, appeals to body and, 83

audience position, x, 1–3; decoder, 26; disaffected Euro-Americans, 29, 57–59; insiders, xi, 11–13, 19–21, 132–33, 136, 139–40; literate readers, 31–32; modern people, 32–33; northern whites, 30–31; observer position, 35–37; outsiders, xi, 21–23, 136, 139–40; participation and empowerment, 143–48; pathos and, 26–28; projection of, 91; science fiction hero as model, 116; as second persona, 35, 36, 57; television, 69–70; television and, 9, 69–70; third person, 92, 94; triple persona and, 94, 132–33; vicarious experience of, 141; Victorian, 71–72; women, 28–29

Augustine, St., 13

authority, appeals to, x–xi; evidence and, 13–16; insider response, 19–21; metonymy and, 129–30; outsider response, 21–23; religious discourse, 11–13

author position, x, 1–3, 9; encoder, 26; ethos and, 26, 27; metaphor and, 141–43, 148; metonymy and, 140–41; Native American perspective, 58–59. *See also* motives

autobiographical rhetoric, 103–6

Autobiography of Malcolm X, The (Malcolm X and Haley), 102, 103–8

awareness, appeals to body and, 83

background of appeal, 28

Bateson, Gregory, 140

Berry, Wendell, 5–7, 10, 41, 42, 44, 92, 124, 134–35, 140

Bible, as metaphor, 12

Bitzer, Lloyd, 26–28

Black Nationalism, 103–4

body, alienation from, 78–79

body, appeals to, xi, 54, 65–66, 98, 106, 116, 156n2; in advertising, 69–70; democracy and, 68–69, 70–73, 82–83; disability and, 78–80; empowerment and, 67, 80–83; identification vs. difference, 83–84; literature of reform, 73–75, 83; metaphor and, 124–26; personification of nature, 63–64, 68; unconscious motives, 80–81; voice metaphor, 79–80, 156n5; war rhetoric, 75–78, 83
body, poetry of, 70–71
body criticism, 156n2
Bookchin, Murray, 118
Boorstin, Daniel, 68
Booth, Wayne, 133, 137, 148
boundaries, 4–5
"Bowling Alone: America's Declining Social Capital" (Putnam), 16–19, 129, 131; responses to, 19–23, 40–41
brain, metaphorical functioning of, 123
Burke, Kenneth, 3, 52–54, 113, 122–23

"Carnal Acts" (Mairs), 78
Carson, Rachel, 68, 100
celebrity memoir, 104
Ceremony (Silko), 59–60, 100, 143
character, 25
cinema, 7–8
civic engagement, 16–19
Civilization and Its Discontents (Freud), 81
"Claiming an Education" (Rich), 28–29
class, hierarchy of, 72–73
classical rhetoric, x, 1–2, 14–15, 24–26, 137, 153n1
Classical Rhetoric for the Modern Student (Corbett), 38–39
Clinton, Bill, 19
cognitive dissonance, 100
coming-of-age narrative, 107

communal ideal, 27, 32
communication triangle, 26, 28
community, 138–40, 142; holistic, 5–6
compensation, law of, 149
complex appeals, 11, 36–37, 39–42, 59, 65
confessional writings, 104
contiguity, 127
conversion narratives, 105–6
Corbett, Edward P. J., 38–39
countercultural perspective, 60–66
Crane, Stephen, 73
cripple, as term, 78
crisis, rhetoric of, 42–44; journey metaphor and, 45–46
critic, rhetorical, 36
critical distance, 134–35
cultural criticism, 5–7

Darwin, Charles, 12–13, 80
data-based arguments, xi, 17, 136, 139, 149; facts as authority, 13–16
decoder (audience), 26
deduction, 14–15
defamiliarization, 141–43
dehumanization, rhetoric of, 100, 104–7, 109–10
deliberative speeches, 25, 38
Deloria, Vine, Jr., 55–58, 98, 118
democracy, rhetoric of, 68–73, 82–83
Democracy in America (Tocqueville), 16
demonization, rhetoric of, 77–78, 100; military rhetoric and, 116–17
denotative discourse, 136, 139
development, concept of, 56–57
Dharma Bums, The (Kerouac), 61
dialectic, 123
Dickinson, Emily, 130
diminishment, rhetoric of, 99–100, 102–3, 116
disability studies, 78
discourse communities, 11
disease metaphor, 74–75, 124–25
distance, 121, 131–34; critical, 134–35

Donne, John, 22
Douglass, Frederick, 30–31, 100, 102–3, 139, 140, 143
dramatic irony, 133
dramatism, 52–53

Ecology of a Cracker Childhood (Ray), 63–66, 117
Emerson, Ralph Waldo, 70
empowerment: appeals to body and, 67, 80–83; appeals to place and, 66–67; participation and, 143–48
encoder (author), 26
Encyclopedia of Rhetoric and Composition, 128, 130
"Enemy Mine" (Longyear), 113–19, 142
Engels, Friedrich, 80
entertainment, 7–8, 137
enthymeme, 15
environmental rhetoric, 46–48, 54, 66–68, 155n2. *See also* Leopold, Aldo
epideictic speeches, 25, 29, 38
ethnographies, 3–4
ethos, 2, 25–26, 27, 97, 115, 153n1
evidence, 13–16
exigence, 26–28, 38, 57

facts, 13–16
falsifiability, 13
Faulkner, William, 43–44
fear, rhetoric of, 77, 81
Female Eunuch, The (Greer), 94–96
Feminine Mystique, The (Friedan), 91–94
feminism: French, 94–95. *See also* Friedan, Betty; gender, appeals to; Greer, Germaine
figures of speech, 121. *See also* tropes
first person, 94
Fisher, Walter, 136
forensic speeches, 25, 38
"For Whom the Ball Rolls" (Pollitt), 21–23
four D's of reporting, 39

"Four Master Tropes" (Burke), 123
Franklin, Benjamin, 46
Freire, Paulo, 119–20
French feminists, 94–95
Freud, Sigmund, 80–81, 138
Friedan, Betty, 91–94, 134
friendship, rhetoric of, 114
Frost, Robert, 42
fulfillment, appeals to, 91–94
futility thesis, 48–49

Gaines, Ernest, 102, 108–13, 142
gender, appeals to, xi, 22, 29, 41, 85–86, 98; body images and stereotyping, 94–96; fulfillment and health, 91–94; liberty and equality rhetoric, 86–87; marketing, 87–91; shifting perspectives, 96–97
genres, classification of, 25, 38
Gettysburg Address (Lincoln), 43, 44, 45, 48–49, 143
"Glimpse of War's Hell-Scenes, A" (Whitman), 77–78
global vs. local perspectives, 58–60
God Is Red (Deloria), 55–58
Grammar of Motives, A (Burke), 52, 122–23
Great Chain of Being, 72–73
Greece, classical, 24, 38
Greek myths, 47, 143
Greer, Germaine, 94–96
ground of appeal, 28

Haley, Alex, 104, 108
health, appeals to, 6, 33–34, 66–67, 73–75, 134–35; gender appeals and, 91–94
"Hearing Voices" (Hogan), 29–30
Hearts and Minds (film), 99–100
Hemingway, Ernest, 75–76, 149
hermaphroditism, 85–86
hierarchy of class, 72–73
Hirschman, Albert, 48–50
history, appeals to, 57–58
Hochschild, Arlie Russell, 88–90, 134, 141

Hogan, Linda, 29–30, 128, 143
holistic community, 5–6
Homer, 47
hooks, bell, 31, 65–66, 155n3
Horace, 143–44
humanistic values, 93, 96
Hunger of Memory (Rodriguez), 31–32
hysterical, as term, 94–95

idealism, 52
identification, 3, 121, 123–26, 141–43, 148
identity politics, xi, 119
"I Have a Dream" speech (King), 45–46, 50, 98, 109, 134–35, 143
"I Heard a Fly Buzz When I Died" (Dickinson), 130
image, rhetoric of, 91, 157n2
imitation, 138
individualism, 18–19, 21, 119; science fiction and, 115–16
individuation, 101, 119
induction, 15
information, 140
instructions, 38
interpretation, 10, 15, 16
introductions, xi, 28–34
irony, 7–8, 22, 89–90, 114, 121, 123, 141–43; as distance, 131–34
"I Sing the Body Electric" (Whitman), 71–72

Jakobson, Roman, 123, 127
jeopardy thesis, 48–49
Johnson, Mark, 123, 124, 126
journey metaphor, 44–48
judgment, 134–35

kairos, 26, 38, 42, 57
Kennedy, George A., 153n1
Kerouac, Jack, 61
Khomeini, Ayatollah, 100
King, Martin Luther, Jr., 45–46, 50, 98, 109, 125, 134–35, 143

Kinneavy, James L., 26, 28
Kozol, Jonathan, 74, 141, 142, 155n3

Laguna Pueblo, 55–56
Lakoff, George, 123, 124, 126
"Land Ethic, The" (Leopold), 46–48, 68, 143
"Landscape, History, and the Pueblo Imagination" (Silko), 55–56, 58, 141
language, 4, 52, 97
"Leaves of Grass" (Whitman), 70–73
Left Hand of Darkness, The (Le Guin), 96–97, 99, 100
Le Guin, Ursula K., 96–97, 99, 100
Leopold, Aldo, 46–48, 68, 100, 143
Lesson Before Dying, A (Gaines), 102, 108–13, 142
"Let My People Go" theme, 143
"Letter from Birmingham Jail" (King), 125
liberty and equality, rhetoric of, 43, 86–87
lifespan metaphor, 43
Lincoln, Abraham, 43, 44, 45, 48–49, 143
listening, 36–37
literacy, 99, 116; dehumanization and, 106–7, 109–10; as humanizing enterprise, 119–20; racial identity and, 101–18; rehumanization and, 108–13; status linked to, 99, 101; theories of as racist, 101–2
literary realism, 149
Locke, John, 134
logos, 2, 25–28, 97, 153n1
Longyear, Barry, 113–19, 142
Lyotard, Jean-François, 136, 139, 140

Mairs, Nancy, 78–80
Malcolm X, 102, 103–8, 141, 157–58n2
manifest destiny, 55
Marx, Karl, 80

materialism, 52–53

Matrix, The, 7–8, 10

McLuhan, Marshall, 5, 69, 101, 116

means, 52

medium of appeal, 1, 4, 5, 28

Melville, Herman, 129

metaphor, 29, 122, 134; author position and, 141–43, 148; as identification, 121, 123–26; as ratio, 124, 125

Metaphors We Live By (Lakoff and Johnson), 123, 124, 126

metonymy, 123; as association, 121, 126–30; author position and, 140–41; cognitive dimension of, 129

military rhetoric, 116–17. *See also* war rhetoric

Moby-Dick (Melville), 129

modernism, 39–40; alienation and, 41, 115–16; conflict between past and present, 41–42; place and, 52–53, 60

modern rhetoric, 26–28, 39, 50–51; tropes and, 121–23

"Modest Proposal, A" (Swift), 131–34, 142

money, equated with time, 40

monotheism, 55

motives, 27, 52–54, 137–40; unconscious, 80–81

movement, concept of, 4, 26–27

Muhammad, Elijah, 106

mythology, 47, 143

narrative, xii, 136–37; compensation in, 149; motivations for storytelling, 137–40; of progress, 55–56; showing vs. telling, 144–48

Narrative of the Life of Frederick Douglass (Douglass), 30–31, 102–3, 139

Nation of Islam, 106, 107

Native American perspective: local vs. global in, 58–60; on time and place, 54–58

Native Americans, literacy and, 101

nautical/navigation imagery, 3–4

neo-Marxists, 119

newness, 39–40

news stories, 39–40

Nietzsche, Friedrich, 80, 122, 129–30

1984 (Orwell), 93

nuclear threat, 44

observer position, 35–37

"Ode to the West Wind" (Shelley), 124

Odyssey (Homer), 47

Ong, Walter, 101

Organization of Afro-American Unity, 107–8

Orwell, George, 32–34, 40–42, 93, 122, 125–26

othering, rhetoric of, 99–101, 114, 116–17

Paine, Thomas, 42, 43, 128

participation, of audience, 143–48

pathos, 2, 25–28, 97, 153n1

patriarchy, 86

Paul, St., 106

pedagogy of the oppressed, 119

persona, 89–90; first person, 94; second person, 35, 36, 57, 94; third person, 92, 94, 132–33; triple, 94, 132–33

personification, 63–64, 68, 100

perspective, 123

perversity thesis, 48–49

Phaedrus (Plato), 72–73, 81–82

place, appeals to, xi, 52–54, 72, 155n2; countercultural perspective, 60–66; local vs. global, 58–60; metonymy and, 128; Native American perspective, 54–58; race and, 98, 113–19; reinhabitation, 54, 59–66, 98; time and, 50–51, 57–58; virtual places, 66–67

Plato, 68, 72–73, 81–82

poetics, 137

Poetics (Aristotle), 137, 138
poetry of the body, 70–71
"Politics and the English Language" (Orwell), 32–34, 40, 41, 122, 125–26
Pollitt, Katha, 21–23, 40–41
"Poor Richard's Almanac" (Franklin), 46
poverty, 73–75
prison memoir, 105–6
proclamation, 13
professional men, gender roles and, 89–91
progress, rhetoric of, 32–33, 39, 48–50, 55–56
proposals, 38
purpose, 52
Putnam, Robert D., 16–23, 40–41, 129, 131

race, appeals to, xi, 54, 65–66, 98–99; dehumanization, 100, 104–7, 109–10; diminishment, 99–100, 102–3; historical context, 109; place and, 98, 113–19; racial identity and literacy, 101–18; rehumanization, 108–13; stereotyping and, 99–101
ratio, 52–53, 56, 124, 125
rational world paradigm, 136
Ray, Janisse, 63–66, 68, 117
reactive rhetoric, 48–50
Reagan, Ronald, 100
realignment, 12
reality (world), 26
reduction, 123, 128
reform, literature of, 73–75
rehumanization, rhetoric of, 108–13
reinhabitation, 54, 59–60, 98; countercultural perspective, 60–66
religious discourse, 11–13
Renaissance, 121–22
renaming, 61
repetition, 95
reports, 38

representation, 121, 123, 130–31
rhetoric, definitions, x, 137
Rhetoric (Aristotle), 1–2, 153n1
"Rhetorical Situation, The" (Bitzer), 26–28
rhetorical situations, x–xi; classical roots, 24–26; complexity of, 36–37; modern contributions, 26–28; simple, 35–36; social situations and, 34–35; storytelling and, 137–38
Rhetoric of Fiction (Booth), 148
Rhetoric of Irony, A (Booth), 133
Rhetoric of Motives, A (Burke), 3, 52
Rhetoric of Reaction, The (Hirschman), 48–50
Rich, Adrienne, 28–29, 35–36
risk, advertising and, 8–10
roadkill metaphor, 62–63
"Road Not Taken, The" (Frost), 42
Rodriguez, Richard, 31–32, 141
Romantic writers, 41, 124

Sand County Almanac (Leopold), 46–48, 68
sarcasm, 132
scene, 52, 53
science fiction, 7–8, 113–19; American vs. European, 114
scientific rhetoric, 136, 139–40
seasons metaphor, 42
second person, 35, 36, 57, 94
Second Shift, The (Hochschild), 88–90, 141
self-realization, otherness and, 116–17
September 11 attacks, 82
sermonic language, 122
Shelley, Percy Bysshe, 124
Sherman, William Tecumseh, 77
signal (text), 26
Silent Spring (Carson), 68, 100
Silko, Leslie Marmon, 55–56, 58, 59–60, 100, 141, 143
similarity, 127

simile, 123
Sinclair, Upton, 73
Skocpol, Theda, 20–21
slave narratives, 102–3
slavery, 71–72
Snyder, Gary, 54, 61–63
social capital, 18, 40
social ecology, 118
social realism, 114
social situations, 34–35
"Song of Myself" (Whitman), 70–71, 140
specialization, 5–7, 15–16, 41, 124–25
Specimen Days (Whitman), 77–78
speech genres, 25, 38
spin, 10
Steinbeck, John, 73
stereotyping, 128; gender and, 94–96; as racist rhetoric, 99–101; shifting perspectives, 96–97
style, 79
substance, 3
substitution, 3, 9–10, 13–16
Swift, Jonathan, 131–34, 142, 143
Symbolic of Motives (Burke), 52
synecdoche, 121, 123, 130–31, 134

technical and business writing, 38
technology, rhetoric of, 66–67, 81–83
television audience, 9, 69–70
Terminator films, 7
terrorism, rhetoric of, 82–83
testimonial stories, 137
text (signal), 26
"Thinking Like a Mountain" (Leopold), 68, 100
third person, 92, 94, 132–33
Thoreau, Henry David, 91
thought experiment, 96
time, appeals to, xi, 38–39, 72, 94, 98, 128, 149; crisis rhetoric, 42–44, 45–46; forward motion, rhetoric of, 44–48; modern, concept of, 40–42; Native American perspec-

tive, 54–58; place and, 50–51, 57–58; progress, resistance to, 48–50; simple and complex, 39–42
Tocqueville, Alexis de, 16, 17, 40, 129
tone, irony and, 132–33
training, storytelling and, 138–39
triangulation, 3–4, 14, 26, 28
triple persona, 94, 132–33
tropes, xi–xii, 121; critical distance and, 134–35; in history of modern rhetoric, 121–23; synecdoche, 121, 123, 130–31, 134. *See also* irony; metaphor; metonymy
Turtle Island (Snyder), 61–63

unconscious motives, 80–81
unmasking strategy, 89–90, 134
Unsettling of America, The: Culture and Agriculture (Berry), 5–7, 10
"Unsolved Mysteries: The Tocqueville Files" (Skocpol), 20–21
urgency, sense of, 26–27, 38–39
utopian vision, 67

value, position of, x, 1–3; logos and, 26, 28; substitution and, 9–10; triple persona, 132–33. *See also individual types of appeal*
Vico, Giambattista, 122–23
virtual reality, 66–67
voice, metaphor of, 79–80, 156n5
Volta, Alessandro, 139

Walden (Thoreau), 91
war rhetoric, 75–78, 83. *See also* military rhetoric
Weaver, Richard, 122
websites, 66
white man's ethos, 55–56
Whitman, Walt, 70–73, 77–78, 98, 127–28, 140
wholeness, 5–6
wilderness ethic, 117–18
winter metaphor, 42
wit, 134–35

witness, bearing, 140–41, 148
women's movement, advertising
    rhetoric and, 87–88
women's rhetoric, 156–57n1
working-class men, gender roles and,
    89–91
world (reality), 26
World War I, 76

M. Jimmie Killingsworth is a professor of English and the director of Writing Programs at Texas A&M University. He is the author or coauthor of over fifty scholarly articles and book chapters and seven books on American rhetoric, literature, and culture.